Leadership,
Equity,
and
School
Effectiveness

Leadership, Equity, and School Effectiveness

edited by
H. Prentice Baptiste, Jr.
Hersholt C. Waxman
Judith Walker de Felix
James E. Anderson

SAGE PUBLICATIONS
The Publishers of Professional Social Science
Newbury Park London New Delhi

For information address:

SAGE Publications, Inc.
2111 West Hillcrest Drive
Newbury Park, California 91320

SAGE Publications Ltd.
28 Banner Street
London EC1Y 8QE
England

SAGE Publications India Pvt. Ltd.
M-32 Market
Greater Kailash I
New Delhi 110 048 India

Printed in the United States of America

Library of Congress Cataloging-in-Publication Data

Main entry under title:

Leadership, equity, and school effectiveness / H. Prentice Baptiste,
    editor . . . [et al.].
        p. cm.
    "Evolved out of the Journal of educational equity and leadership"-
-Pref.
    Includes bibliographical references.
    ISBN 0-8039-3466-1. — ISBN 0-8039-3467-X (pbk.)
    1. Educational equalization — United States.   2. Minorities —
Education — United States.   I. Baptiste, H. Prentice.   II. Journal
of educational equity and leadership.
LC213.2.L43   1990
370-19'342 — dc20   89-37459
                                                                    CIP

FIRST PRINTING, 1990

Contents

Preface   7

1. Equity and Excellence in Educational Leadership:
A Necessary Nexus
MARTHA M. McCARTHY and L. DEAN WEBB   9

I. Leadership and Equity

2. Introduction: Lessons from the Past and
Directions for the Future
JAMES E. ANDERSON   17
3. Equity and the Educational Practitioner:
A Leadership Model
BARBARA A. SIZEMORE   21
4. Facilitating Equity Through the School Superintendency
J. JEROME HARRIS and MAE A. KENDALL   45
5. The Quest for Equity: Imperatives for Administrators
in Higher Education
HUGH J. SCOTT   59

II. Educational Environments That Promote Equity

6. Introduction: Research on Equity in
Learning Environments
JUDITH WALKER de FELIX   79
7. Productivity and Equity
HERBERT J. WALBERG   83
8. Compassion and Equity: Culture and English Literacy
for Linguistic Minority Children
HENRY T. TRUEBA   97
9. Classroom Language Use and Educational Equity:
Toward Interactive Pedagogy
CHRISTIAN FALTIS   109

III. Instruction That Enhances Equity

10. Introduction: Classroom Instruction
That Enhances Equity
HERSHOLT C. WAXMAN   127
11. Programs That Promote Educational Equity
MARGARET WANG   132

12. Instructional Organizational Practices
    That Affect Equity
    ADAM GAMORAN   155
13. Linguistic and Cultural Influences
    on Classroom Instruction
    YOLANDA N. PADRON and STEPHANIE L. KNIGHT   173
14. Teacher Effectiveness Research and Equity Issues
    JANE A. STALLINGS and JANE McCARTHY   186

IV. Educational Preparation for Equity

15. Introduction: The Challenge of Preparing for Equity
    H. PRENTICE BAPTISTE, Jr.   209
16. Administrative Preparation for Equity
    CHAROL SHAKESHAFT   213
17. Teacher Preparation for Equity
    GENEVA GAY   224
18. Teacher Education That Enhances Equity
    JAMES B. BOYER   244
19. Educating Society for Equity
    CARLOS E. CORTÉS   259

    About the Authors   273

Preface

The *Leadership, Equity, and School Effectiveness* yearbook evolved out of the *Journal of Educational Equity and Leadership* (JEEL). When it became apparent that the publication of JEEL must cease for financial reasons, its editors began searching for a viable alternative to continue its philosophy and to maintain its forum for the education community. Several months of discussions led to the idea of a series of yearbooks focusing on equity and leadership issues. The editors saw this as the most appropriate means for continuing the purposes set forth in JEEL for directing the enhancement of equity for African Americans, American Indians, Asian Americans, Hispanics, women, and other excluded groups. The purposes of *Leadership, Equity, and School Effectiveness*, as first stated in JEEL, are to

- provide educational leaders with ideas for advancing educational equity;
- stimulate research and innovative thinking on educational equity;
- facilitate communication across differing groups with equity-related needs; and
- provide a forum for examining philosophical positions, research findings, and emergent practices on equity.

The editors of this yearbook wish to express specific thanks to the contributors who prepared manuscripts for this initial volume. Special appreciation is extended to Patrick B. Forsyth, executive director, University Council for Educational Administration, and Mitch Allen, Sage Publications, for their support and encouragement during the development of this project. A special thanks to Martha McCarthy for her untiring support and willingness to contribute to the development of JEEL's yearbook. Finally, sincere appreciation must be extended to Grace Castor and Susan Gauthier for editing and typing services provided in the preparation of this manuscript.

H. Prentice Baptiste, Jr.
Hersholt C. Waxman
Judith Walker de Felix
James E. Anderson

1

Equity and Excellence
in Educational Leadership:
A Necessary Nexus

MARTHA M. McCARTHY
Indiana University

L. DEAN WEBB
Arizona State University

During the twentieth century, researchers have addressed the topic of educational leadership from various perspectives. Within the past few decades, the concept of educational equity (i.e., fairness, impartiality) also has been the subject of inquiry, although most of the research has focused on student concerns. The intersection between equity issues and educational leadership has received insufficient attention in the literature and, when it has been addressed, the researchers have usually been members of underrepresented groups.

The beneficiaries of efforts to attain equity in educational opportunities or employment traditionally have been viewed too narrowly as only the discrimination victims. Under the social justice theory, those who have been disadvantaged (e.g., women, members of racial and ethnic minority groups, and individuals with disabilities) deserve compensation in terms of equitable treatment or, in some cases, special treatment to address their needs. While the social justice theory alone could provide sufficient justification for a national priority on achieving educational equity, the continuation of discriminatory practices hurts society as a whole. For example, while few would contest that we want the most intelligent, most creative, and best qualified individuals leading our schools, the talents of women and members of minority groups have been underutilized in leadership roles. As a result, the entire educational enterprise has suffered. Ensuring gender, racial, and ethnic diversity can provide role models for an increasingly heterogeneous student population and allow us to draw on a wider range of perspectives in developing theories of effective leadership. Our contention is that equity is a prerequisite of educational excellence. These are complementary, rather than mutually exclusive, concepts.

Complicated and not yet fully understood factors have precluded us from achieving equity and excellence in educational leadership. Educational administration has evolved as a field dominated by White males. The separation of the educational profession into teachers and managers, accompanied by gender segregation, is long-standing (Ortiz & Marshall, 1988). Various explanations have been offered for this condition, from the heavy reliance on sponsorship to sex-role stereotyping to the evolution of schools as control-oriented bureaucracies. Access to the field as well as contributions to the knowledge base traditionally have been controlled by "powerful elders" who have discouraged new perspectives and "questions about the fundamental structure of the field" (Ortiz & Marshall, 1988, p. 138). In short, equity concerns have systematically been excluded from the study of educational administration (Shakeshaft, 1987; Yeakey, Johnston, & Adkison, 1986).

The challenges associated with achieving gender equity in educational leadership differ somewhat from the problems of attaining racial equity. No longer can the lack of women in leadership positions be attributed to the male-dominated candidate pool. Women now constitute half or more of the graduate students in educational administration. But female students find few female professors to serve as role models; less than 12% of educational administration professors are women (McCarthy, Kuh, Newell, & Iacona, 1988). Also, in comparison with their male counterparts, female students are given less opportunity to engage in research and have fewer support systems available to them (Webb, Stout, & Metha, 1987). Female students also are often subjected to inappropriate treatment by male faculty members and students (e.g., sexist comments, devaluation of their contributions in class discussions).

Once graduated from administrative preparation programs, women face discrimination in hiring and promotion practices and remain sorely underrepresented in line administrative positions. Women hold only 5% of the superintendencies nationwide and only 3% of the high school principalships (Heller, Conway, & Jacobson, 1988). And those women who have been able to secure administrative roles often have felt uncomfortable operating in hierarchical, bureaucratized schools.

The second wave of school reform efforts in the 1980s may offer hope for increasing sex equity in educational leadership. The themes of teacher empowerment and instructional leadership, for example, are consistent with and may give legitimacy to the leadership styles of women. Studies have indicated that women are more likely to use collaborative decision making, attend more to community building, and play a more assertive role in instructional leadership (Shakeshaft, 1987). Perhaps the recent interest in systemic changes in the delivery of educational services will result in more than lip service to fundamental restructuring of schools, which in turn will make leadership positions more attractive to and congruent with characteristics of female administrators. Instead of women feeling that they have to model male behavior, educational leadership may be reconceptualized with women's abilities more highly valued (Ortiz & Marshall, 1988).

While minority men have fared better than women in securing line leadership roles in school districts, the small pool of minority candidates is a very serious problem. Unlike women, the portion of minorities in graduate educational administration programs is not increasing; in fact, Black representation among recipients of doctorates in education has declined during the past decade (National Center for Education Statistics, 1988). As with women, minorities do not encounter supportive environments in educational administration graduate programs. Minority women have experienced particular feelings of isolation as they "suffer the double bind of laboring under two negative statuses" (Yeakey et al., 1986).

Minorities who complete college are often pursuing jobs outside education, where opportunities for advancement and remuneration appear more promising. Only 3% of the superintendencies nationwide are held by non-Whites; less than 8% of principalships are held by Blacks, and 3% are held by Hispanics (Heller et al., 1988). Minority representation is only 8% in the educational administration professoriate, and there are no signs that this percentage will increase in the near future (McCarthy et al., 1988). Creativity is sorely needed in designing incentive programs (e.g., fellowships, loan forgiveness plans) for minorities who will make a commitment upon graduation to serve a designated number of years in educational roles.

Not only are efforts needed to curb discriminatory practices and ensure gender and racial diversity in educational leadership roles, but fundamental changes are needed in administrative preparation programs. Preparation programs need to emphasize the identification of socialization patterns and subtle discriminatory practices that perpetuate gender and racial stereotypes. Only if educational leaders develop greater sensitivity to equity concerns and instill such sensitivity in their staffs and students can systemic changes occur in our schools and in the values that are reinforced through schooling.

Some contend that civil rights legislation and court rulings during the latter 1960s and 1970s have assured equal employment and educational opportunities, and therefore continued attention to equity concerns is no longer needed. The evidence belies this contention. And the strides that have been made through affirmative action programs are currently threatened by the federal government's lack of aggressive support of equity concerns. A recent report written by the House Education and Labor Committee chair accuses the Education Department of failing to enforce civil rights laws, particularly those barring race and gender discrimination ("Education Committee Chief," 1989). The report contends that schools merely promising to change discriminatory practices have been considered in compliance with legal requirements. Richards (1988) has argued that "the prospects for improvement are in the mid-1980s threatened as much by structural factors and benign neglect as by overt discrimination" (p. 165).

We will not significantly enhance educational leadership and the delivery of educational services until we reconceptualize leadership in a broader perspective that gives appropriate consideration to the contributions of women and ethnic and racial minorities. While education is currently quite visible on state political agendas, attention to strengthening standards and ensuring accountability will have little long-term payoff in improving education in our nation unless reforms are grounded in a commitment to achieving educational equity.

As we look toward the next century, the development of new paradigms for schooling will be a major challenge. Will these paradigms alter our perceptions of educational leadership, authority relationships, and school effectiveness? How should leadership preparation be changed, and how might alternative models to prepare and certify school administrators affect the representation of women and minorities in leadership positions? Can educational excellence and equity be achieved in an environmental context characterized by increasing demands on public schools to meet the needs of all children with limited resources? Are changes needed in the basic governance structure of public education? This book is designed to facilitate the much-needed dialogue about these and related issues that must be addressed by educators and policymakers in the coming decade.

References

Education committee chief criticizes ed's civil rights enforcement record. (1989, February 17). *Education Daily*, pp. 1-2.

Heller, R. W., Conway, J. A., & Jacobson, S. L. (1988). Here's your blunt critique of administrator preparation. *Executive Educator, 10*(9), 18-22.

McCarthy, M., Kuh, G., Newell, L. J., & Iacona, C. (1988). *Under scrutiny: The educational administration professoriate.* Tempe, AZ: University Council for Educational Administration.

National Center for Education Statistics. (1988). *Survey of earned doctorates 1982-1986.* Washington, DC: U.S. Department of Education.

Ortiz, F., & Marshall, C. (1988). Women in educational administration. In N. Boyan (Ed.), *Handbook of research on educational administration* (pp. 123-141). New York: Longman.

Richards, C. (1988). The search for equity in educational administration: A commentary. In N. Boyan (Ed.), *Handbook of research on educational administration* (pp. 159-168). New York: Longman.

Shakeshaft, C. (1987). *Women in educational administration.* Newbury Park, CA: Sage.

Webb, L. D., Stout, R., & Metha, A. (1987). *Overcoming sex disequity in educational administration.* Tempe, AZ: University Council for Educational Administration.

Yeakey, C., Johnston, G., & Adkison, J. (1986). In pursuit of equity: A review of research on minorities and women in educational administration. *Educational Administration Quarterly, 22*, 110-149.

PART I

LEADERSHIP AND EQUITY

2

Introduction:
Lessons from the Past and
Directions for the Future

JAMES E. ANDERSON

University of Houston

For most of our history in the United States, social institutions, including education, have been defined and organized by conditions of social consensus. Historically, these conditions have often reflected advantaged positions in our society, based on racial, ethnic, gender, socioeconomic, religious, and political identities. The result of these conditions of social consensus and advantaged positions has been that nearly all social institutions, again including education, have been structured and operated by ensuing power arrangements that reflect a bias for the advantaged majorities over the minorities. Dodson (1974), in his discerning analysis titled "Authority, Power, and Education," describes this phenomenon, noting that these power arrangements are monolithic and monocultural and that, in many instances, the children of the minorities, the poor, and the powerless are discriminated against.

For society, this history of consensus, built on preferred majority ethnic and social group identities in power arrangements, has been contrary, in a sense, to democratic traditions and our proclaimed and acknowledged societal values. For education, this history clearly indicates that learning has not been an equitable enterprise for all the citizens of America. For schools and other institutions of learning it has

17

meant that they have been inadequate in meeting the academic and social needs of the students they must serve.

The bottom line is that education has not provided equal opportunities for quality involvement that would result in comparable beneficial outcomes across various groups in our society (Austin, 1985, p. 81). In essence, equity remains an unfulfilled right in the democratic tradition and an unmet challenge in the social institution called education.

While multiethnic histories related to the social dynamics of America have provided penetrating insights as to why equity has not been fully realized in education, as well as in other sectors of the society, languishing in the past is nonproductive. In today's society it is clear that the historical conditions of the past are not in question. In many instances, these conditions are undergoing change. Instead of power arrangements in education that have been traditionally dominated by majoritarian middle- and upper-class males reflecting conservative ideologies, we are now seeing a broadening of power bases with respect to minorities and women with economically diverse perspectives.

Thus the important questions related to achieving excellence and equity in today's social context and educational environment deal with issues of how this will be done. The authors in this section have taken the position that responsible and aggressive leadership is central to the issue. Correspondingly, they have directed themselves to describing and interpreting the essential dimensions of the roles, tasks, and functions necessary to meet this challenge.

Barbara A. Sizemore's work focuses on the relationship between educational practitioners, at various levels of the educational enterprise, and the task of achieving equity as facilitated through their leadership roles. She asks three important questions. The first relates to whether or not there is a process or model and/or exemplar of the kind of leadership necessary to elevate achievement and eliminate achievement gaps between African Americans and white Americans. The point she makes is that equity should be tied to improving achievement and attaining excellence. The second question relates to what styles and types of leadership are needed in various educational environments. In answering this query, she uses the African American experience in a case-study framework and meticulously chronicles exemplars of leadership that have emerged out of that historical context. The third question posed is concerned with what the leadership dimension has looked like as demonstrated by various role models and individuals who have had significant impact related to equity issues. Among the practitioner groups addressed are teachers, principals, superintendents, and college professors.

In summing up the leaders she has chosen, Sizemore describes lessons that have been learned from leadership models. She illustrates the position taken by many that color, for racial minorities, remains a significant problem in achieving an impartial and just educational system. She declares that in order to achieve equity, a nationally integrated leadership will need to develop a curriculum and an agenda that reflects the newly configuring national culture that is emerging out of today's developing social contexts.

Chapter 4, by J. Jerome Harris and Mae A. Kendall, centers on the significance of demonstrating leadership for equity in the role of the superintendency in public schools. These authors begin their discussion by clearly articulating both the professional responsibility inherent in the superintendency's prescribed role and the social and moral responsibility that emerges out of the historical and current social context of education. The discussion then moves to the complexities of issues surrounding equity, such as how we determine what amount of resources are to be directed toward achieving this goal or to what degree affirmative action will be utilized. The point that Harris and Kendall emphasize at this juncture is that the superintendent is the central figure in creating solutions to these problems.

Throughout this work, Harris and Kendall lay an aggressive foundation that is supported with a detailed framework of tasks that are to be enacted by the superintendent. According to these authors, "The superintendency ought to be the central nervous system, the intractable force for the establishment of equity in the school district."

Hugh J. Scott's contribution to this volume addresses the imperatives in higher education that must be attended to by administrators in order to facilitate more responsive and equitable environments. Within the context of higher education, Scott traces the relatively recent development of this concept and notes that the underrepresentation of minorities in all sectors of higher education and the lack of enthusiastic support for equal access and affirmative action are inextricably linked to the inequities often experienced by minorities. He continues this penetrating analysis by pointing out that there has always been a reluctance on the part of predominantly White colleges to embrace the minority experience in any form.

In his focus on imperatives for administrators, he begins by declaring that change of any type in higher education will be resisted and will come slowly. For equity to become an established condition, administrators will need to be prepared to act out their leadership commitment through effective management of conflict and meaningful translation of social events into institutional policy. Among the areas of obligatory actions and duties that Scott addresses are institutional practices and policies and their relationship to pluralism, modification of curricula to include minorities, racism in higher education, affirmative action, admissions, minority faculty, testing, and financial assistance.

Without a doubt, the authors in Part I agree that the necessary conditions for equitable educational environments, whether at the K-12 level or in higher education, will not come easily. A key to achieving fair play in education is greatly dependent on education accepting the responsibility of aggressively demonstrating its commitment to this concept through the strength of its actions. It is not that equity goes unarticulated in our institutions; it is more likely that it has not been articulated well in the institutions of education. It is not that equity goes unarticulated in the institutions in this society; rather, it is apparent that the individuals and groups responsible for the institutions have not been held accountable. It is the position of the authors of the chapters in Part I that leadership is the key to equity.

References

Austin, A. (1985). *Achieving educational excellence.* San Francisco: Jossey-Bass.
Dodson, D. (1974). Authority, power, and education. In Association for the Supervision and Curriculum Development Yearbook, *Education for an open society.* Washington, DC: Association for the Supervision and Curriculum Development Yearbook.

3

Equity and the Educational Practitioner: A Leadership Model

BARBARA A. SIZEMORE
University of Pittsburgh

Recently, concern has been expressed in many quarters regarding the academic achievement of American youth, especially in competition with international students (Wattenberg, 1989, p. 50), where American youth fare poorly in comparison. In explaining this phenomenon, a Japanese official stressed the impact of African American and minority student achievement on this poor performance. While Ravitch, in *The Troubled Crusade* (1983), notes that inequitable funding, poverty, and racism presented severe problems for public education during the years from 1945 through 1980, she also notes the following:

> The debate about standards that had been initiated as a result of the decline in SAT scores produced evidence that other standardized test scores had been dropping, beginning in about the fifth grade; that enrollments in advanced courses in mathematics and science in high school had fallen steadily since the mid-1960s; that widely-used textbooks had reduced their reading levels in order to adjust to falling verbal abilities; that homework assignments had been sharply curtailed and that grade inflation was common; that large numbers of easy or nonverbal electives had been added to the schools' curricula as substitutes for demanding courses; that writing skills had declined, at least in part because writing was not systematically emphasized as a part of learning and thinking, and because short-answer quizzes and standardized tests had gained a place alongside of, or in place of, the essay. (p. 326)

21

Therefore, American leaders needed to determine a solution not only for the achievement gap between African Americans and White Americans, but also for that between Americans and other nationals.

This chapter is devoted to the following questions: Is there a process or model and/or exemplars of the kind of leadership necessary to elevate achievement and eliminate these achievement gaps? What is the nature, style, and type of leadership that is needed for such learning environments and schools? What does this leadership look like as it works through and with practitioners to create equity in learning environments? First, an attempt will be made to define leadership and equity. Next, a brief history will be given to show how American leadership has tried in the past to solve this problem. Finally, an effort will be made to describe the leadership of educators who have closed the achievement gap in their schools and the kind of leadership that is needed to develop a national culture.

What Is a Leader?

A leader is one who shows the way, who guides and directs, or who goes in front. Heller (1988) notes that an essential ingredient is a clear sense of mission and followership, without which there is no leader. Describing leadership qualities, he cites problem-solving ability, decisiveness, and judgment as necessary, but he says that the essence of leadership is wise decision making. Whether or not decision making is wise is determined by outcomes rather than by intentions. Therefore, decision making is wise when the goals are achieved. Lastly, Heller points out that the leader must face pressures, analyze trade-offs, be aware of political implications of his or her actions, face consequences, and present the type of image deemed appropriate by followers and employers.

According to Thompson (1963), all definitions of leadership agree on at least two interrelated points:

> One, the leader is one who initiates, stimulates, coordinates and directs the activities of others, his followers, in the solution of some common problem or the achievement of some specific social (as opposed to individual) goal. And, two, those who achieve high positions, or meet with notable success in any group, are likely to be individuals who can be identified as champions of the group's basic values and who symbolize

norms that the group accepts as essential for its survival at a particular time and location, and in a given situation. (p. 3)

Additionally, a leader must have a vision of the future and must be able to develop a consensus among the members of the group. Here consensus is a means whereby all involved accept the result of the process because they have participated meaningfully in the discussion preceding the making of the decision. The idea is to motivate everyone to accept a position on which all can agree. Such leadership involves the generation of a common dialogue through a national culture.

Leadership Models and How They Developed

American leadership models have developed out of notions of reform, which has come to mean the improvement of whatever is wrong with, corrupt in, or unsatisfactory about public education. The African American struggle epitomizes the reform effort well. It has passed through four phases: entry, egress, equity, and excellence. During the entry phase the leadership waged the struggle to be accepted into public schools from two different vantage points: one for the free African Americans and the other for the slaves (Sizemore, 1986, p. 181). From 1619 through 1865, the goal was to determine whether Africans would have the right to attend public schools or have the right of access. In the South it was against the law to educate the African. In South Carolina, for example, in 1740, a law was enacted that decreed that "all and every person and persons whatsoever, who shall hereafter teach, or cause any slave or slaves to be taught to write or shall use or employ any slave as a scribe in any manner of writing whatsoever, hereafter taught to write; every such person or persons shall, for every offense, forfeit the sum of one hundred pounds current money" (Berry & Blassingame, 1982, p. 262).

For free Africans in the South during this period, whatever education was achieved came through self-effort and White philanthropy at great risks. Berry and Blassingame report that Christopher McPherson opened a school in Richmond, Virginia, in 1811 and hired a White schoolmaster who was run out of town. When McPherson continued his efforts, he was jailed and sent to the Williamsburg Lunatic Asylum. In the North, conditions varied. In Chicago, public school policy toward African American children shifted from exclusion to integration to segregation to mixed schools after 1865. Illinois allocated no public funds to educate Africans and public schools were restricted to Whites in 1835 and 1837 by law. Local ordinances of 1849 and 1851 removed the racial bar and granted all children access to the public schools. For more than ten years, Africans attended classes with Whites even though state education funds for Chicago were based solely on the city's White enrollment (Berry & Blassingame, 1982, p. 45; Herrick, 1971, pp. 24, 400; Homel, 1984, p. 1; Sizemore, 1986, p. 182). Free Africans lived a precarious existence where rights were unclear (Sizemore, 1986, p. 181).

In the mid-nineteenth century, free Africans were forming self-help groups in the North. Martin R. Delaney, John Vashon, and Lewis Woodson formed the African Education Society in 1832 in Pittsburgh. Their school was located in a church. It moved around for several years before African children were accepted into the ward schools. Usually, African Americans demanded integrated schools for their children if and when they were admitted. Benjamin Roberts sued in court because his daughter, Sarah, was excluded from attending the neighborhood school and forced to walk a distance to the segregated school in 1849 in Boston. Although he lost this case, abolitionists petitioned the state legislature, which ended separate schools throughout the state in 1855 (Berry & Blassingame, 1982, p. 46; Franklin, 1947, pp. 160-161). Mostly, free Africans acquired their education after overcoming many adversities and hurdling numerous obstacles. When their children were mistreated in public schools, they dropped out. Often, they sent their children to private schools.

During the First Reconstruction Period, 1865-1876, the Freedmen's Bureau, White philanthropy, and self-efforts established African American schools throughout the South. Southern public schools were a direct result of Reconstruction governments and legislation. According to Du Bois (1935), the first great mass movement for public education at the expense of the state in the South came from Negroes (p. 641). Berry and Blassingame (1982) report that there were 79 northern aid societies supporting African schools in the South by 1869, and by 1870 4,239 schools with 9,300 teachers and 247,000 pupils had been established by the Freedmen's Bureau (p. 262).

The firm belief that African education would upset White supremacy resulted in a strong White backlash. By the 1870s, an agreement had been reached concerning the kind of education considered acceptable to prepare African Americans for their subservient place in the segregated socioeconomic mainstream created by Hayes's betrayal and removal of the military from the six districts in the South (Anderson, 1988, p. 23). Soon after the Civil War, African Americans began establishing their own institutions of higher education. While African Americans adopted the classical liberal arts curriculum as the kind that would prepare their leadership, the southern Whites chose the Hampton Institute model created by Samuel Chapman Armstrong and promoted by his star pupil, Booker T. Washington.

According to Anderson (1988), the newly freed Africans struggled to acquire an education that would be appropriate for the defense of their recently won civil and political rights and one that challenged the social power of the returning southern planters. On the other hand, Anderson says that Armstrong "developed a pedagogy and ideology designed to avoid such confrontations and to maintain within the South a social consensus that did not challenge traditional inequalities of wealth and power" (p. 33). The debate over these two ideologies continued for over 50 years, until Hampton and Tuskegee changed their curricula to conform more generally with the African American ideal (p. 33).

According to Anderson (1988), Armstrong advocated "the removal of African American people from any effective role in southern politics; wrote about the immorality and irresponsibility of African American voters; excoriated African American politicians and labeled the freedmen's enfranchisement as dangerous to the South and the nation" (p. 37). His curriculum, and, later Washington's at Tuskegee, employed a manual labor routine and an ideology of self-help as the foundation of the teacher training process. The primary goal was to "work the prospective teachers long and hard so that they would embody, accept and preach an ethic of hard toil or the dignity of labor."

Morality rather than intelligence was the basis for admission to the Institute. Anderson (1988) comments upon this curriculum:

> The students with good labor records were thought the best potential exponents of the Hampton Idea. Vice-Principal H. B. Frissell, after visiting Hampton graduates in the field, reported in 1885 "that very frequently the dull plodder at Hampton is the real leader of his people toward better things, while the bright scholar who was our pride and delight at school, because of his mental acuteness, either yields to temptation or leaves school work for the more tempting offers of clerkships or political appointments." Similarly, Armstrong argued that "the plodding ones make good teachers." (p. 49)

African Americans, however, chose the New England classical liberal curriculum for their post-Civil War elementary, normal, and collegiate schools, and what they taught there did not differ too much from what was taught in northern White schools. They saw this education providing them with the best intellectual traditions of their time and the best means of understanding their own historical development and sociological essence (Anderson, 1988, pp. 28-29). Therefore, in 1868, when Du Bois was born, the die had been cast for his future debate.

Du Bois believed in the New England education that he had received. His vision for the future was a "Talented Tenth": the African American leadership group that would direct and guide the African into the socioeconomic mainstream of American life on an equal basis. He did not believe that the African could protect an economic gain without political, civil, and social rights; therefore, he disagreed with Washington's Hampton model. Du Bois wanted the classical liberal arts model:

> I believed in the higher education of the Talented Tenth, who through their knowledge of modern culture could guide the American Negro into higher civilization. I knew that without this the Negro would have to accept white leadership, and that such leadership could not always be trusted to guide this group into self-realization and to its highest cultural possibilities. (Du Bois, 1940, p. 70)

Yet this education received by the Talented Tenth at all colleges was questioned, especially by Carter G. Woodson in 1932:

> The so called modern education, with all its defects, however, does others so much more good than it does the Negro, because it has been worked out in conformity to the needs of those who enslaved and oppressed weaker peoples. For example, the philosophy and ethics resulting from our educational system have justified slavery, peonage, segregation and lynching. The oppressor has the right to exploit, to handicap, and to kill the oppressed. Negroes daily educated in the tenets of such a religion of the strong have accepted the status of the weak as divinely ordained, and during the last three generations of their nominal freedom they have done practically nothing to change it. (p. xxxii)

Woodson argued for an education based on the careful study of the Negro himself and the life that he is forced to lead in order to teach him to think and do for himself (p. xxx).

During the First Jim Crow Period, 1876-1954, dual, separate but unequal, school systems proliferated throughout the country. Berry and Blassingame (1982) state that southern Whites wanted to limit African American education to elementary schools where the chief focus was on industrial education, teaching trades, and manual skills. These African American schools were organized around the labor needs of southern planters and consequently closed during planting and harvesting times (pp. 264-265).

As a result, African American public schools in the South never developed educational quality. Berry and Blassingame (1982) point out that native-born Whites were placed in charge of these schools and that the funding for them was drastically reduced in the 1880s (pp. 264-265). Egress (exit out of subservient roles and into teaching) was achieved in the South and in some northern states such as Indiana and Ohio, where separate schools existed. African American teachers were expected to teach African Americans in the South, but not so everywhere in the North, although places differed. In Pittsburgh no African American teachers were hired between 1867 and 1933. Applicants were told to go South to look for teaching jobs. Little progress could be made because the African American community was divided on the strategy to be used to attain this goal.

The Pittsburgh School Board did consider hiring African American teachers for the Watt Street School (later renamed Robert L. Vann School) early in the twentieth century, but a part of the African American community could not agree to such a segregated approach, so no one was hired. In Philadelphia, however, the school board segregated African Americans, forming a dual school system that hired African American teachers and principals, but for the segregated schools only (Sizemore, 1986, p. 186). Throughout the nation, African American leadership agitated for access to jobs, positions, and resources within public schools and for equal facilities and treatment in them. African American protest of White control of African American institutions reached its peak in the 1920s. This agitation for African American leadership of these institutions was rewarded with Mordecai Johnson's elevation to the position of president of Howard University in 1926.

Nearly a decade later, in 1935, Homer A. Brown, state legislator, was the first African American board member appointed to the Pittsburgh Board of Education by the 15 judges of the Court of Common Pleas; John P. Turner, a medical doctor, was appointed by the same process as a member of the Philadelphia Board of Education in the same year, after 7 years of active lobbying. After more than 30 years of lobbying, in 1938, Midian O. Bousfield was the first African American appointed to the Chicago Board of Education by the mayor. For the most part, African American board members fought for access to jobs, positions, and resources. In Pittsburgh, Brown, while a state legislator, created a committee to investigate the hiring practices of the Pittsburgh School Board. Turner agitated for the school board to end its policy of segregating African American teachers in the Philadelphia system, and it did (Franklin, 1979, p. 122; Sizemore, 1986, p. 188). On the other hand, Bousfield had a dismal record of defending the race and advancing its interests (Homel, 1984, pp. 163-164; Sizemore, 1986, p. 188). Bousfield, an integrationist, identified with the school administration rather than with the constituency that he was expected to represent.

These contradictory positions concerning the goal of integration and the need for separatist institutions to attain it, especially the Black college, have survived down to the present day, completely confounding the problem of equity, which is fairness and justice, a condition where no one is favored over others. First, because there is no consensus among the White majority regarding full citizenship rights for African Americans, there has been little support for funding their education from 1619 until the present. Whites have continually been favored, and, as a consequence, African Americans have had little success in achieving their goals in either integrated or segregated settings; however, in the latter they have had more control and the outcomes have been more dependable, if not always utilitarian.

Because the National Association for the Advancement of Colored People (NAACP) saw integration as the solution to the problem of African American inequality, anything all-African was anathema. The NAACP's vision called for the elimination of all segregated institutions. But did this include the Black church? The Black college? The Black family? Here was the crux of the problem. Without resolving this dilemma, the NAACP concentrated on graduate and professional education in the South first – because most southern states did not provide such training for African Americans, and this was prima facie evidence that the facilities were not equal. Cases seeking the elimination of segregation in institutions of higher education in the South began with Donald Murray, who integrated the University of Maryland Law School in 1935, and Lloyd Gaines at the University of Missouri Law School in 1938 (Sizemore, 1986, p. 188).

Before these cases were won, Du Bois had left the NAACP because of a dispute over the proper course to follow to achieve the social rights of African Americans. Du Bois felt that the NAACP did not have an economic self-help program for the relief of poverty among African Americans. In 1934, Du Bois had come full circle to support part of the Washington plan for African American success. He criticized the NAACP program in this way:

> This program of organized opposition to the action and attitude of the dominant white group, includes ceaseless agitation and insistent demand for equality: the equal right to work, civic and political equality, and social equality. It involves the use of force of every sort: moral suasion, propaganda and where possible even physical resistance. . . .

> There are, however, manifest difficulties about such a program. First of all it is not a program that envisages any direct action of Negroes themselves for the uplift of their socially depressed masses; in the very conception of the program, such work is to be attended to by the nation and Negroes are to be the subjects of uplift forces and agencies to the extent of their numbers and need. (Du Bois, 1940, pp. 192-193)

Thus in 1940 Du Bois was arguing self-help.

> It is not then the theory but a fact that faces the Negro in education. He has group education in large proportion and he must organize and plan these segregated schools so that they become efficient, well-housed, well-equipped, with the best of teachers and with the best results on the children so that the illiteracy and bad manners and criminal tendencies of young Negroes can be quickly and effectively reduced. Most Negroes would prefer a good school with properly paid colored teachers for educating their children, to forcing their children into white schools which met them with injustice and humiliation and discouraged their efforts to progress. (p. 201)

Du Bois summed up his theoretical position in this way:

> The Negro needs neither segregated schools nor mixed schools. What he needs is Education. What he must remember is that there is no magic, either in mixed schools or in segregated schools. A mixed school with poor and unsympathetic teachers, with hostile public opinion, and no teaching of truth concerning black folk, is bad. A segregated school with ignorant placeholders, inadequate equipment, poor salaries, and wretched housing is equally bad. (quoted in Cruse, 1987, pp. 193-194)

The Emergence of Black Power
and Community Control

Neither Martin Luther King, Jr., nor any other civil rights leaders were able to resolve this massive contradiction: the desire for integration and, at the same time, the retention of African American institutions — the Black church, the Black family, and the Black college. The White backlash against busing closed the schools in Prince Edward County, Virginia, and generated the White Academy, which resegregated the public school system there. In cities like Washington, D.C., Baltimore, Richmond, and Newark, Whites fled the public schools, leaving them majority African American; Eisenhower sent troops to protect African Americans trying to integrate Central High School in Little Rock, Arkansas. While desegregation occurred without such fanfare in many places, "deliberate speed" generally meant not at all.

At this point the Black power movement exploded on the African American scene, and the demand for community control was generated by this movement. What African Americans said in actuality was this: If the schools cannot be desegregated, then give us the power to make the policy decisions that will affect the life chances of our children. The most widely known experiment was Ocean Hill-Brownsville in Brooklyn, New York. When the board and superintendent tried to fire 19 teachers for incompetence, the United Federation of Teachers struck the schools in 1968. At that point community control ended for all practical purposes, although the Adams-Morgan School and the Anacostia Community Schools in Washington, D.C., and the Woodlawn Experimental Schools Project in Chicago continued until the mid-1970s (Sizemore, 1981, pp. 44-49).

Essentially, advocates of community control were saying that African American students can learn if someone will put in place the policies and practices that will teach them the things they need to know. What the teachers' strike taught these advocates was the political nature of the answer. Even though we did know what was necessary to teach these children, teachers and principals would have to be *made* to do it with *power*. What was further evident at that time was that *Black power* could not accomplish this in New York City.

Although Washington, D.C., is a colony where the laws are made by residents elected to political office, these laws can be vetoed by the U.S. Congress and/or the president within 30 days. Although the citizens of the District can vote for the president, they do not vote for the members of Congress and their nonvoting delegate votes only in committee. Yet, the two budget committees of the House and Senate determine how the citizens will spend their own tax monies. In the District, there is taxation without representation and the government is *not* of, by, or for the people.

It was here that two of the most important community control experiments were executed. Here, unlike in New York City, the largely African American union supported the projects. Yet, here as well as in Chicago, little progress was made in eliminating the achievement gap between African American and White students. In Chicago, one glaring reason was the emphasis placed on jobs instead of student achievement. In all of these community control efforts, career ladders were formed for professional aides to become teachers and for community organizers and similar types to work in the schools as ancillary service workers and researchers. Title I programs, Office of Economic Opportunity projects, and Head Start mandated parental and/or community involvement and greatly expanded this role in the school. Additionally, teachers and principals were often the choices of the board members and the system was used for patronage.

In Washington, D.C., the Board of Education and the superintendent argued over the way the community would be involved in the decentralization of that school system. In this case, the paternalist board faction wanted to control the selection of community leaders, while the superintendent and the populist faction of the board wanted the community to do so. Congress had no intention of funding either of these approaches, so the superintendent finally decentralized by administrative fiat without funding and incurred the board's wrath, even though she had been hired to do just that. However, in neither of these options was student achievement the overriding goal; the paternalist faction was committed to educational alternatives in the private domain. Control and power were the issues (Arnez, 1981, pp. 101-102; Sizemore, 1981, pp. 353-423).

The African American Superintendent as a Model of Leadership

It was during this time that the African American superintendent flourished in public schools. Moody (1971, p. 3; Sizemore, 1986, p. 189) was the first to study the African American superintendent in depth. He

saw the emergence of this administrator as an outgrowth of the desegregation struggle. Moody (1971), Jones (1985), and Scott (1980) agree
that the increase in African American superintendencies was due, in
part, to the appointment of many African Americans to urban school
systems with high percentages of minority students. Moreover, Scott,
the first African American superintendent in the Washington, D.C.,
schools, predicted that there would be an increase in the number of
African American superintendencies in school districts with high minority populations because of critical financial conditions and educational problems accrued through years of neglect and deprivation.

The emergence of the African American superintendent can be viewed
as another stage in the long struggle for equity and excellence in public
schools (Sizemore, 1986, p. 189). In earlier work, I have commented
regarding the importance of the struggle up to this date:

> Schools are resources, and power is the central core concept in politics.
> If politics is a management of the conflict that occurs when groups war
> over scarce resources, African Americans need to do two things for more
> effective struggle: (1) develop some kind of consensus on what kind of
> education is desirable for African American youngsters — industrial or
> liberal arts, desegregated or segregated, Afrocentric (as advocated by
> Woodson) or Eurocentric; and (2) use this consensus in a more effective
> way to gain power over the governing structure of public schools.
>
> Ocean-Hill Brownsville taught the importance of union power and the
> problem that existed when another ethnic group controlled the teaching
> process even though the governing structure was in the hands of African
> Americans. Adams-Morgan and Anacostia taught the lesson of colonial-
> ism. When the decision-making structure is controlled by another legisla-
> tive body, lines of influence become more powerful decision-making
> mechanisms than the legal structures created for this purpose (Arnez,
> 1981; Sizemore, 1981). The Woodlawn Experimental Schools District's
> outcomes taught the powerful interrelationship and conflict between
> African Americans who wanted jobs and positions in the public schools
> and those who sought student outcomes (i.e., the elevation of student
> achievement and the improvement of student discipline). Power in public
> schools is vested in the school board.
>
> It is also practiced by the superintendent and the unions. To determine
> decision-making, control over these entities is necessary, although not
> sufficient as Washington D.C. certainly instructs (Arnez, 1981, pp. 649-
> 656). (Sizemore, 1986, p. 190)

As Scott (1980) predicted, the lack of financial support and resistance to change contributed the most obdurate obstacles to the success of African American superintendents:

> In urban school districts with a high concentration of disadvantaged students, school officials and other school personnel will not have the resources to improve the quality of life and the level of academic achievement without more assistance from other essential service institutions.
>
> Significant increases in the number of black superintendents will reflect continued societal deterioration and increased racial isolation rather than decisions by school boards to comply with the principle of equal employment opportunity. (p. 184)

Furthermore, while Scott concludes that the inadequacies of socioeconomic support, not poor instructional and related services, put high numbers of Black students in the low percentiles on reading and mathematics achievement tests (p. 185), Ron Edmonds (1979) argues that, in fact, poor instruction does indeed contribute to low achievement. During the 1980s the effective schools movement caught fire as a result of Edmonds's research, reignited the community control flames of discontent, and continued the reform movement.

Du Bois, Washington, and Carter G. Woodson provided leadership models for educators who were convinced that all children could learn and that whether or not a school is racially isolated should not determine the academic achievement of the student body attending. In a way this was a continuation of the progressive education movement, although segregated education seldom reflected Dewey's theories, which rejected the lockstep system, uniform curriculum, and stress on passive learning and rote memorization and drill found in public schools in the nineteenth and twentieth centuries (Ravitch, 1983, p. 47). Ravitch (1983) notes that

> teachers in a progressive school had to be extraordinarily talented and well educated; they needed both a perceptive understanding of children and a wide knowledge of the disciplines in order to recognize when the child was ready to move through an experience to a new understanding, be it in history or science or mathematics or the arts. (p. 47)

Even though the *Cardinal Principles of Secondary Education* (U.S. Bureau of Education, 1918) promoted pedagogical progressivism in the organized education profession, according to Ravitch, this did not permeate African American education since there were very few high schools available for African Americans at that time. As a model, progressivism failed to "assert leadership on the already explosive racial issue and remained blind to the social implications of their separation of children into academic, general and vocational curricula" (p. 78). Inequality persisted and equity became the prerequisite of excellence.

The Effective Schools Leadership Model

In the struggle for excellence, a reform model for leadership is the effective schools movement. Fredericksen and Edmonds (1978) classify ineffective schools as general, having effects regardless of race and class, and as discriminatory, having effects because of race and class. But effective schools are only general. Their research does not include discriminatory effective schools, those that perform well because effective leadership could make them do so for poor African American students (Sizemore, 1985, p. 275).

Weber (1971) illustrates his concept of "strong leadership" with a principal who was instrumental in setting the tone of the school, helping with decision making on instructional strategies, and organizing and distributing the school's resources. Edmonds has said that strong administrative leadership is indispensable in effective schools to hold the disparate elements of good schools together.

A review of the effective schools literature reveals the following leadership model:

> Mackenzie lists three dimensions of effective schooling found in the research: leadership, efficacy and efficiency. Under each dimension are listed core and facilitating elements. Under leadership core elements are: positive climate and overall atmosphere, goal-focused activities toward clear attainable and relevant objectives, teacher-directed classroom management and decision-making and inservice staff training for effective teaching. Facilitating elements are: shared consensus on values and goals, long range planning and coordination, stability and continuity of key staff and district level support for school improvement. (Sizemore, 1985, p. 276)

In my study of effective African American elementary schools, I found that leadership was the most important factor in the creation of these high-achieving, predominantly African American schools. This model can be replicated in all schools to improve academic achievement. First, the principals were convinced that all children could learn and that African American children, in particular, could learn. School actors were influenced to adopt cause-belief statements that attributed African American low achievement to ineffective school routines and practices and not to African American families, culture, or communities. Consensus was developed around high achievement as the highest priority in the school, and routines that would guarantee success were carefully implemented.

Schools leaders had high expectations for students and teachers and acted on these beliefs. They often counteracted decisions that had been made by their superiors regarding goals, instruction, curriculum, coordination, and control that they considered counterproductive. Sometimes they worked within constraints and sometimes they simply ignored them. They believed that school systems should be effective and devoted to the mission of educating all children; therefore, African American life, history, and culture were integrated into the regular curriculum. Moreover, these principals felt strongly that they could make a difference in the lives of their students. They were intensely self-reliant.

Principals in high-achieving African American public elementary schools were willing to take risks to accomplish their goal, high achievement for African American students. One of these risks was choosing routines, scenarios, and processes that differed from those of the system. Such a routine was the refusal to accept incompetent or uncredentialed teachers assigned to their schools by the Department of Personnel in the school system's central office. Another was the willingness to evaluate teachers as unsatisfactory in spite of the system's hostility to such practices because of union opposition and contracts. Another was the development of consensus around high achievement as the highest priority goal in the school.

Once the high-achieving African American school was in place, it became an abashing anomaly, raising questions about low-achieving African American schools. Because they did not cooperate with routines that produced low-achieving African American schools, principals of high-achieving African American public schools tended to cause problems in the system by raising these questions. Since the system strove to preserve a steady state, any actor who disturbed it was not a team player and was considered a troublemaker. This label impeded recommendations for promotion within the system; therefore, most of these principals had resigned themselves to remaining in their present positions long before my study commenced.

These leaders developed routines that improved the quality of the teaching force by constant and continuous staff development, which was implemented to assist teachers in the improvement of instruction. Principals monitored teacher and student performance regularly to be certain that the routines necessary for the acceleration of growth and the elevation of academic achievement were in place. Achievement was measured to determine whether or not goals were met.

These principals had clear discipline routines and supervised the implementation of those routines themselves. They did not pass the buck. Clearly in charge in their schools, they viewed themselves as moderately authoritarian. Students and parents knew what to expect. Discipline was administered consistently and fairly. Parents, students, and teachers were involved in the resolution of severe discipline problems, but the principal was by far the most important factor.

In the study of African American effective schools, structure is important. The leader assumes responsibility for establishing an environment conducive to learning. There is rigorous supervision of both student and teacher performance and the principal makes daily visits to the classrooms. There is consistent monitoring of students' academic progress and the supervision of instruction is directed toward the mastery of these skills. Conferences are held to discuss the pacing routines necessary to put students who are far behind back on schedule. Measurement routines provide feedback data to teachers on a regular basis so that they can determine whether or not they are successful in reaching their goals.

Principals and teachers select teaching strategies and materials on the basis of a fit between the content and the students' needs. For example, in one school, the basic text that was being used did not fit. The African American children needed more phonics in their instructional program, according to the teachers' diagnosis. The principal of this school requested the right to deviate from the system's prescription to experiment with a text with more phonics material in it. When the phonics approach appeared successful, the system changed to a phonics text.

Teachers' ideas and knowledge are respected in high-achieving schools, but my research did not support a widespread desire among teachers for inclusion in all decision making. Teachers in high-achieving African American schools want to be consulted, to be able to disagree, to have their views respected and seriously considered, and to be able to participate in decision making; but the matters that are of greatest concern to them are student discipline and classroom pedagogy. Teachers in these studies wanted the principal to be in charge of student discipline and parental conflict. In exchange for this action, teachers were willing to give the principal the authority to monitor their teaching.

There are routines for parental involvement in high-achieving African American elementary schools, but when this does not or cannot occur, school actors assume these responsibilities. The fact that a student's parent may be imprisoned, chemically dependent, or indifferent does not prevent him or her from achieving (Sizemore, 1988).

School board leadership is an important variable and proved effective in one city. In 1978, there were only two African American members on this board. One of them voted most of the time with the White conservative majority. The other was usually in the minority in an 8 to 1 vote. Frustrated by this continual disregard for the best interests of his community, the minority board member took his case to the people and exposed the other African American member, who was defeated in the next election. Then there were two. These two worked together to recapture a seat lost to a White conservative because of voter apathy and disinterest. Then there were three. These three then united with the two White liberals on the board and progress began. The superintendent was fired and a new superintendent was selected, after which the elimination of the achievement gap was voted as the highest priority of this school system. During this period the African American who had provided the leadership for these accomplishments was elected president of the Board of Education and served as such for five years.

A division in the African American community occurred during this time much like that of Du Bois's and Washington's time. The middle-class African American faction supported the retention of some African Americans in jobs even though they were not effectively working for the elevation of achievement. Others wanted competence as well as race. They felt that these people should have to perform in order to keep their positions. On one occasion, an African American principal who had served in a low-achieving school for 13 years was demoted. In his defense, one African American supervisor said, "But I feel he was treated unfairly. The White assistant superintendent should have helped him to improve his work." African American school board members saw it differently. They said that any African American who needs to have a White person tell him how and when to do his job educating African American children is in deep trouble. These men on the school board formed a majority that generated a school improvement program designed to assist schools in the institutionalization of the routines necessary for goal accomplishment. By making African American student achievement the highest priority of the school system, they made it possible for principals who wanted to create high-achieving schools to do so without penalty. Since the education of African American children is so political and subversive, African Americans face an uphill battle, fighting against school systems and against segments of their own community. This takes a special kind of leadership, one that can persist and proceed without rewards and recognition (Sizemore, 1987, 1988).

Professors as Practitioners of Equity

In higher education, the African American professor is often called on to serve as counselor, special friend, tutor, and surrogate parent to African American students, especially in White universities. They, too, make a sacrifice, because teaching is not what results in getting tenure in the large university setting. Serving students takes time away from research and publications, which are what really count.

At the same time African American professors are trying to meet their scholarly obligations, they are moved to serve the larger African American community through fighting against racism, sexism, and poverty. In the African American colleges they studied in 1964, Gurin and Epps (1975) found the students highly motivated for individual achievement, persistent in finishing college, desirous of advanced education beyond the baccalaureate, ready to work and borrow to further their education, and committed to professional careers. They did not see any evidence of rising individual aspirations and expectations during the period of the mid- to late 1960s, but did see an effect on students' collective commitments, and often they saw a marriage of individual achievement and collective commitment. According to Gurin and Epps (1975):

> The major way in which activists differed academically from other students was in their relationships with faculty. Activists repeatedly reported more outside contact with faculty members. This contact was not exclusively political. At the college we studied intensively for four years, more of the activists not only reported contact with more faculty members and more often listed a faculty person as one of their friends but also

reported as seniors that they had gone to a faculty member to talk about their futures and to get help with graduate school or job planning. (p. 334)

This condition often characterizes departments and programs of Black studies, where the mission is to define, defend, and advance the interests of the African on the continent, in the diaspora, and in the United States. In these departments and programs, the multidisciplinary academic effort is often tarred with an image of inferiority. Students want to know, "What can I do with Black studies?" as though they can do anything more with sociology. Moreover, athletes and marginal students often are counseled to take Black studies for an "easy A."

Black studies professors then must tutor and provide extra services for these students in order for them to be successful. One professor has study groups for students who are failing weekly quizzes that are given to determine whether or not they are doing the work and understanding the concepts and facts. Another has weekly conferences with students who are not in good standing with the university. Generally, the achievement of African American students depends on the interest and willingness of educators to teach them.

University officers often have responsibilities for fighting the effects of racism on the campus. At one university the African American assistant to the provost must frequently find money and/or jobs for students who run out of funds in the middle of the year. In recent months, overt acts of racism against African American students and faculty have occurred. Addressing these acts has become an increasingly heavy burden on African American university faculty and officials, especially when the university fails to act expeditiously against the perpetrators of such offenses.

Lessons Learned from Leadership Models

In describing the condition of education after World War II, Ravitch (1983) says:

The essence of racism was the belief that differences in skin color represented real and substantial differences among people; that "whites" and "Negroes" were essentially different kinds of people; and that people who were "Negro" or "white" should be dealt with by the state as group members rather than as individuals. To give legal meaning to racism, southern state laws contained various definitions of "Negro" such as

Arkansas' declaration that a Negro is "any person who has in his or her veins any Negro blood whatever," or Alabama's explanation that "the word 'mulatto' or term 'person of color' means a person of mixed blood descended in part of the father or mother from Negro ancestors, without reference to or limit of time or number of generations removed." Black people were at the bottom of a system that was designed to keep them there, and the prospect of upending this system must have seemed as unlikely as a summer snowstorm in Mississippi. (pp. 115-116)

For the most part, in 1989 African Americans are still at the bottom. Du Bois said that the problem of the twentieth century is the problem of the color line. It will continue to be so in the twenty-first century unless we change what we teach our students. Leadership for efforts to integrate the diverse cultures of our country into a national curriculum is now imperative. Once again this leadership must face national resistance from groups that the curriculum now exalts at the expense of other groups. Because the U.S. Constitution does not protect group rights, groups such as the Democratic and Republican parties must be organized to so do.

For African Americans and other visible minorities, the political parties do not always afford them equal participation. Cruse (1987) describes this dilemma:

The United States is racially, ethnically and culturally a plural society. The legal and judicial problem is that the American Constitution was never conceived, written, amended or otherwise interpreted either to reflect, accommodate or otherwise acknowledge the pluralistic composition of American society. . . .

If the Bill of Rights, the 14th and 19th Amendments are not sufficient guarantees for the full economic, political, and social equality of women as women, then neither are the 14th and 15th Amendments and their judicial reinforcements, sufficient guarantees for the full economic, political and cultural equality of nonwhite minorities. (pp. 38, 67)

Cruse argues, therefore, that the social determinant of leadership for African Americans is that it must make its followers more conscious of their innate potential. Quoting another theorist, Cruse says, "It does not dictate; rather it engages the fundamental needs and wants, aspirations and expectations of the followers" (p. 209). This leadership must help the group internally organize the African American infrastructure of economic, cultural, political, social welfare, educational, and self-help efforts to broaden the range and effectiveness of the new African American political leadership (p. 201).

Nationally, an integrated American leadership must change the curriculum so that the national culture is more diverse and includes the events, issues, and contributions of all ethnic and racial groups. In 1967 Cruse noted that the most crucial requirement for the American society was a complete democratization of the national cultural ethos. Banks (1981) calls for such reforms also in his book, *Multiethnic Education.* He says that an ethnic group is an involuntary cultural group with several distinguishing characteristics: It shares a common ancestry, culture, history, tradition, and sense of peoplehood, and is a political and economic interest group (p. 53). He calls for curriculum reform that incorporates ethnic content into the mainstream curriculum that is experienced by all students (p. 57), and says, "We need to redefine what the common culture actually is and make sure that our new conceptualization reflects the social realities within this nation and that it is not a mythical and idealized view of American life and culture."

Our present Eurocentric curriculum promotes White European supremacy, male superiority, and the superiority of the wealthy — our institutional values — through omissions, distortions, and half-truths. Leadership is needed to construct a national culture that is the whole body of efforts made by all of the people in the sphere of thought to describe, justify, and praise the action through which those people have created themselves and keep themselves in existence (Fanon, 1963). As Cruse (1967) put it more than 20 years ago:

> As long as the Negro's cultural identity is in question, or open to self-doubts, then there can be no positive identification with the real demands of his political and economic existence. Further than that, without a cultural identity that adequately defines himself, the Negro cannot even identify with the American nation as a whole. He is left in the limbo of social marginality, alienated and directionless on the landscape of America, in a variegated nation of whites who have not yet decided on their own identity. The fact of the matter is that American whites, as a whole, are just as much in doubt about their nationality, their cultural identity, as are Negroes. Thus the problem of Negro cultural identity is an unsolved problem within the context of an American nation that is still in process of formation. (pp. 12-13)

For the practitioner, leadership must appear at all levels of education, for inadequate leadership at any level affects the work at all others.

If equity is to be achieved in the American socioeconomic main-stream, a two-tiered model of leadership is required. On the one hand, national educational leaders must strive for a curriculum that is plural but equal. The struggle for survival and liberation of all racial, ethnic, and religious groups must be represented in terms of their contribu-tions: issues, important events, heroes and heroines. An admission must be made about the centrality of Africa to civilization and the humaniza-tion of homo sapiens. There must be no more lies, omissions, distor-tions, and fantasy. On the other hand, minority leadership must rise to the occasion to construct self-help organizations and institutions that uplift the group. Cruse (1987) puts it this way:

> No matter how competing political, economic, educational, and minority establishments care to interpret the meaning of traditions, history, and constitutional legality, the United States still has a rendezvous with both the past and the future of its destiny as a nation. In the future context, the blacks must struggle to save themselves because allies are not promised. In organizing to save themselves, any political allegiance blacks would consider extending to other minorities would have to be purely condition-al. Despite the false promises of the most recent civil rights cycle of the Sixties and Seventies, American blacks still represent the most crucial minority group, the most strategically positioned to impact on the institu-tional structures of the total society. What is lacking is the quality of black leadership capable of harnessing black potential. (p. 391)

This model so aptly described by Cruse is the same as that prescribed so long ago by Washington, Du Bois, and Woodson. To achieve equity it should be implemented. Equity and excellence are the two sides of the coin of leadership in American education.

References

Anderson, J. D. (1988).*The education of Blacks in the South 1860-1935.* Chapel Hill: University of North Carolina Press.

Arnez, N. L. (1981). *The besieged school superintendent: A case study of school super-intendent-school board relations in Washington, D.C., 1973-1975.* Lanham, MD: University Press of America.

Banks, J. A. (1981). *Multiethnic education: Theory and practice.* Boston: Allyn & Bacon.

Berry, M. F., & Blassingame, J. W. (1982). *Long memory: The Black experience in America.* New York: Oxford University Press.

Cruse, H. W. (1967). *The crisis of the Negro intellectual: From its origins to the present.* New York: William Morrow.

Cruse, H. W. (1987). *Plural but equal: A critical study of Blacks and minorities and America's plural society.* New York: William Morrow.

Du Bois, W.E.B. (1935). *Black reconstruction: An essay toward a history of the part which Black folk played in the attempt to reconstruct democracy in America, 1860-1880.* New York: Harcourt, Brace.

Du Bois, W.E.B. (1940). *Dusk at dawn: An essay toward an autobiography of a race concept.* New York: Schocken.

Edmonds, R. R. (1979, March-April). Some schools work and more can. *Social Policy, 9,* 28-32.

Fanon, F. (1963). *Wretched of the earth.* New York: Grove.

Franklin, J. H. (1947). *From slavery to freedom: A history of Negro Americans.* New York: Alfred A. Knopf.

Franklin, V. P. (1979). *The education of Black Philadelphia.* State College: Pennsylvania State University Press.

Fredericksen, J. R., & Edmonds, R. R. (1978). *Search for effective schools: The identification and analysis of city schools that are instructionally effective for poor children.* Unpublished manuscript, New York City Public Schools. Office of Educational Evaluation.

Gurin, P., & Epps, E. (1975). *Black consciousness, identity and achievement: A study of students in historically Black colleges.* New York: John Wiley.

Heller, M. (1988). Leadership. In R. A. Groton, G. T. Schneider, & J. C. Fisher (Eds.), *Encyclopedia of school administration and supervision.* Phoenix, AZ. Oryx.

Herrick, M. J. (1971). *The Chicago schools: A social and political history.* Beverly Hills, CA: Sage.

Homel, M. W. (1984). *Down from equality: Black Chicagoans and the public schools, 1920-1941.* Urbana: University of Illinois Press.

Jones, E. (1985). A survey of the problems and characteristics of school districts administered by Black superintendents (Doctoral dissertation, George Washington University, 1985). *Dissertation Abstracts International, 46,* 35.

Mackenzie, D. E. (1983). Research for school improvement: An appraisal of some recent trends. *Educational Researcher, 12,* 8.

Moody, C. D. (1971). Black superintendents in public school districts: Trends and conditions (Doctoral dissertation, Northwestern University, 1971). *Dissertation Abstracts International, 32,* 2965A.

Ravitch. D. (1983). *The troubled crusade: American education 1945-1960.* New York: Basic Books.

Scott, H. J. (1980). *The Black superintendent: Messiah or scapegoat?* Washington, DC: Howard University Press.

Sizemore, B. A. (1981). *The ruptured diamond: The politics of the decentralization of the District of Columbia Public Schools.* Lanham, MD: University Press of America.

Sizemore, B. A. (1985). The pitfalls and promises of effective schools research. *Journal of Negro Education, 54*(3), 269-288.

Sizemore, B. A. (1986). The limits of the Black superintendency: A review of the literature. *Journal of Educational Equity and Leadership, 6*(3), 180-208.

Sizemore, B. A. (1987). The effective African American elementary school. In G. W. Noblit & W. T. Pink (Eds.), *Schooling in social context: Qualitative studies* (pp. 175-202). Norwood, NJ: Ablex.

Sizemore, B. A. (1988). The Madison school: A turnaround case. *Journal of Negro Education, 57*(3), 243-266.

Thompson, D. C. (1963). *The Negro leadership class.* Englewood Cliffs, NJ: Prentice-Hall.

U.S. Bureau of Education. (1918). *Cardinal principles of secondary education: A report of the Commission on the Reorganization of Secondary Education* (commission appointed by the National Education Association). Washington, DC: Government Printing Office.

Wattenberg, B. J. (1989, March 20). Is education as bad as ever? *U.S. News & World Report*, p. 50.

Weber, G. (1971). *Inner city children can be taught to read: Four successful schools* (Occasional Paper No. 18). Washington, DC: Council for Basic Education.

Woodson, C. G. (1932). *The miseducation of the Negro.* Washington, DC: Associated.

4

Facilitating Equity
Through the School Superintendency

J. JEROME HARRIS
MAE A. KENDALL

Atlanta Public Schools

It is curious that so vital a word as *equity*, so frequently invoked, still eludes the understanding and commitment to daily duty of institutionalized educational practitioners. The fact is that if educational justice for our nation's children of African American heritage is to become the dream realized, the quest must become relentless. Those at the nerve center, those designing the battle plan, must be guided by dedicated leaders — more specifically, by dedicated superintendents. Recognition of the superintendent role as key suggests that there must be symbiotic relationships among the expressed mission, the functional mission, and the daily behavior of the superintendent. This person must not only give lip service, but must be willing to become the embodiment of, and act upon, the belief that all children can learn and will learn in an environment where the landscape has been so arranged as to disturb the inertia of indifferent traditionalism.

Accordingly, in pursuit of equity and excellence for every child, the school superintendent must be willing and prepared to make sweeping changes in educational directions within the local school district. Translated, this posture requires the determination to act to accomplish the following:

45

- Mobilize and place resources so that the best possible goals for all children are met with equal and adequate support.
- Restructure often entrenched, nonproductive, provincial dynasties that may have evolved out of a sense of nothing more than the selfish intent to perpetuate their own kind, their own motives. Often, no concern for equity of outcome or opportunity for all has ever been evident or planned.
- Move to rectify historical wrongs, and make this real by insisting upon high but attainable standards of excellence and capability.
- Act boldly to screen and select the most capable, articulate, and representative staff available. This is especially crucial at the administrative and cabinet levels.

Equity Defined

Equity, or total freedom of opportunity, in its most noble, achievable, and healing form, will thrive in a richly planned and well-developed setting. Equity is the freedom, the fairness, the justice, the unbiased opportunity to become that must be extended to every child and every staff member. Its branches must extend far beyond ordinary, traditional underpinnings and practices. It is the primary responsibility of the superintendent to stand at the helm and lead the revolutions that must take place.

The school superintendent cannot afford to relegate to anyone the assurance that every child will be the recipient of the benefits inherent in educational equity. These requisites, selections, and possibilities must be served as a daily menu of offerings to every child, every day, all day. Therefore, the school superintendent must seize every opportunity to deliver on the promise and the responsibility of preparing our children for the twenty-first century. The nature and basic elements of this important principle, this inalienable right, must never again be left to flounder in destructive and broken promises as it has been.

Traditional methods and materials used in most schools and classrooms are class-bound, White, Anglo-Saxon, male, Protestant, racist, and Western. Ronald Edmonds (1979) is indeed correct when he notes that the "inequity of American education derives from our failure to educate the children of the poor." There can be no equity until all schools commit themselves to the absolute removal of faulty policies, practices, and behaviors that have been the major causes of the literacy deficiencies found in too many of our students. Educational equity must finally be judged on the results of pupil outcomes. In order to produce equity of outcomes, one must start with adequate resources and programs for all students according to their needs. We must rid our schools of the historical inequities and mind-sets that work against educational equity for all pupils.

The historical "solution" presented for pupils of the inner city, the Black and the poor, have been filled with negative and racist assumptions that guarantee failure. Title I, based on Coleman's research, assumed that pupils were culturally deprived and that this condition could be corrected by Title I.

Moynihan (1969), followed by Jensen's (1972) research, concluded that all pupils were not educable and that the school could do little to overcome problems of the home, community, and even the genetic makeup of inner-city pupils. Educators have "searched" with great eagerness for the causes of our pupils' failure. The search always focuses outside the school — that is, on the home, the environment, the child, or the family. Attention must be directed at the school: what the schools teach, and how the schools teach. Rather than blame the learner, educators should look at the factors under their control. After all, schools have the pupils 6½ hours every day, 5 days a week, 180 days per year, for 12 years. Surely schools should be able to teach charges in that span of time. Pupils are, for the most part, in a clean, safe, orderly environment. The behavior of the school is critical in determining the quality of education. Schools are the major influence on the life of students. There has never been a time in the life of the American public school when we have not known all we needed to know in order to teach all those whom we choose to teach. Educators would rather blame the student or the family, thus absolving themselves of their professional responsibilities to be instructionally effective.

If educational equity is to come from within the school system, it is the role of the superintendent to direct that reform. It is now known that there is a clear relationship between effective schools and an active, visible principal who is an instructional leader. We have found that the effective school correlates provide solid direction for a superintendent. Thus a superintendent should focus on instructional planning and development.

Murphy and Hallinger (1986), in an examination of the leadership of 12 school districts found to be instructionally effective, report that superintendents were key to the success. In these *instructionally effective school districts*, superintendents were actively involved in managing and directing technical core activities. They used a variety of both

direct and indirect leadership tools, controlled the development of
goals both at the district and schools levels, were influential in establishing procedures for the selection of staff, took personal responsibility for the supervision and evaluation of principals, and established
and regularly monitored a districtwide instructional and curricular
focus.

Wissler and Ortiz (1989) suggest that recognition of the superintendent's importance in school reform may be just around the corner.
According to these authors, "First and foremost, superintendents are
the primary and most important persons engaged in comprehensive
school district reform efforts." This position constitutes some powerful
and significant policy and delivery implications:

- The issue of school reform should be lodged in the office of the superintendent.
- School reform must encompass the entire school organization that makes
  up a school district. Targeting separate schools for reform is not sufficient.
- The process of change in organizations is a long one, and it requires a
  leader's continuous attention from inception to completion.

For true change to occur, for equity to take its place in the school, the
superintendent must strive, daily, to make equity vigorously obvious.

The Substance of the Battle for Equity

The issues of importance in equity are complex, many, often frustrating, and, yet, exciting. The placing of equity at the top of the
superintendent's agenda must become a concentrated, multifaceted
undertaking to bridge the equity gap. It can have cataclysmic and
contagious results. In moving to treat the paucity of research and
concomitant outcomes that exist around the superintendent's ability to
integrate powerful organizational constructs into programs for children, equity has to be an absolute objective.

Rowan (1983) calls for obtaining much richer details about how
districts will organize such instructionally critical areas of systems
operations as staffing, curriculum, resource allocation, and interpersonal deficits or attributes. It is implied that only persistent dreaming
and studied, direct, unrelenting, scientific action should compose the
critical elements to make things happen. Though the dreaming is not

new, the challenge to the superintendency for decisive and direct action is a current phenomenon.

More than a decade ago, Alvin Toffler, author of the then controversial *Future Shock* (1970) and *Learning for Tomorrow* (1974) warned, "The basic assumption draining American education, one that is both dangerous and deceptive, is that the future will be like the past and the present. Schools are preparing children for a society that no longer exists." During the same period, Toffler's observations lent support to the conclusion drawn by Gerald E. Levy (1970) that there was every reason to believe that present-day educators, like many researchers, lack the necessary familiarity with the social and cultural needs of culturally distinct populations for pedagogical and life-planning purposes.

During the past decade, the academic community has continued to see convulsive periods of sweeping accusations, charges, countercharges, reviews, and limited innovations. A long series of acrid publications assaulted the equality ills of our educational potpourri. One author suggested that children would be better off on the streets than in the impossible inner-city classrooms they are now forced to attend. Jonathan Kozol (1967), James Herndon (1978), and Ivan Illich (1971) all sounded similar death knells to teachers, schools, curricula, and teacher training programs that were out of step and out of tune with the needs of children, especially the needs of children of a dark and different hue.

As we review history of the debates, facts, and charges related to educational equality and the plight of minority children, we must constantly remind ourselves to look also at the tepid flow of history in terms of treatment of certain crimes against races and social classes, and the universal lack of concern for the rights of minorities. These factors alone place educational equity at a crucially pivotal point in the annals of historical importance. Thus the recognition of equity's stature is set in history.

In July 1975, in an address to the members of the Teacher Corps Development Conference in Washington, D.C., Senator Edward M. Kennedy made declarations that ring with truth today:

> We must recognize that in inner city schools . . . there still are children marking time for today and losing their chance for tomorrow. We must recognize that in parts of my own state of Massachusetts, in poor black neighborhoods and in poor white neighborhoods, there are schools where the promise of equality in education remains a distant dream. We must

recognize that in the rural outposts of America, on Indian reservations and in migrant communities, a decent education remains the exception and not the rule. There are some who argue that these failures must be expected in a nation so large, in an educational institution so vast, and in a society so complex. I will not accept that argument. And I do not believe you will accept it either. We can change those schools. We can improve the quality of teaching, the quality of the environment, and the quality of learning in those classrooms. And we can fulfill not just the ten-year-old promise of President Johnson, but the 200-year-old promise of our founders. For if there are some children in this land — whether because they are black or because they were born on a reservation or because they speak a different language or because they are poor — if there are some children who do not have an equal opportunity for a quality education then there are some children who are not free.

Look into the faces of young students, and tell them that new promises were made to them. It is our contention that the school superintendent, especially the school superintendent of African American descent, ought to make certain these promises are kept.

According to Goodman (1964), the educational system that prepares children of minority heritage must hold onto and value elements that are the foundations of basic principles and promises upon which democracy must be based. If differences and talents are to be respected and valued, it becomes crucial that the superintendent support, advocate for, respect, and teach acceptance of those creative talents found among inner-city children.

If the view that superintendency support for educational change to the benefit of inner-city children is a revolutionary concept, then it is a phenomenon that must gain energetic acceptance in many quarters. The superintendent cannot afford to lend presence and substance to those educators unwilling to keep fighting until the fortresses surrounding institutionalized mockery of the talents and intelligence of, and due process for, inner-city children have fallen. Why are more superintendents — Black and White — not committing themselves to the guarantee of a fair deal for children of African American heritage? There is a lost connection between this absence of indignation to foster true understanding of the importance of equity and the will to act, to create a kind of training ground that will prepare educators for acting to ensure "real-world" equity for the inner-city child.

One possible explanation of the relative absence of intense effort to take up the challenge of the importance of equity is that there are different conceptions of the challenge itself: the alternatives to the status quo, the possible results of the facilitation of equity through the superintendency, and, finally, fear about the consequences of the revolution. There are no real models for the revolution. There is no widely accepted, painless approach to change and renewal.

No one with the power to bring about real change in the educational system has moved to act profoundly; no one has come forth — with meaning — to quell the dissonance. No one has called a true halt to the unfair and inequitable banishing of poor kids into special education cells and compartments; no one has called a halt to the unfair labeling and treatment of minority learners; no one has come to lead the necessary revolution. In short, the ambiguity with which superintendents have addressed the challenge and the lack of real dedication and commitment to the struggle by educators in powerful positions have tended to weaken the effectiveness of efforts to sound the call to action.

A second possible cause of the apparent absence of understanding of the importance of equity is ignorance. To some, the challenge to change educational behaviors to fit the needs of the child to be taught is strange and frustrating. Social class, economic differences, and racial attitudes have combined forces to create a gap. The differences in life and learning styles of many minority children and the ignorance and coldness of many who teach them combine to perpetuate a sickening alienation from the mainstream of American life. For these, the change, the revolution, the struggle implies too profound a revision for a future where educational equity prevails. Such a future is simply too difficult to envision, too threatening to entrenched beliefs.

The lack of a clear and centralized national mandate for general and equal education of all children has created levels of "safety" — escape routes for many teachers currently teaching in the American educational establishment. The lack of consensus among the powerful who could mandate radical change in the educational establishment has allowed the seekers of the "safe" levels to join forces to ensure that the ranks are not broken. The school superintendent is, perhaps, the most powerful force able to set in motion the vehicle for change that must defeat the forces.

From a more rational perspective, unless the basic issues are explicated, and people with power (i.e., school superintendents) push for universal advocacy of the equitable education of all children and grapple with the implementation of some lasting and rewarding alternatives, the issues will soon ulcerate, become rotten, and smell foul — or they will dry up, like "a raisin in the sun." The dissonance is growing louder, is becoming more irritating. Children are withering on the intellectual vine.

This need not happen. There is some time left. The challenge can be accepted; the alternatives can be implemented. Change can be realized — it must be realized. The following elements of the challenge and the characteristics of the alternatives suggest action points and the importance of equity:

- The present educational establishment reflects a value system that emphasizes rejection of behavioral and intellectual differences, values, and attitudes that do not conform to the so-called norm. Learning and living is pervasive — there is no norm. Therefore, the challenge is to be aware of and accept all humanistic values and attitudes and to reject those ideas that spell personal harm, inhumaneness, or violation of personal rights or civil law.
- The concepts relevant to educational equity transcend matters of race. The challenge is to reject any arguments of a one-to-one correlation between race and culture and race and intelligence. The evidence simply does not support the theory.
- The educational revolution cannot be composed of a new methodology grafted to the old establishment. The concept inherent in this challenge is the need to implement alternatives that are different. This challenge is to take a different view of responsibility, a more lucid vision of society and education than what currently exists in some school districts. Changes in pedagogical characteristics and approaches must be recognized throughout school districts as crucial to the establishment of equity.
- A change in the educational state of affairs calls for equal acceptance, treatment, pay, promotion, and application of all policies for all concerned. A monocultural faculty and student population, the hiring or retention of mediocre personnel to lessen the competition, the relegation of competent personnel to lesser assignments, and monocultural curricula will not achieve the kind of change that must become real.
- The educational revolution for equity, to be real and lasting, cannot be one that is devoid of tension and conflict. The superintendent must be prepared and willing to face these conflicts. Differing cultures, folkways, and styles do not always complement one another.

The challenges of today explicitly reject the historical ideal of the model American education archetype. They also reject the ideal of assimilation with the existing educational conditions, the elusiveness of true educational equity for the blessed few, pseudoeducation for the masses, and the perpetuated dictum that poor folks and their children are dumb — that nobody owes poor folks any equality of education. One might suggest that any such hue and cry ought to generate indignation and hostility. Ordinarily, indignation and hostility give rise to battle; however, to date, such reactions to this flavor of change are primarily isolated and surprisingly infrequent. It appears that those who hold values associated with maintaining the educational status quo have yielded no ground to pedagogical revolution, nor have they come out to fight. If the fight were to surface, each side could declare respective issues. Further, the evidence does not even support the contention of some who believe with trepidation that real revolution and acceptance of change are occurring — although gradually. The superintendent must define new standards of professional effectiveness and must demand and forge new and brave journeys.

Equity and Quality Education

Without equity, there can never be true quality and excellence in education. *A Nation at Risk* (National Commission on Excellence in Education, 1983) loudly proclaimed among its basic assumptions:

- Learning is lifelong.
- Quality and equality are not mutually exclusive.
- Diversity, meeting individual needs, is still a value.
- Education is tied to larger societal goals and issues.

The report warns of a "rising tide of mediocrity" unless we provide necessary leadership for bringing about needed reforms, and specifically cites principals and superintendents as having major roles to perform in developing school and community support for reforms. It is through the office of the superintendent that the pursuit of educational enlightenment must continue to take shape, must give vitality to the urging of *A Nation at Risk* to sustain the push for equality.

The superintendent must lead the way in attending to every facet of the reform movement. For example, wherever the school superintendent finds unclear policies, incompetence, or ineffective instructional practices, he or she should act to correct the situation with all deliberate speed. All disturbing problems and frightening chasms, no matter how bothersome, must be pursued. The superintendent must give vigorous support and presence to closing the painful gaps between true reform and unstable, impermanent results.

If superintendents continue to fail in efforts to educate children of African American heritage equitably, they will continue to contribute to the destruction and the wasting of the minds of millions of young people, our most valuable resource. As admonished in *A Nation at Risk*, superintendents must make time available to learn. They must also find additional time to assist students who are experiencing difficulties in the regular classroom, time to counsel, cajole, and support those students. Fair salaries, promotions, enriched programs, tenure, instructional management, dropouts, community and corporate involvement, certification, turfdom, and resistance to change are all issues akin to the aforementioned; they are both relevant and interrelated. None of these can be ignored.

How can the superintendent act profoundly to cultivate believers and doers? It may be useful, at this point, to share with you portions of Harris's (1988) "A Districtwide Application of the Effective Schools Research":

> Blacks are now serving as superintendents in over one hundred school districts throughout the country. There are Black superintendents in big cities, such as Oakland, Atlanta, Chicago, Baltimore, and Detroit, and in smaller areas, e.g., Perris, California; Port Gibson, Mississippi; and Moscow, Arkansas. When Blacks are appointed superintendents or even principals, we can generally make certain assumptions about the nature of the district or school. We can generally assume that the district or school is in a perilous condition, plagued with low student achievement, poor pupil discipline, bureaucratic inefficiency, and financial problems. It is not so much that Blacks gained control of a district or school, but rather that Whites have abandoned it. We generally become administrators of schools and districts with a myriad of problems. Blacks inherit the "husk" of the educational system.

> As administrators, we generally bring improvement in the school climate of our district and schools, but academic excellence often eludes us. As a group, Black educators have not yet been able to produce districts or schools that have high pupil achievement. We have yet to develop models of administration that lead to effective schools that mass produce students who are able to shine and excel in the real world.

> Too often we choose to become Black copies of our White predecessors. We have modeled our leadership styles after failures. It should be clear to us that if our White predecessors had not failed, we would not be here. There is a need for new models, and we must develop those models.

Let us examine the assumptions upon which this position is based. The assumptions are:

1. The schools we administer are less effective than we would like them to be: student achievement is low, discipline is poor, the public image of our organization is negative and community support is also low.
2. Changing leadership from White to Black will not in itself improve the schools.
3. A Black administrator should have a "head start" in resolving the kinds of problems found in the poor, low-achieving district they inherit. Black administrators can and must make a difference.
4. Changing the administrative style of the leadership is the best method to improve the school's academic performance.
5. Over 25 percent of the Black students in the country are in schools administered by a Black principal or superintendent who should be doing a better job.

It remains unacceptable that Black and minority leaders continue to accept failure. It is essential that the effective superintendent live by the principles that one must have confidence in and believe in all children, and one must expect all children to learn. Further, superintendents must demand that each staff member treat every child as though that child were his or her own, and that child is expected to learn.

Clearly, there is merit to believing all children can learn. The argument may be that the fix usually takes time. It is often very difficult to overtake such a mind-set. As mentioned above, this is the route by which some educators have satiated their egotistical and intellectual thirsts. The superintendent must study, understand, and act to override such callousness as well as be prepared to take on different shapes and forms to lead the struggle against wrong and inequality.

Ronald Edmonds (1979) and his colleagues at Harvard University began to crystallize some of the impediments and circumstances for superintendents and began clearing pathways for successfully educating our nation's poor children. Edmonds provided guidelines for understanding that changing our schools is not a bland, clinical, bloodless event. In other words, we must speak loud, long, and with hollow sounds about innovation, improvement, and renewal — we cannot afford to wait. Edmonds admonishes us that, while we may not know the best possible way of doing what needs to be done, we should know what *not* to do. We are compelled to use, right now, everything we know in order to make education the kind of instrument for equity that this nation needs.

Edmonds was fairly certain that not everyone was ready for, or wanted to jump up and fully subscribe to, this position. As father of the effective schools movement, however, Edmonds provided a model that, when successfully followed, will result in effective schools.

How Superintendents Facilitate Equity

How a superintendent translates beliefs into actions (i.e., where the true intent is to do something about inequality) will determine an energetic life or a slow death for a school system. To borrow a phrase from Murphy and Hallinger (1986), a superintendent who is "hip-deep in change" must first focus his or her vision essentially on some specific organizational elements. While possibly time-consuming, active pursuit of these needs cannot be left to happenstance:

- The superintendent must first lead the school district in establishing clearly defined, realistic, creative, learned, critically analyzed curriculum goals and objectives.
- The superintendent must then affirm and continuously reaffirm, at all organizational levels, belief in the convictions that all children can learn, and that children must be provided with the best resources affordable.
- The superintendent must surround him- or herself with top- and central-level administrators who share and practice that philosophy.
- The superintendent ought to know curriculum and instruction and be able to demonstrate and spread that knowledge through teaching, observing others teaching, and providing clear, direct, no-nonsense feedback to those observed.
- The superintendent, while using political savvy, cannot surrender personal commitment and integrity when inequities are found. While the political realities are often lucidly profound, the superintendent must find a way, or make one, to correct observed inequities.
- The superintendent, while giving basic amenities to staff, must be the personification of support for students, their parents, and the broader community, as they are the superintendent's raison d'être.
- The superintendent must consistently display, with urgency, the demand and need for every staff member, from central level to classroom, from food service to maintenance, to give children hope, every day. This behavior may be as simple as speaking to children pleasantly, or it may involve working to guarantee that every child leaves school, daily, feeling that he or she has experienced success.
- The superintendent must build and maintain strong ties between the school district and business, agencies, state and local government, and all others who seek to help legitimate safe passage into life for the children.

- The superintendent's goals of quality and equality must sometimes stretch across the dark, treacherous, and frightening depths of incompetence and indifference. He or she must be brave enough to intervene; to organize or reorganize until key decision-making positions are clearly and profoundly controlled by trusted, highly trained, caring, creative individuals with well-furnished minds.
- The superintendent must be highly visible and available to the total community. Such a strategy includes making the presence of the superintendent felt at church, political, social, and community functions, cultural affairs, and parent-school activities.
- The superintendent must be fearless, truthful, frank, and demanding, of him- or herself as well as of other district personnel. He or she should recognize capable personnel, and make them a significant part of a highly visible, trusted team of informed, delegate managers.

In conclusion, the superintendency can and ought to be the central nervous system, the intractable force for the establishment of an unshakable system of equality in the school district. The occupancy of the superintendent's chair by a member of a minority group ought to be so deeply rooted, so enclosed in equity and excellence for every child, that not even a cosmic upheaval of universal proportion can unsettle its foundations. There must burn within the superintendent a zeal to part the waters and make way for children to cross over into the promised land of educational well-being.

Whether a school district succeeds or fails in what ought to be its highest mission, to assist every child in becoming all that he or she is capable of becoming, is contingent upon one basic factor: the willingness of the superintendent to be at the head of the battle. Superintendents must take on the challenge to make the position one that proves that schools can solve some of our nation's problems. What would really happen if this country were pushed into addressing the question: What good can come out of truly and equally educating all the children? The existence of one school of excellence means it is realistic to expect that all schools can be excellent. According to Edmonds (1980), whether or not our social order ever faces the decision to make education the instrument for equity depends largely upon how we feel about the fact that we have not done that so far.

Superintendents can no longer afford to be members of the silent majority; they must speak out and act decisively. Unless they do so, equity issues will get lost in the shuffle and the major functions of effectiveness as set forth by Murphy and Hallinger (1986) will become sterile.

Balancing staff commitment, student achievement, goals, expectations, standards, curriculum focus, and instruction monitoring is very
difficult where equity is a missing ingredient. Unless the superintendent attends to the well-being of equality and excellence, the crisis will
worsen, and children will go on dying, literally. Sweeping improvements in urban schools can and must occur, but change will come only
when the nation wills it. The greater the delay, the greater the cost
(Carnegie Foundation for the Advancement of Teaching, 1988). The
school superintendent must proceed with all deliberate speed.

References

Carnegie Foundation for the Advancement of Teaching. (1988). *An imperiled generation: Saving urban schools*. Princeton, NJ: Author.

Edmonds, R. (1979). Effective schools for the urban poor. *Educational Leadership, 37*, 15-17.

Edmonds, R. (1980). *Developing effective schools*. Paper presented at the Year's End Conference of the New England Teacher Corps Network, Newton, MA.

Goodman, P. (1964). *Compulsory mis-education*. New York: Vintage.

Harris, J. J. (1988). A districtwide application of the effective schools research. *Journal of Negro Education, 57*, 292-306.

Herndon, J. (1978). *The way its spozed to be*. New York: Bantam.

Illich, I. (1971, June 19). We can disestablish schools or we can de-school culture. *Saturday Review*.

Jensen, A. R. (1972). *Genetics and education*. New York: Harper & Row.

Kennedy, E. M. (1975). *The promise*. Address presented at the Teacher Corps Development Conference, Washington, DC.

Kozol, J. (1967). *Death at an early age*. Boston: Houghton Mifflin.

Levy, G. E. (1970). *Ghetto school: Class warfare in an elementary school*. New York: Western.

Moynihan, D. P. (1969). *Maximum feasible misunderstanding: Community action in the War on Poverty*. New York: Free Press.

Murphy, J., & Hallinger, P. (1986). The superintendent as instructional leader: Findings from effective school districts. *Journal of Educational Administration, 24*.

National Commission on Excellence in Education. (1983). *A Nation at Risk: The Imperative for Educational Reform*. Washington, DC: Author.

Rowan, B. (1983). *Instructional effectiveness in school districts: A conceptual framework*. San Francisco: Far West Laboratory for Research and Development.

Toffler, A. (1970). *Future shock*. New York: Random House.

Toffler, A. (1974). *Learning for tomorrow*. New York: Vintage.

Wissler, D., & Ortiz, F. (1989). *The superintendent's leadership in school reform*. New York: Falmer.

5

The Quest for Equity: Imperatives for Administrators in Higher Education

HUGH J. SCOTT

Hunter College of the City University of New York

Higher education in America is an extraordinary venture. For 1986-1987, the nation's 3,406 colleges and universities had 12,500,798 students and 390,731 full-time faculty ("Nation," 1988). Higher education in our pluralistic democracy is an enterprise that is unmatched by any other nation in the quality of its research and teaching, in the size of its enrollment, in the proportion of the nation's youth that it serves, and in the diversity of its institutions and offerings. Yet, the concept of equal educational opportunity is relatively new in American education. For the greater part of its history in America, higher education existed for the elite. Access to a college education was significantly expanded when Congress established the foundations of the public land-grant universities in the 1860s. Open enrollment in higher education probably began with the establishment of a national complex of land-grant institutions. Between 1890 and 1925, enrollments in higher education grew four to seven times as fast as the population. Vacarro (1975) notes that the American ideal of democratic higher education began to be realized in the early 1900s, when what was once an elitist system of higher education suddenly lunged headlong toward the egalitarian ideal.

Chancellor Joseph Murphy of the City University of New York (CUNY) — the nation's largest and most diverse urban university —

identified higher education as the most important avenue of social mobility for the working class, women, and minorities (cited in CUNY, 1984). It was not until the 1950s and 1960s that America's colleges and universities became deeply involved in the press for upward social and economic mobility. The period of the 1950s and 1960s witnessed significant increases in minority enrollments in higher education, with this influx producing dramatic changes in college curricula, financial practices, admission standards, and other rules and regulations (Vacarro, 1975). Murphy asserts that the view that higher education is essentially the privilege of the academic and economic elite has been superseded in the past few decades by the growing conviction that going to college should be an option for every American (quoted in CUNY, 1984).

Gone are the days when higher education in the United States meant private, ivy-covered institutions reserved mainly for White males studying for the ministry (Bauer, 1988). Gone are the days when the unspoken assumption in most colleges and universities was that the education of White students should be undertaken, for the most part, in isolation from students of color (Visiting Committee on Minority Life and Education at Brown University, 1986). Higher education has indeed become less elitist, more democratic, more accessible, and less homogeneous (Shalala, 1985). Higher education in America will never return to what it used to be, and that reality, in major respects, is not movement in the wrong direction. Whatever has been lost in higher education by no longer opting to provide the very best for a special few has been more than adequately compensated for by seeking to do a good job for a larger and more widely heterogeneous representation of the population.

Undeniably, higher education in the United States has undergone marked changes in its expectations about the relationships that should exist between racial minority and racial majority students and the values that should be attached to minority and majority experiences in higher education. But as the decade of the 1980s moves toward its conclusion, the goals of diversity and equity in higher education have begun to wear thin. After more than a decade of effort to increase the proportion of minority population enrolling in colleges and universities, the nation's attention has turned elsewhere; the rate of college attendance for Blacks and Hispanics has slowly begun to sink (Reeves, 1985). Black enrollment in higher education dropped 11% during the period from 1975 to 1982, but more Blacks graduated from high school in 1982 than in 1975. Although the high school graduation rate for

Hispanics increased 38% from 1975 to 1982, Hispanic college enrollment declined 16% ("All One System," 1986).

The American Council on Education reports that not only has there been a loss of momentum since the earlier minority progress, there have been actual reversals in the drive to achieve full equality among minority students ("Minority Changes," 1984). The American Council on Education (ACE) Office of Minority Concerns (1986) reports that while minorities are growing in numbers and proportion of the population, they remain underrepresented in higher education, while Whites remain overrepresented. The problem of underrepresentation of Blacks and Hispanics in higher education is exacerbated by their concentration in a relatively small number of institutions ("Racial and Ethnic Makeup," 1986). Niara Sudarkasa (1988), president of Lincoln University, comments on the trend in enrollments:

> From 1976 to 1986, . . . African American enrollment in higher education dropped precipitously. The rate of growth for Hispanic enrollment also declined, although the number and proportion of Hispanics in higher education continued to rise. Throughout the period, Native American enrollment increased, but their numbers and percentages remained minuscule. What gains there were in minority enrollments over the decade between 1976 and 1986 were attributable to the almost meteoric rise in the number of Asian Americans in colleges and universities. (p. 23)

Reginald Wilson, director of the ACE's Office of Minority Concerns, notes that for the 1988-89 academic year, figures tend to indicate an increase in Black enrollment (cited in Farrell, 1988). Wilson stresses that ACE and other organizations are in part responsible for the increase in Black enrollment because of their efforts to stop the decline. The circumstances cited below highlight the problem of underrepresentation of minorities in higher education and the socioeconomic consequences of such:

- Minorities continue to be the most underrepresented at four-year institutions and are often in programs that will not necessarily give credit toward a baccalaureate degree.
- The attrition rates in higher education for Blacks and Hispanics are about twice those of Whites.
- Black, Hispanic, and American Indian participation in graduate and professional schools remains exceptionally low.
- The percentage of minorities taking college preparatory classes in high school is considerably lower than that of Whites.

- More and more states are using standard performance tests to rank and set graduation standards for students; due to cultural differences and historically inferior education, Blacks and Hispanics tend to do poorly on these tests.
- The significant majority of persons who occupy status positions in this society will have attended and/or graduated from institutions of higher education; higher education functions as a principal device for channeling literally millions of Americans into a wide variety of professions and higher-level occupations.

Even in the best of times, White Americans were never enthusiastic about equal access and affirmative action for Black Americans. Blacks and other minorities made their greatest advancements in higher education at a time in the nation's history when the quality of life and education for White Americans were significantly advanced. Resurfacing in an up-and-down economy is a strong conservative attitude among many White Americans that communicates a "shortsighted and uncharitable spirit" (Pifer, 1975) toward Blacks and other minorities. Many White Americans believe that minority advancement needs no further assistance from the courts and government. Financial woes have served as convenient justification for withdrawing from the fragile social promises on which prior commitments to equal educational opportunity and affirmative action were based.

Notwithstanding proclamations to the contrary, higher education in America does not provide equal educational opportunity for all regardless of "genetic structure, condition of birth, race, or color, or previous condition of servitude." Higher education — along with elementary and secondary education — is conducted in a manner that reflects a belief among many majority Americans that certain groups and social classes deserve better treatment than others (Oakes, 1985). It is not by happenstance that higher education mirrors the social and economic hierarchy of our society. Nor is it any accident that the racial and socioeconomic discrimination that regulates entry into education and affects the response of educational institutions is a reflection of the discrimination that separates race and class in our social hierarchy. Fields (1988) notes that higher education institutions are creatures of the society that spawns them and that while many colleges and universities espouse inclusiveness of all groups, in reality the decisions affecting the operational aspects of higher education are and have been the sine qua non of White America.

Integrally linked to the problem of underrepresentation of minorities in higher education is the concern that predominantly White colleges and universities tend to demonstrate a reluctance or unwillingness to embrace the minority experience. Diversity on most campuses is still measured by numbers and percentages rather than by revising the map of the White majority's intellectual terrain (Visiting Committee on Minority Life and Education at Brown University, 1986). Minority students and faculty are voicing increased resentment and protest about "too little reflection of their cultural heritage and history within the curriculum and a seeming indifference to their presence." The alarming increase in overt intimidating and harassing behavior directed toward minority students on predominantly White campuses has embarrassed college and university officials, but too few administrators have been willing to look inside their institutions and question whether or not minority students are receiving equal treatment.

Imperatives for Administrators

Elam (1975) poses the question: "Could colleges and universities respond to the needs of the masses?" He responds: "Some could, some didn't want to, and quite a few didn't recognize the problem." The reformation of higher education aimed at making colleges and universities more inclusive of minorities with regard to their student profiles, to the composition of their faculties and staffs, and to the content and importance of the pluralist ideal in curriculum must start at the top with the president. Also, changes promoted in response to the quest for equity and pluralism in higher education must be understood, supported, and catalyzed by those in key administrative positions: presidents, vice presidents, deans, and department heads. Administrators in higher education cannot wait for other social or political forces to remedy this social ill. Fundamental changes in higher education do not occur solely or primarily as the result of an administrator's letter of support or intent. Presidents, vice presidents, deans, department heads, and so on must be prepared to communicate their support for pluralism and equity in what they do as well as in what they say (Striner, 1983). In the quest for equity and pluralism, every higher education administrator should have two signs behind his or her desk for all to take notice. The signs should read: "The Buck Stops Here" and "The Buck Starts Here."

There are at least two certainties about change in higher education: It will be resisted, and it will come slowly. Higher education is noted for the complexities, contradictions, and traditions that affect the governance and administration of colleges and universities. Faculty participate extensively in the determination of the affairs of a college or university, but faculty rarely carry a commensurate share of the responsibility for the consequences of their institutional decisions. Many faculty often complain about what is and demonstrate an equally negative disposition toward proposals to change or reshape what is current. It is not uncommon among the ranks of faculty to find many who perceive the academy as an enclave that ought to be independent from the "trials and tribulations" that "alter and illuminate" the lives of those who work outside the academy.

Faculty in higher education long ago established the principles that the professor must have control over his or her teaching and that the autonomy of the collective faculty must prevail with respect to central educational decisions within the institution, particularly as they relate to curriculum and academic personnel. On the matter of the independence of faculty in higher education, the Visiting Committee on Minority Life and Education at Brown University (1986) notes:

> Each discipline in a college or university tends to function as a colony of its professional associations rather than a cell of that particular institution. Further, each professor tends to be a free-standing professional entity with wide-ranging discretionary authority over what materials he or she will include in a syllabus. It is a challenge to get the sum of departments or the aggregation of professors to function as a faculty when presented with a problem like the curriculum or the paucity of minority membership in the faculty as a whole. (p. 3)

Granted that in many colleges and universities some essential administrative matters are overly democratized and that the line between the prerogatives of the administration and those of the faculty is often blurred or invisible. But the effectiveness of any organization is dependent on the quality of its leadership. While fundamental decisions about admissions, retention, curriculum, and academic personnel are made only after significant faculty input, a college or university needs leadership from its top administrators to help it take form and direction in its goals and commitment to action. Leadership is what causes individuals and groups to perform in a manner that maximizes their contributions to the goals and objectives of the organization. Leadership is the quality that enables an individual within a setting to motivate and inspire others to adopt, achieve, and maintain organizational and individual goals (Gutherie & Reed, 1986). The challenges inherent in the quest for equity and pluralism in higher education require leadership from higher education administrators.

The higher education administrator's behavior is not simply a function of formal expectations, individual needs, and organizational goals; he or she brings to the college or university a host of unique attributes, sentiments, values, and motives (Hoy & Miskel, 1987). The beliefs and decisions of administrators, particularly as they relate to issues of equity and pluralism, are affected by their sociological values and understandings of the problems and needs faced by majority and minority group members in their pursuits of life, liberty, and happiness. The higher education administrator's educational priorities and strategies are derived from his or her pervasive beliefs and principal educational assumptions.

One of the most demanding requirements of leadership in an institutional setting that has a significant impact on the lives of individuals and groups is that major and quite often controversial decisions have to be made. The higher education administrator should be an effective manager of conflict; he or she should be an interpreter and translator of social events into institutional policy. Dodson has stated that change produces conflict and tension, but without such there is very little opportunity for growth (cited in Chicago Urban League, 1968). The plight of minorities in higher education requires that colleges and universities examine themselves, with the appraisal focusing upon the extent to which they provide higher intellectual development; professional and occupational training; development of research capabilities; cultivation of breadth, flexibility, and autonomy of mind; and a questioning, even skeptical spirit that will best prepare all students to meet the demanding responsibilities of democratic citizenship in a rapidly changing nation and world (Pifer, 1975). The quest for equity in higher education requires higher education administrators to come to grips with the question of whether the ideals of pluralism and equity can find working expression in institutions that are deeply grounded in the traditions of White America (Visiting Committee on Minority Life and Education at Brown University, 1986).

Higher education administrators are not all-powerful in the academy. It is conceded that the positive consequences of the influence of their leadership in the engagement of the challenges inherent in the quest for equity will range from tangential to significant. Nevertheless, the pervasive nature of leadership (Heyns, 1973) makes it essential that higher education administrators communicate to faculty, staff, and students their support of the premise that the academy's true purpose is to prepare its students for "lives of usefulness and reputation," with the focus on building a social framework of decency and fairness, in which all races and ethnic groups contribute to the sum of human knowledge and the advancement of human welfare.

Leadership imperatives in the quest for equity in higher education are actions taken by presidents, vice presidents, deans, department chairpersons, and the like that directly and indirectly contribute to making higher education more inclusive and supportive of minorities with regard to student profiles; the composition of faculties, staffs, and administrations; and the incorporation of and respect for the pluralist ideal in curriculum. There are numerous imperatives that compel the attention and action of higher education administrators in the quest for equity. Ten imperatives are presented here as examples of actions that individually and collectively can make our colleges and universities more inclusive of the minority presence and minority history and culture. Each of the imperatives is supported by a companion comment.

Pluralism and Higher Education

Imperative: Colleges and universities must examine the interrelationships that exist on campuses between minority and majority persons to determine which institutional practices, policies, and traditions impede or negate social conditions that permit ethnic, religious, and racial groups to live side by side, willing to affirm each other's dignity, ready to benefit from each other's experience, and quick to acknowledge each other's contributions to the common welfare.

Comment: The unique diversity of cultural heritages and backgrounds of this nation should be recognized in higher education as a valuable asset, to be cherished and shared (National Alliance of Black School Educators, 1984). Leadership in higher education should commit itself to finding ways for majority and minority members alike to work together in a productive, harmonious, and mutually supportive manner; this must be accomplished without requiring complete agreement on what is good, just, and worthy and without any requirement that we all be the same (Council of Presidents' Ad Hoc Committee on Pluralism and the City University, 1988). Integration is not only racial but cultural, a coming together of different peoples in a social, aesthetic, emotional, and philosophical manner — not a mechanical juxtaposition, but pluralism rather than assimilation, based on respect for difference rather than a desire for amalgamation. Pluralism is a compromise between the extremes of segregation and assimilation and is a recognition of the fact that the United States is a nation of minorities, each emphasizing its race, its language, its culture, its national origin, or some combination of these (Howe, 1980).

The Curriculum

Imperative: Administrators must accept their obligation to encourage and support efforts to modify the curriculum in order to give better attention to the domestic history of racial groups in the United States, to develop curriculum that embraces an understanding of cultures worldwide, and to broaden students' understanding of arts, humanities, and social sciences beyond the traditional Western cultural courses.

Comment: Higher education should comprise the best that has been thought and said in the world (Gilliam, 1988), but in the United States it has been influenced by the ubiquitous human tendency toward egocentrism and ethnocentrism (Hamburg, 1984). The nation's colleges and universities tend to base their curricula on culture, traditions, and values inherited from Western Europe. We need to examine our traditional values, beliefs, and goals and revise them so that they become more inclusive and reflect positively the cultures and races of all people. Pluralism begins with the curriculum; by what it elects to include in the research it supports and the courses it offers, the institution implies something about what is worth knowing (Visiting Committee on Minority Life and Education at Brown University, 1986). Faculty should be appreciative of and adaptable to the acquired experiential backgrounds that students from minority groups bring with them into the institution and should accommodate and capitalize on the life-styles of students from different ethnic and racial groups by adopting a multicultural base and by changing those assumptions and practices that are antithetical to that concept.

Racism in Higher Education

Imperative: In order to preserve the moral endowment of the academy, colleges and universities must take immediate and decisive action through education, rule enforcement, and policy initiatives to state clearly that behavior of administrators, faculty, staff, or students that debases, degrades, inflicts injury on, or promotes animosity against minority groups will not be tolerated and will result in swift and severe punishment.

Comment: Higher education should aim to free individuals and groups from the burdens and impediments caused by ignorance and irrationality. Racism is a manifestation of ignorance and irrationality. Colleges and universities tend to presume that racism is the product of other institutions, but colleges and universities must deal with racism in their student bodies, in their own personnel, and in at least some of the presumptions that drive the curriculum and shape the allocation of resources (Visiting Committee on Minority Life and Education at Brown University, 1986). We no longer have the luxury of indulging in prejudice and ethnocentric extremes; these are anachronisms grounded in our ancient past (Hamburg, 1984). Some administrators and faculty — whether consciously or unconsciously — do not expect students from certain minority groups to achieve; such expectations can have a profoundly negative effect on student behavior and performance in higher education. Of special concern is the need to make certain that those in administrative and instructional positions do not have the power to support their prejudices.

Affirmative Action

Imperative: Affirmative action must be approached as a policy that enhances minority access and strengthens the institution's ability to fulfill its mission, with the ultimate responsibility for its success, although shared by all officials who make personnel decisions, residing with the president, who must establish goals, monitor progress toward these goals, and ensure their attainment.

Comment: Justice Blackmun (1978) has declared: "In order to get beyond racism we must first take account of race. . . . In order to treat some persons equally, we must treat them differently." John F. Kennedy first used the term *affirmative action* in Executive Order 10925 in 1961 in proclaiming that the nation must take affirmative action to seek to overcome the present effects of past racial discrimination. Lim (1984) notes that affirmative action is normally associated with programs designed to assist minority groups that have been discriminated against and left behind in the course of the development of a society. Vincent (1987) notes that affirmative action remains widely misunderstood, poorly administered, and selectively enforced, and that in academia affirmative action often gets little more than lip service. Murphy rejects the argument that affirmative action goals are in fact discriminatory:

If the purpose of the policy is to advance the interest of those who have been previously damaged, or to remove the effects of previously enforced invidious practices from an institution, then such a policy cannot be considered equivalent to something whose explicit purpose is to damage the already-hurt further. (cited in CUNY, 1986, p. 3)

Minority Faculty

Imperative: Each administrator must take appropriate administrative measures to ensure that units under his or her administration implement nothing less than a good-faith effort to recruit minority faculty in at least as great a proportion as those faculty exist in the pool of qualified candidates, with such efforts characterized by a wide recruitment net, an aggressive search, and results that indicate a strong effort and deep commitment.

Comment: Minorities are not only significantly underrepresented in faculty positions in higher education, their underrepresentation is made more serious by the fact of the high attrition rate among minority faculty (Madrid, 1988). Minority faculty experience greater difficulty in obtaining tenure-track positions and in being promoted ("Cross-Racial Collegiality," 1988). On predominantly White campuses, minority faculty face difficult and more numerous pressures than White faculty, and minority faculty confront greater difficulties in seeking to reconcile their professional aspirations, their community obligations, and their scholarly responsibilities (O'Brien, 1988b). The competence of minority faculty is often unfairly questioned by their White counterparts (Pigford, 1988), and racial and cultural biases serve to downgrade and demean research conducted by minority faculty, particularly when such research is focused on minority issues. The underrepresentation of minority faculty serves to signal to White students inadvertently that most minority persons are intellectually incapable of meeting the intellectual standards set by White institutions (Visiting Committee on Minority Life and Education at Brown University, 1986).

Academic Freedom

Imperative: Academic administrators, in their oversight of matters pertaining to curriculum and academic personnel, must make certain that appropriate checks and balances are operative to ensure that the protection of academic freedom is not permitted to serve as a cover for institutional violations of the rights of minority faculty and students.

Comment: Colleges and universities should be experiment stations, where new ideas may germinate and be allowed to grow, if they will, into part of the accepted intellectual food of the nation or of the world (Committee A on Academic Freedom and Tenure, 1986). Academic freedom has been used to embrace both the individual freedom of the professor and the freedom of the academic institution from external control, but it also has been used to protect perceived institutional or individual rights to discriminate and to promote a series of special privileges unrelated to academic freedom (Gray, 1982). Griffiths (1982) notes that a society concerned with social justice will not readily concede the academy's claim to be the guardian of its own gate. As U.S. District Judge Duross Fitzpatrick has declared: "If academic freedom or tenure gives one the right to use expressions in public that are patently offensive to a particular group . . . then quite possibly the boundaries of proper conduct should be redrawn" ("Judge Refuses," 1988).

Admissions

Imperative: Admissions policies and practices with respect to minority students should be responsive to the reality that high school performance today does not adequately indicate the creativity latent in many high school graduates and that each high school graduate has within him or her potential for growth and development that is unknown until society has bent every effort to provide the maximum opportunity for that individual to achieve that potential.

Comment: Determining the admissibility of higher education applicants has always been more of an art than a science. About a third of the ability of this nation is wasted or underused because of the failure of educational institutions to measure and recognize the real ability of the damaged victims of adverse prior discrimination. No group in the United States or in any other nation finds itself lacking in innate capacities solely on the basis of race, color, or socioeconomic status. Many minority students approach the narrow gate of higher education admission with the heavy burdens of inadequate prior schooling, lower test scores, and smaller income. Healy (1969) asserts that higher education standards ought to refer to what an institution does for its students, rather than to their opening handicap. As Soldwedel (1971) observes: "Higher education shall not be higher by virtue of serving the rich, the well-born, the academically able and advantaged or those destined to fill the academic ranks; rather it shall be 'higher' because it takes an adult or near adult beyond his present level toward a fuller realization of his powers to be" (p. 107).

Testing

Imperative: Colleges and universities must end the tendency toward overreliance on tests as the single or the dominant predictor of a student's potential to cope satisfactorily with the academic rigors of undergraduate or graduate education and should incorporate other predictors such as the student's grade point average and the strength of his or her academic program with a commitment to recognize potential in ways that might not always be obvious.

Comment: O'Brien (1988c) notes that minority students consistently score lower than majority students on college admissions tests. Gifford states that testing, when at its best, is a valuable method of identifying talent, but test misuse has the potential to harm individuals for a lifetime ("New Commission Focuses," 1988). Admissions tests have been accorded a higher regard than their history warrants (Bond, 1986). Tests tend to reveal what students do not know, not what they can learn. Tests also provide dramatic documentation of the negative consequences of discrimination and deprivation. Tests are often the instruments of politics rather than of science (National Alliance of Black School Educators, 1984). Gifford notes that when the incorrect use of tests is incorporated into public policies, the results can be devastating to the social fabric of society ("New Commission Focuses," 1988).

Remedial/Development Assistance

Imperative: Equity in access to higher education for minority students must include the provision of a structured program of special assistance to selected students who require and can utilize such assistance to overcome educational, economic, and social disadvantages in order to achieve a college education and to expand their social and career capabilities.

Comment: The higher education experience is not only different but demanding. The successful negotiation of the academic, social, economic, and psychological difficulties that students encounter in the pursuit of a college degree are consequential even for students who are well prepared in high school. The challenges are often herculean and, under certain circumstances, insurmountable for students who enter college with serious deficiencies in their prior education and levels of academic and social maturity. Equity in admission to higher education must include coordinated efforts to ensure that a high school graduate is not prevented by his or her past performance, financial situation, or other socioeconomic factors from receiving an education. In concert with the principle that education is the instrument by which the poor and disadvantaged must enter the mainstream of American economic and social life, compensatory and other programs aimed at achieving equality for the disadvantaged should include all who are disadvantaged by their economic condition regardless of their ethnic origin (Council for Economic Development, 1987).

Financial Assistance

Imperative: Administrators must be champions of and effective advocates for the premise that no public policy is more important to retaining access to and choice in public higher education than the maintenance of the lowest possible tuition level and a supplemental comprehensive system of tuition assistance for students unable to meet even modestly priced tuition.

Comment: The high cost of tuition, combined with uncertainty over the status of federal financial-aid programs and the poor state of the economy, is keeping many majority and minority students from attending college or from having educational choices. Most minority students do not have the range of sources of support that are available to most White students. Also, White students often have family resources and greater access to nonfederal sources of support, such as bank or private loans and fellowships and assistantships ("Black Graduate Students Decline," 1987). Minority students bring to higher education their ambitions, dreams, and ideals, but they are often burdened by the fragile nature of their economic circumstances (CUNY, Office of University Relations, 1987). Murphy calls for support from the Congress to make postsecondary education available to lift as many people as possible off the welfare rolls and out of the cycle of poverty (cited in CUNY, Office of University Relations, 1987). Cross sees financial aid as a means to "help process human potential, which bitter experience has shown us is all too often wasted" (cited in Higher Education Service Corporation, 1985). Financial aid should be available to all students who otherwise would be unable to pursue a college education and should meet the differences, or needs, that exist between the cost of education and the expected family or individual contribution.

Conclusion

Every institution of higher education worthy of its designation as a college or university should measure up to high standards of ethnic sensitivity and racial civility. All colleges and universities should be committed to engendering values and implementing policies that will enhance respect for individuals and their cultures with an acceptance of the premise that the nation's cultural, racial, ethnic diversity — America's pluralism — is one of the most valued, significant, and important characteristics of our democracy (Council of Presidents' Ad Hoc Committee on Pluralism and the City University, 1988). In the quest for equity in higher education, administrators must recognize that understanding is a condition of, not a synonym for, solutions (Visiting Committee on Minority Life and Education at Brown University, 1986), and that anything that counteracts progress toward equity must inevitably become a factor in diluting the scope and impact of the pluralist ideal in higher education.

References

All one system: Demographics of education. (1986, February 1). *Black Issues in Higher Education*, p. 7.

American Council on Education, Office of Minority Concerns. (1986). *Minorities in higher education: Fifth annual status report*. Washington, DC: Author.

Bauer, B., et al. (1988, October 10). America's best colleges. *U.S. News & World Report*, pp. c3-c32.

Black graduate students decline. (1987, July 1). *Black Issues in Higher Education*, pp. 1, 3.

Blackmun, H. B. (1978). Concurring in part in *Bakke v. Regents of California* 438 U.S. 265, 307.

Bond, L. (1986). On new horizons in testing. In University of Pittsburgh, *Learning and research and development center: A twentieth anniversary profile* (pp. 21-24). Pittsburgh: University of Pittsburgh.

Chicago Urban League. (1968, May 28-30). *The principal in the new world*. Chicago: Author.

City University of New York. (1984). *1984 master plan*. New York: Author.

City University of New York. (1986). *An anniversary for access to excellence*. New York: Author.

City University of New York, Office of University Relations. (1987, Fall). *City University news*. New York: Author.

College Entrance Examination Board. (1985). *Equality and excellence: The educational status of black Americans*. New York: Author.

Committee A on Academic Freedom and Tenure, American Council on Education. (1986, January/February). Some observations on ideology, competence, and faculty selection. *Academe, 72*(1), 1a-10a.

Council for Economic Development. (1987). *Children in need: Investment strategies for the educationally disadvantaged.* New York: Author.

Council of Presidents' Ad Hoc Committee on Pluralism and the City University. (1988, January 20). [Report]. Unpublished manuscript, City University of New York.

Cross-racial collegiality: Trouble in academe. (1988, November 10). *Black Issues in Higher Education,* p. 84.

Elam, S. M. (1975, February). Brief look at higher education. *Phi Delta Kappan, 56*(6), 386.

Farrell, C. S. (1988, November 10). Black student enrollment on the rise. *Black Issues in Higher Education,* p. 48.

Fields, C. A. (1988, August 15). Institutional responsibility and minority students. *Black Issues in Higher Education,* p. 48.

Gardner, J. W. (1986). *The nature of leadership: Introductory considerations.* Washington, DC: Independent Sector.

Gilliam, D. (1988, June 1). A backward trend. *Black Issues in Higher Education,* p. 7.

Gray, M. (1982). Academic freedom: A symposium. *New York University Education Quarterly, 13*(3), 6-9.

Griffiths, D. D. (1982). Freedom of, freedom to, freedom from . . . . *New York University Education Quarterly, 13*(3), i.

Gutherie, J. W., & Reed, R. J. (1986). *Educational administration and policy.* Englewood Cliffs, NJ: Prentice-Hall.

Hamburg, D. A. (1984). *Prejudice, ethnocentrism, and violence in an age of high technology.* New York: Carnegie Corporation of New York.

Healy, T. S. (1969, September 20). Will everyman destroy the university? *Saturday Review,* pp. 54, 70.

Heyns, R. G. (1973). Leadership lessons from Watergate. *Educational Record, 54,* 172-174.

Higher Education Service Corporation. (1985). *Annual report 1984-85.* New York: Author.

Howe, H., II. (1980). Pluralism, the Brown decision and the schools in the 1980s. *College Board Review, 115,* 18-23, 36, 37.

Hoy, W. K., & Miskel, C. G. (1987). *Educational administration: Theory, research and practice.* New York: Random House.

Judge refuses to lift suspension of Georgia professor for racist remark. (1988, September 29). *Black Issues in Higher Education,* p. 3.

Lim, M. H. (1984, May). Affirmative action in Malaysia. In *International perspectives on affirmative action: A Bellagio conference, August 16-20, 1982* (pp. 1-41). New York: Rockefeller Foundation.

Madrid, A. (1984, November 5). Where we are; and where we need to go. *Higher Education & National Affairs,* p. 7.

Madrid, A. (1988, May 1). Diversity and its discontents. *Higher Education & National Affairs,* pp. 10, 11, 16.

Minority changes hold major implications for U.S. (1984, March 9). *Higher Education & National Affairs,* p. 8.

Murphy, J. S. (1986, May 20). *Statement on affirmative action.* Paper presented at the 148th Plenary Session of the University Faculty Senate of the City University of New York.

Nation. (1988, September 1). *Chronicle of Higher Education,* p. 3.

National Alliance of Black School Educators. (1984). *Saving the African American child.* Washington, DC: Author.

New commission focuses on testing and public policy. (1988, February 1). *Black Issues in Higher Education,* pp. 1, 5.

Oakes, J. (1985). *Keeping track: How schools structure inequality.* New Haven, CT: Yale University Press.

O'Brien, E. M. (1988a, March 1). Succeeding on predominantly white campuses: Black administrators' advice to minority faculty. *Black Issues in Higher Education,* pp. 3, 4.

O'Brien, E. M. (1988b, May 15). More research needed on minorities' performance, apprehension of standardized tests. *Black Issues in Higher Education,* pp. 1, 4.

O'Brien, E. M. (1988c, November 10). Blacks' upward mobility stymied by racial discrimination, economic changes, conferees told. *Black Issues in Higher Education,* pp. 9, 11.

Pifer, A. (1975). *Black progress: Achievement, failure and an uncertain future.* New York: Carnegie Corporation.

Pigford, A. B. (1988, November 24). Being a black faculty member on a white campus: My reality. *Black Issues in Higher Education,* p. 76.

Policy trends erode minority gains in education. (1985, April 8). *Higher Education & National Affairs,* pp. 1, 4.

Racial and ethnic makeup of college and university enrollments. (1986, July 23). *Chronicle of Higher Education,* p. 25.

Reeves, M. S. (1985, April 17). Minorities and college: "A time bomb." *Education Week,* pp. 1, 12, 13.

Shalala, D. E. (1985, November 11). Nontraditional students in higher education. *Higher Education & National Affairs,* p. 5.

Soldwedel, B. J. (1971). Whoever wants it needs it. In W. T. Furniss (Ed.), *Higher education for everybody?* Washington, DC: American Council on Education.

Striner, H. E. (1983, Fall). The changing economy and its implications for postsecondary curricula. *Educational Record, 64,* 38.

Sudarkasa, N. (1988, September/October). Can we afford equity and excellence? Can we afford less? *Academe, 74*(5), 23-26.

Vacarro, L. C. (1975, February). The future look at American education. *Phi Delta Kappan, 56*(6), 387-389.

Vincent, W. E. (1987, April 20). Affirmative action: A mandate to more. *Higher Education & National Affairs,* p. 7.

Visiting Committee on Minority Life and Education at Brown University. (1986, May). *The American university and the pluralist ideal.* Providence, RI: Brown University.

PART II

EDUCATIONAL ENVIRONMENTS THAT PROMOTE EQUITY

6

Introduction:
Research on Equity
in Learning Environments

JUDITH WALKER de FELIX

University of Houston

Recent educational thought has emphasized the importance of the school environment for promoting equity. Replacing the body of literature that tended to blame the victims of poor schooling for their own academic failure, current research is attempting to discover the school variables that promote effective learning.

At the same time, the work of the schools is becoming more challenging as students are increasingly more heterogeneous and society's needs change. U.S. classrooms now are filled with culturally, physically, and linguistically diverse children. The ages in one classroom may even vary greatly, as states restrict social promotion and immigrant children arrive in the United States without prior schooling. The chapters in this section demonstrate that equitable education means schooling that is far from merely equal. Individual children need distinct learning environments. The chapters in this section describe theories and practices upon which educational leaders can draw for innovations in both research and practice.

The first chapter, by Herbert J. Walberg, reviews studies of effective classroom environments. He warns, however, that this research is just a beginning. Students are still failing, and there is evidence that even America's most gifted are trailing the gifted in other countries.

To emphasize his point, Walberg presents dictionary definitions of the term *equity*, then makes an interesting contrast between the definitions of educational equity in the United States and in Japan. In the United States *equity* has been used to describe the educational parity expected in a democratic society. Since the official recognition in 1954, with *Brown v. Board of Education*, that separate educational facilities are inherently unequal, U.S. educators have attempted to design learning environments in which children have equal access to educational institutions. Japan, on the other hand, has been severely criticized for its treatment of its ethnic minorities. Korean-Japanese, for example, have separate, unequal schools. Walberg, however, points out an important aspect of the word *equity* that the Japanese have perfected. To the Japanese, equity is the value of an investment. It is Walberg's opinion that American education will suffer unless we consider this double meaning of *equity*.

One consistently effective environment for academic achievement consists of school-parent partnerships. Walberg describes one program in which children normally assumed to be "at risk" and hence incapable of achieving made academic gains similar to middle-class children when their parents were involved in the children's education.

In Chapter 8, Henry T. Trueba draws from psychological and anthropological theories to explain why school-home partnerships work: They draw together the three aspects of culture — cognition, affect, and action. Trueba also describes a successful project, one that increased teacher expectations of educationally vulnerable students while increasing students' writing achievement.

Trueba's study suggests a difficulty that leaders in the development of educational equity must confront: the labeling of children who need more attention in schools than they are currently receiving. Previously called "culturally deprived" or "economically disadvantaged," the children of poor ethnic, racial, and linguistic minority families are currently called "at risk." Statistically, this is an appropriate term. Most school leavers are from the lower economic strata in the United States. Researchers and administrators need a descriptive term to study and plan effective environments for students who may not be served in traditional settings. For the individual student, however, this term may be the negative equivalent of the Pygmalion in the classroom: a self-fulfilling prophecy. Teachers know the risks that poor children run. Often they fail to expect at-risk students to achieve. As Trueba points out, once teacher expectations — and consequently their classroom practices — change, students can begin to achieve.

In the past we have simply changed terminology to avoid negative expectations. Many who decry labeling children realize that funding and societal attention result from catchy phrases that are easily cited in the newspapers and in Congress. Scholarly journals are not immune to the power of the word, either; they frequently feature theme issues that center on the current catch phrase. How to identify children to serve their specific needs without labeling them with a term that later becomes negative is an issue with which we may continue to struggle for a long time.

Trueba's chapter has an additional dimension. He reviews one of his earlier studies in light of a different theoretical perspective. Frequently, educational research has depended on a monocultural interpretation. Student achievement, for example, is measured by tests manufactured for dominant-culture students. By discovering why normally vulnerable students achieve, scholars will be better equipped to develop effective environments.

Dropout and failure rates indicate that it is especially limited English proficient (LEP) students who suffer from inappropriate classroom environments. In his chapter, Christian Faltis summarizes research that describes the usual classroom as being teacher oriented. Instead, Faltis, like Trueba and Walberg, proposes a Vygotskian perspective of educational development. Faltis synthesizes research on effective classrooms for LEP students in particular to propose an interactive environment. While some may contend that such an environment is needed for all children, Faltis presents compelling cultural and psychological arguments regarding the need for such an environment for heritage-language students.

Most classroom environments, however, do not have the kinds of cognitive, affective, physical, and parental involvement described by Walberg, Trueba, and Faltis. As Walberg points out, we know a great deal about effective environments, but we seem to lack the economic and moral commitment to implement them; that is, we are not protecting our investment. The consequences are that school attrition rates are alarmingly high in the world's most technologically advanced country, and even the most gifted students in this country cannot compete well on tests on subjects basic to technological development.

There are abundant critics of U.S. schools and their leaders. Schools are condemned for reproducing society's current inequities. Bright students, especially girls, in the United States are falling behind students in other countries. Whole groups of young people are alienated from schools' values. Yet the chapters in Part II demonstrate that there is, to use Trueba's words, compassion and a desire for equity and productivity among prominent educational researchers. More practically, these researchers also have described successful, equitable practices that school leaders can implement with confidence.

7

Productivity and Equity

HERBERT J. WALBERG

University of Illinois at Chicago

Equity: "a right, claim, or interest existing or valid in equity; . . . the money value of a property or of an interest in a property in excess of claims or liens against it; . . . a risk interest or ownership right in property."

(WEBSTER'S NINTH NEW COLLEGIATE DICTIONARY, 1988, p. 421)

In *A Nation at Risk*, the National Commission on Excellence in Education (1983) pointed out that American students' achievement was, by international standards, mediocre at best. The United States was spending enormous sums on schools, but its accumulating human capital — in particular, its investment equity in youth — lagged. In the view of many citizens, parents, and legislators, the quality and quantity of educational services was fundamentally uncompetitive, which jeopardized both effectiveness and equity (Walberg, 1986). Hence ensued a colossal wave of educational reform.

The past decade of statistics from the National Assessment of Educational Progress shows improved achievement in the standard school subjects, but much remains to be done. For example, recent scores on the mathematics achievement of the top 5% of students in industrialized countries show U.S. students in last place. Achievement scores in science show advanced placement high school students below those in Europe and Japan and tied with those in Third World countries (Walberg, 1989).

Japanese Equity

In an important paper on American, Japanese, and Taiwanese elementary mathematics learning, Stevenson, Lee, and Stigler (1986) show some of the reasons for our poor national rankings. As these authors report, IQ test scores reveal that all three groups were equally able at the start of schooling. Each year, however, Asian students drew further ahead in achievement. A small achievement advantage at the end of the first grade grew ever larger, so that by fifth grade, the worst Asian class sample exceeded the best U.S. class.

The Asian students had a far more rigorous curriculum and worked at a faster pace; they studied more at school and, with their parents' encouragement, at home. In the United States, parents attributed success to luck or ability more often than to hard work; in Asia, parents attributed success to hard work. A U.S. Department of Education (1987a) study also shows that Japanese students muster effort both inside and outside school. The number of hours spent in class, on homework, and in special evening tutoring schools, as well as the number of school days per year, are all substantially higher than in the United States. My observations in Japan indicate that the time students spend in class and in outside study is also used more efficiently than among the top U.S. students.

By contrast, U.S. high school students average 28 hours of television per week and only 4 or 5 weekly hours of homework (Walberg, 1984b). Japanese students may be getting twice as much annual study time as our own. A Japanese high school diploma, indeed, may indicate more learning than an American baccalaureate degree. Even aside from other advantages, the ratio of Japanese to U.S. school days per year $(240/180 = 1.33)$ suggests that the Japanese learn in 12 years what would take a U.S. time equivalent of 16 years.

Nine Productivity Factors

Educational researchers have accumulated many findings that show how education can be made more productive, even though the nation has yet to implement them intensively and extensively. Analyses of large-scale educational surveys and syntheses of thousands of educational research results have been conducted (see Fraser, Walberg,

Table 7.1 Nine Educational Productivity Factors

Student Aptitude
  (1) *ability* or preferably *prior achievement* as measured by the usual achievement tests
  (2) *development* as indexed by chronological age or stage of maturation
  (3) *motivation* or self-concept as indicated by personality tests or the student's willingness to persevere intensively on learning tasks

Instruction
  (4) *amount* of time students engage in learning
  (5) *quality* of the instructional experience, including method (psychological) and curricular (content) aspects

Psychological Environments
  (6) *curriculum of the home*
  (7) *morale* of classroom social group
  (8) *peer group* outside school
  (9) minimum leisure-time *television* viewing

Welch, & Hattie, 1987; Walberg, 1984b, 1989). These surveys and syntheses show that nine factors increase learning. Potent, consistent, and widely generalizable, these nine factors fall into the three groups shown in Table 7.1.

Collectively, the various studies suggest that the nine factors are powerful and consistent in influencing learning. An early synthesis of about 2,575 studies suggests that these generalizable factors are the chief influences on academic achievement and, more broadly, school-related cognitive, affective, and behavioral learning. Many aspects of these factors, especially the amount and quality of instruction, can be altered by educators; these deserve our attention, especially in improving educational opportunities for at-risk youth.

Each of the first five factors — prior achievement, development, motivation, and the quantity and quality of instruction — seems necessary for learning in school; without at least a small amount of each, the student can learn little. Large amounts of instruction and high degrees of ability, for example, may count for little if students are unmotivated or instruction is unsuitable. Although most students can gain much from the alterable instructional factors, policymakers increasingly realize that, among the environmental factors, the home environment is crucial for increased performance among at-risk children and youth, especially in the early years of childhood and schooling.

The Curriculum of the Home

What has been called "the curriculum of the home" is constituted by informed parent-child conversations regarding school and the day's events, encouragement and discussion of leisure reading, monitoring and joint critical analysis of television viewing and peer activities, deferral of immediate gratifications to the accomplishment of long-term human-capital goals, expressions of affection and interest in the child's academic and other progress as a person, and perhaps, among such unremitting efforts, laughter, caprice, and serendipity. Such "home teaching" may extend for 20 years with the same teacher and learner — apart from instances of family disruption. In contrast, school offers a different teacher each new academic year of elementary school and multiple teachers in secondary schools.

Cooperative efforts by parents and teachers to modify alterable educative conditions in the home have strong, beneficial effects on learning. In a review and synthesis of 29 controlled studies conducted between 1963 and 1980, 91% of the comparisons favored children in experimental groups (Graue, Weinstein, & Walberg, 1983). The programs favored children on measures of mathematics, reading and language achievement, and affective development. Even though the average effect was twice that of socioeconomic status, some programs had effects 10 times as large. The programs, moreover, seem to benefit older as well as younger students.

Since few of the programs lasted more than a semester, the potential for those sustained over years of schooling is great. Educators, however, cannot implement such programs in a vacuum; the cooperation of teachers, as well as that of parents and students, is essential. Hence the term *partnership*.

The parents' role can be both supplementary and complementary to the school efforts (Barth, 1979; Walberg, Bole, & Waxman, 1980). Home intervention programs may extend or increase the quality and quantity of academic instruction beyond the school day, stimulate children to be more motivated and receptive to school lessons, decrease the number of hours children spend watching television (which may be detrimental to academic learning), and promote closer, more constructive family relations (Graue et al., 1983).

The Matthew Effect

Students who are slow in starting often continue at a slower rate; those who start ahead often gain at a faster rate — a results that has been called the "Matthew effect" of the academically rich getting richer (as originally noted in the Bible: "For unto every one that hath shall be given, and he shall have abundance; but from him that hath not shall be taken away even that which he hath"; Matthew, 25:29, KJV). This effect characterizes school learning, family influences on development, and socioeconomic advantages in communication among adults (Walberg & Tsai, 1983), as well as the development of reading comprehension and verbal literacy (Stanovitch, 1987).

Ironically, although improved instructional programs may benefit all students, they may confer greater advantages on those who are initially advantaged. For this reason, the first six years of life and the curriculum of the home are decisively influential in academic achievement (U.S. Department of Education, 1986; Walberg, 1984a). This Matthew effect of the educationally rich getting richer has been observed in many U.S. studies (Walberg & Tsai, 1983), and its pervasiveness is one reason educators and policymakers are inaugurating parent partnership programs before and during the school years.

Changes in families bode ill for youth and provide another important reason to strengthen home-school ties. During the century from 1860 to 1960, for example, the divorce rate in the United States held at between 30 and 35 per 1,000 marriages; but fertility declined after 1960, non-marital cohabiting relations rose dramatically, and divorces increased to unprecedented levels. At current rates, about one-third of all American children will see the dissolution of their parents' marriages. The percentage of working wives, moreover, rose from 32% in 1960 to 56% in 1981 (Cherlin, 1983). It is hardly the poor alone who are at risk for the Matthew effect.

Parent Partnerships

Even our best and brightest could be doing much better. The schools, in partnership with other institutions, can reach out to families in specific and proven ways to extend and improve learning time. The

U.S. Department of Education's *What Works* (1986), for example, makes several suggestions regarding what parents can do:

(1) Conversation is important. Children learn to read, reason, and understand things better when their parents read, talk, and listen to them; tell them stories, play games, share hobbies, and discuss news, TV programs, and special events.

(2) Enrich the curriculum of the home by providing books, supplies, and special places for studying; ensure regularity in mealtimes, bedtimes, and homework times; and monitor the amount of time children spend watching TV and doing after-school jobs.

(3) Parents stay aware of their children's lives at school when they discuss school events, help children meet deadlines, and talk with their children about school problems and successes.

Chester Finn (1987), former U.S. assistant secretary of education, elaborates: "Parents can do a lot to buttress the impact of schooling, they can encourage their children to read, make sure they do their homework, regulate the amount of television they watch, and display a lively interest in their academic performance" (p. 65).

A Model Program in Chicago

Chicago educators and parents developed an exemplary early parent-education program for grades 1-6. Operation Higher Achievement, at the Grant School in Chicago's severely depressed near Westside, illustrates what educators can do in inner-city public schools with parent partners (Walberg et al., 1980).

A joint school staff-parent steering committee at Grant initially formulated seven program goals such as "increasing parents' awareness of the reading process" and "improving parent-school-community relations." Seven 10-member staff-parent committees met periodically to plan and guide the accomplishment of each goal. The goals were based on parent surveys that showed that they wanted closer school-parent cooperation, stricter school discipline, and more educational activities conducted in the school and community for their children.

The committees wrote staff-parent-child agreements to be followed during the school year. The district superintendent, principal, and teachers signed contracts for educational services to be provided to each child. The parents pledged such things as providing a quiet, well-lit place for study each day; informing themselves about and encouraging their children's progress; and cooperating with teachers on matters of school-work, discipline, and attendance. The children also signed improvement pledges. Small business merchants in the community raised funds to provide book exchange fairs and other school activities.

Evaluation of this program, along with other research, shows that inner-city children can make middle-class progress in achievement. To help them, educators need to sustain active cooperation with parents on joint goals.

Although parent-teacher work on specific goals shows the greatest learning effects, David Williams and others at the Southwest Educational Development Laboratory in Austin, Texas, describe other constructive roles for parent partners in school programs: as an audience for their children's work, as home tutors, as colearners with their children, as school program supporters, as advocates before school boards and other officials, as school committee members, and as volunteers or paid school aides.

Efficacious Teaching and Instruction

What teachers and instructional systems do can also substantially affect how much students learn. An Australian-U.S. team recently assessed 134 reviews of 7,827 field studies and several large-scale U.S. and international surveys of learning (Fraser et al., 1987). I will draw from my recent summary of this work (Walberg, 1989) in addition to more recent compilations to indicate the scope of the findings.

Specific Effects on Learning

Table 7.2 shows that empirical studies of classroom learning can be divided up in at least 15 ways. One may begin, for example, with the effects of the psychological elements of teaching and then turn to methods and patterns of teaching—all of which can be accomplished by a single teacher without unusual arrangements and equipment. Systems of instruction require special planning, student grouping, and materials. Next are effects that are unique to reading, writing, science, and mathematics. The remaining results concern special students and techniques, and effects of training on teachers.

The compilation of effects allows us to compare educational means with one another—including some effective ones that are no longer

Table 7.2 Fifteen Areas of Synthesized Research on Teaching and Instruction

Psychological elements of teaching
Methods of teaching
Patterns of teaching
Learner autonomy in science
Open education
Instructional systems
Computer-assisted instruction
Student grouping
Social environment
Reading effects
Writing effects
Science effects
Mathematics effects
Special populations and techniques
Effects on teachers

popular. We can see that some techniques have enormous effects, while others confer only trivial advantages or even harm learning. To plan and evaluate programs, we can examine the findings in the light of personal experience. In practice, however, educators might attain results half or twice as good as the average estimates reported below. Success will depend not only on care in implementation but on purposes; the best saw swung as a hammer may do little good.

Psychological Elements of Teaching

A little history will help us understand the evolution of psychological research on teaching. Psychologists have often emphasized thought, feeling, or behavior at the expense of one another — even though educators require balance. Today, thinking or cognition is sovereign in psychology, but a half century ago, behaviorists insisted on specific operational definitions — a standard still required.

In particular, Yale psychologists Neal Miller and John Dollard, stimulated by E. L. Thorndike and B. F. Skinner, wrote about cues, responses, and positive reinforcement, especially in psychotherapy. Later, Dollard and Miller emphasized three components of teaching — cues, engagement, and reinforcement — similar to input, process, and output in physiology. Their influential ideas stimulated research on what teachers do rather than their age, experience, certification, college degrees, and other characteristics unconnected with what their students learn.

The behavioral model emphasized the quality of instructional cues impinging on the learner, the learner's active engagement in the process, and reinforcements or rewards that encourage continuing effort over time. Benjamin Bloom recognized, however, that learners may fail the first time or even repeatedly in cycles of cues and effort; if they make no progress, they may practice incorrect behavior, and they cannot be reinforced. Therefore, he introduced the ideas of feedback to correct errors and frequent testing to check progress. Inspired by John Carroll's model of school learning, Bloom also emphasized engaged learning time, and that some learners require much more time than others.

Cues, as operationalized, show what is to be learned and explain how to learn it. Their quality can be seen in the clarity, salience, and meaningfulness of explanations and directions provided by teacher, instructional materials, or both. Ideally, as learners gain confidence, the salience and numbers of cues can be reduced.

Engagement is the extent to which learners actively and persistently participate until appropriate responses are firmly entrenched in their repertoires. Such participation can be indexed by the extent to which the teacher engages students in overt or covert activity — indicated by absence of irrelevant behavior, concentration on tasks, enthusiastic contributions to group discussion, and lengthy study.

Corrective feedback remedies errors in oral or written responses. Ideally, students waste little time on incorrect responses, and teachers rapidly detect and remedy difficulties by reteaching or using alternate methods; when necessary, they also provide additional time needed for practice.

The immense effort elicited by athletics, games, and other cooperative and competitive activities illustrates the power of immediate and direct *reinforcement*, and how some activities are intrinsically rewarding in themselves. By comparison, classroom reinforcement may seem crass or jejune. The usual classroom reinforcers are acknowledgment of correctness and social approval, say, in the form of a smile or praise. More unusual reinforcers include contingent activity — allowing, for example, a music lesson or other enjoyable activity for 90% correctness on a math test. Other reinforcers include tokens or check marks accumulated for steps accomplished and later exchanged for tangible reinforcers such as cookies, trinkets, or toys.

In special education programs, students have been reinforced not only for achievement but also for minutes of reading, attempts to learn, and accuracy of task performance in special programs. When the environment can be rigorously controlled, and when teachers are able to gear reinforcement to performance accurately, as in programs for unruly or emotionally disturbed students, the results have been impressive. Improved behavior and achievement, however, often fail to extend past the period of reinforcement or beyond the special environment.

Educators ordinarily confine reinforcement to marks, grades, and awards because they must assume that students work for intangible, long-term goals such as pleasing parents, further education, adult success, and (one hopes) for an ultimate aim of education — the intrinsic reward of learning itself. Even so, when corrective feedback and reinforcement are clear, rapid, and appropriate, they can powerfully affect learning by signaling the student what to do next without wasting time. In ordinary classrooms, then, the chief value of reinforcement is in providing information rather than incentive.

Patterns of Teaching

Methods and patterns of teaching enact or combine more fundamental psychological elements. Two recent formulations, explicit teaching and comprehension instruction, follow the evolution of psychological research on education: Behavioral research evolved in the 1950s from psychological laboratories to short-term, controlled experiments on one element at a time in classrooms. In the 1970s, educational researchers tried to find patterns of effective practices from observations of ordinary teaching.

Thus behaviorists traded educational realism for theoretical parsimony and scientific rigor; later, psychologists preferred realism until their insights were experimentally confirmed. Fortunately, the results from both approaches appear to converge. It seems possible, moreover, to incorporate the work of cognitive psychologists of the 1980s into an enlarged understanding of teaching.

Explicit Teaching

Explicit teaching can be viewed as traditional or conventional whole-group teaching done well. Since most teaching has changed little in the last three-quarters of a century and may not soon change substantially, it is worthwhile to know how the usual practice can excel. Since it has evolved from ordinary practice, explicit teaching is easy to carry out and does not disrupt conventional institutions and expectations. It can, moreover, incorporate many previously discussed elements and methods.

Systematic research was initiated about 1960 by N. L. Gage, Donald Medley, and others who employed "process-product" investigations of the association between what teachers do and how much their students learn. Jere Brophy, Carolyn Evertson, Thomas Good, and Jane Stallings later contributed substantially to this effort. Walter Doyle, Penelope Peterson, and Lee Shulman put results in a psychological, particularly cognitive, context. Barak Rosenshine has periodically reviewed the research; Nate Gage and Margaret Needels, in forthcoming work, made actual estimates of the effects of explicit teaching.

The various contributors to this research do not completely agree about the essential components of explicit teaching, and they refer to it by different names: explicit, process-product, direct, active, and effective teaching. The contributors, moreover, weigh their own results heavily; however, Rosenshine, as a long-standing and comprehensive reviewer, has taken an eagle's-eye view of the results.

In his early reviews of correlation studies, Rosenshine discussed the traits of effective teachers, including clarity, task orientation, enthusiasm, and flexibility, as well as tendencies to structure presentations and occasionally use student ideas. From later observational and control-group research, Rosenshine and Stevens (1986) have identified six phased functions of explicit teaching: (a) daily review, homework check, and, if necessary, reteaching; (b) rapid presentation of new content and skills in small steps; (c) guided student practice with close teacher monitoring; (d) corrective feedback and instructional reinforcement; (e) independent practice in seatwork and homework with a high, more than 90%, success rate; and (f) weekly and monthly review.

Comprehension Instruction

The descendants of Aristotle and the Anglo-American tradition of Bacon, Locke, Thorndike, and Skinner objected to philosophical "armchair" opinions; midcentury behaviorists, particularly John Watson, constructively insisted on hard empirical facts about learning. But they also saw the child's mind as a blank tablet, and seemed to encourage active teaching and passive acquisition of isolated facts. Reacting to such atomism and William James's "bucket" metaphor around 1980, cognitive psychologists revived research on student-centered learning and "higher mental processes," in the tradition of Plato, Socrates, Kant, Rousseau, Dewey, Freud, and Piaget. In American hands, however, this

Central European tradition can lead to vacuity and permissiveness, as in the extremes of the "progressive education" movement of the 1930s.

Oddly, Russian psychologist Lev Vygotsky hit on an influential compromise: Emphasizing the two-way nature of teaching, he identified a "zone of proximal development" extending from what learners can do independently to the maximum they can do with the teacher's help. Accordingly, teachers should set up "scaffolding" for building knowledge, and remove it when it becomes unnecessary. In mathematics, for example, the teacher can give hints and examples, foster independent use, and then remove support. This approach is similar to the "prompting" and "fading" of the behavioral cues and to common sense, but it sufficed to revive interest in transferring some autonomy to students.

Pearson (1985), for example, outlines three phases much like explicit teaching functions: (a) modeling, in which the teacher exhibits the desired behavior; (b) guided practice, in which students perform with help from the teacher; and (c) application, in which students perform independently of the teacher. Palincsar and Brown (1984), moreover, describe a program of "reciprocal teaching" to foster comprehension by having students take turns in leading dialogues on pertinent features of the text. By assuming planning and executive control ordinarily exercised by teachers, students learn planning, structuring, and self-management. Perhaps that is why tutors learn from teaching, and why we say to learn something well, teach it.

Comprehension instruction encourages readers to measure their progress toward explicit goals. If necessary, they can reallocate time for different activities. In this way, self-awareness, personal control, and positive self-evaluation can be enlarged, and research shows strong effects on comprehension measures (Haller, Child, & Walberg, in press).

Conclusion

Psychological research provides first-order estimates of the effects of family and instructional means on educational ends under various conditions. But some practices may be costly — not in dollars, but in new or complicated arrangements that may be difficult for some parents and teachers to begin and continue. Thus the estimates of effects are only one basis for decision making; we need to consider productivity or values of effects in relation to total costs, including the time and energies of educators, parents, and students.

Psychology alone cannot suffice to prescribe practices, since different means bring about different ends. In their attempt to enlarge educational effectiveness and equity, educators must choose among student, teacher, and curriculum direction of effort; facts and ideas; breadth and depth; short- and long-term ends; academic knowledge and real-world application; equal opportunity and equal results; and Plato's triumvirate of thinking, feeling, and acting. Once these choices are made, the estimates of effects can provide one of the bases for choosing the most productive practices.

References

Barth, R. (1979). Home-based reinforcement of school behavior. *Review of Education Research, 49*, 306-315.

Cherlin, A. (1983). Changing family and household. In R. D. Turner & J. F. Short (Eds.), *Annual review of sociology* (Vol. 9). Palo Alto, CA: Annual Reviews.

Comer, J. P. (1984). Home-school relationships as they affect the academic success of children. *Education and Urban Society, 16*(3), 323-337.

Epstein, J. L., & Becker, H. J. (1982). Teachers' reported practices of parent involvement: Problems and possibilities. *Elementary School Journal, 83*(2), 103-112.

Finn, C. E. (1987, September). Education that works: Make the schools complete. *Harvard Business Review*, pp. 63-68.

Fraser, B. J., Walberg, H. J., Welch, W. W., & Hattie, J. A. (1987). Synthesis of educational productivity research. *International Journal of Educational Research, 11*(2), 147-252.

Graue, N. E., Weinstein, T., & Walberg, H. J. (1983). School-based home instruction and learning: A quantitative synthesis, *Journal of Educational Research, 76*(6), 351-360.

Haller, E., Child, D., & Walberg, H. J. (in press). Can comprehension be taught? A quantitative synthesis of meta-cognitive studies. *Educational Researcher.*

National Commission on Excellence in Education. (1983). *A nation at risk: The imperative for educational reform.* Washington, DC: Government Printing Office.

Palincsar, A., & Brown, A. (1984). Reciprocal teaching of comprehension-fostering and comprehension-monitoring activities. *Cognition and Instruction, 1* 117-176.

Pearson, D. (1985). Reading comprehension instruction. *Reading Teacher, 38*, 724-738.

Rich, D. (1988). *Mega skills.* Boston: Houghton Mifflin.

Rosenshine, B., & Stevens, R. (1986). Teaching functions. In M. C. Wittrock (Ed.), *Handbook of research on teaching.* New York: Macmillan.

Stanovitch, K. E. (1986). Matthew effects in reading: Some consequences of individual differences in the acquisitions of literacy. *Reading Research Quarterly, 21*, 360-407.

Stevenson, H. W., Lee, S. Y., & Stigler, J. W. (1986). Mathematics achievement of Chinese, Japanese, and American children. *Science, 231*, 693-699.

U.S. Department of Education. (1986). *What works: Research about teaching and learning.* Washington DC: Government Printing Office.

U.S. Department of Education. (1987a). *Japanese education today.* Washington, DC: Government Printing Office.

U.S. Department of Education. (1987b). *Schools that work: Educating disadvantaged children.* Washington, DC: Government Printing Office.

Walberg, H. J. (1983). Scientific illiteracy and economic productivity in international perspective. *Daedalus, 112,* 1-28.

Walberg, H. J. (1984a). Families as partners in educational productivity. *Phi Delta Kappan, 65,* 397-400.

Walberg, H. J. (1984b). Improving the productivity of America's schools. *Educational Leadership, 41,* 19-27.

Walberg, H. J. (1986). Synthesis of research on teaching. In M. C. Wittrock (Ed.), *Handbook of research on teaching.* New York: Macmillan.

Walberg, H. J. (1989). Science, mathematics and national welfare: Retrospective and prospective achievement. In A. C. Purves (Ed.), *International perspectives on education,.* Alexandria, VA: Association for Supervision and Curriculum Development.

Walberg, H. J. (in press). Productive teaching and instruction: Assessing the knowledge base. *Phi Delta Kappan.*

Walberg, H. J., Bole, R. E., & Waxman, H. C. (1980). School-based family socialization and achievement in the inner city. *Psychology in the Schools,* pp. 509-514.

Walberg, H. J., & Tsai, S. L. (1983). Matthew effects in education. *American Educational Research Journal, 20,* 359-373.

White, K. R. (1985). Efficacy of early intervention. *Journal of Special Education, 19*(4), 401-416.

8

Compassion and Equity: Culture and English Literacy for Linguistic Minority Children

HENRY T. TRUEBA
University of California, Santa Barbara

This chapter illustrates the usefulness of an interdisciplinary approach in analyzing the role of culture in English literacy acquisition for linguistic minorities. Soviet psychologists led by Vygotsky, and both European and American neo-Vygotskians (see Tharp & Gallimore, 1989) have provided us with forceful arguments to link the development of higher mental functions to social activities, and to view language as critically important for the development of cognitive structures. Furthermore, Vygotsky's view of the learner's role in determining his or her area of greatest possible cognitive development ("zone of proximal development") is intimately related to the role that culture plays in development.

Wertsch, one of the best known experts on Vygotsky's socially based theory of "assisted performance" for cognitive development, feels that the role of culture in the selection and use of specific symbolic systems for the organization of cognitive tasks is essential. He indicates that "people privilege the use of one mediational means over others" (Wertsch, 1987, p. 21); that is, they select specific communicative and symbolic instruments and systems in accordance with the cultural values and patterns they have acquired. He adds that ultimately "we need to combine the analysis of collectively organized mediational means with the analysis of interpsychological functioning," and consequently, "if choice of mediational means is a major determinant of how thinking and speaking can proceed, then processes whereby groups make decisions (either implicitly or explicitly) about these means should become a focus of our research" (p. 20).

In brief, Wertsch (1987) views culture as highly instrumental in either determining or facilitating a conscious, collective choice of mediational means. Consequently, "if we are to take the study of memory, thinking, attention, or any other aspect of human consciousness seriously, we must begin by recognizing the sociohistorical and cultural embeddedness of the subjects as well as investigators involved" (pp. 21-22).

The theoretical framework of Vygotsky (1962, 1978) and neo-Vygotskians (Cole & D'Andrade, 1982; Cole & Griffin, 1983; Wertsch, 1985) has focused on the development of the higher psychological functions, which are naturally related to school achievement. One of the common assumptions is that linguistic, sociocultural, and communicative competencies are critical for the development of higher-order thinking skills. Furthermore, both linguistic and social skills are viewed as developing within the microsociological units in which children grow, such as family and peer group. Most neo-Vygotskians would view culture as an essential aspect of the process of learning. For Vygotsky (1962, 1978), cognitive development consists of an increased ability to manipulate cultural symbols (particularly language) in intra- and interpsychological activities (Wertsch, 1985). Symbolic systems are, according to neo-Vygotskians, presumed to mediate between the mind and outside reality (Tharp & Gallimore, 1989). That reality, however, is determined by cultural knowledge transferred from one generation to another and by universal psychological principles that go beyond the individual.

One can argue that effective English literacy instruction requires the transmission of cultural values and skills as much as the academic knowledge associated with mainstream American culture. Work by Gumperz and Hymes (1972), Gumperz (1982, 1986), and Cook-Gumperz (1986) has forced us to reflect on the relationship between communication and literacy as part of a broader symbolic system dynamically changing along with people's cultural contexts.

Literacy, in its broadest sense as a "socially constructed phenomenon" (Cook-Gumperz, 1986, p. 1) consisting of arbitrary symbols developed for communicative purposes, is intimately related to the economic and political contexts determining power structures and access to information. In this sense, technological, economic, and military development go hand in hand with overall levels of literacy and determine the nature of schools and curricula.

Freire's (1973) notion of literacy, "reading the word and reading the world," is not an esoteric philosophy, but a logical position in the face of stratified societies in which educational institutions are controlled by those who hold power. His notion gets at the heart of continued illiteracy problems in our country: Access to resources is not equal. The per capita expenditure in U.S. schools reflects clearly the socioeconomic strata existing in our society. Academic failure of minority children is clearly related to the role of culture in literacy acquisition.

Gumperz and Cook-Gumperz view literacy as a phenomenon intimately related to interpretive processes within specific cultural contexts. Literacy requires not only technical skills for encoding or decoding, "but also a set of prescripts about using knowledge" (Cook-Gumperz, 1986, p. 1). Reading and writing are inseparable from the sociocultural knowledge we need to function appropriately in society. How can linguistic minority children, especially if they are socially isolated, living in poverty, and moving from one sociocultural environment to another, acquire this essential knowledge?

Researchers with the Kamehameha Project have documented the success of Hawaiian children in instructional activities organized on the premise that cultural congruence enhances literacy acquisition (Au & Jordan, 1981; Tharp & Gallimore, 1989), but more recent events in that project have invited reflection on the nature of cultural congruence and its formal requirements. Can we re-create in the classroom the sociocultural organization of the home, or the discourse and participation patterns of the home, for example, the Hawaiian talk story?

First, let us take the concept of culture in the traditional anthropological sense used by Goodenough (1976):

> The culture of any society is made up of the concepts, beliefs, and principles of action and organization that an ethnographer has found could be attributed successfully to the members of that society in the context of his dealing with them. (p. 5)

Second, let us reflect on what Frake (1964) calls the requirements for a good understanding of another culture:

> The problem is not to state what someone did but to specify the conditions under which it is culturally appropriate to anticipate that he, or persons occupying his role, will render an equivalent performance. (p. 112)

A good understanding of a culture implies a good theory of cultural behavior in a particular society. In other words, cultural knowledge is the basis of reasoning, inferencing, and selecting meaning from myriad competing interpretations.

To understand the role of cultural knowledge in the acquisition of literacy skills — that is, the skills necessary to understand text and what text stands for — including the "concepts, beliefs, and principles of action" alluded to by Goodenough, cultural knowledge, or the cognitive dimensions of culture, must not be confused with the cultural values (the normative dimensions of culture) required to engage in literacy activities and obtain desired academic knowledge and cognitive skills. To what extent is academic underachievement a function of conflicting cultural values? To study the role of culture in literacy acquisition, we need to pursue explanations of observed behaviors in literacy activities beyond traditional boundaries of task performance in the broader psychological, social, and historical context.

An interdisciplinary perspective can enhance the study of social, economic, educational, and political factors affecting the educational performance of minority groups (Spindler & Spindler, 1987a, 1987b; Trueba, 1989a; Trueba & Delgado-Gaitan, 1988). In addition, educational anthropologists have produced a number of studies using interdisciplinary approaches based on work by DeVos and by Spindler and Spindler.

DeVos (1973, 1982, 1983) pioneered the use of projective techniques in combination with ethnographic methods to penetrate complex layers of personality structure and motivational processes (see also DeVos & Wagatsuma, 1966). As a result, he has offered insightful explanations of achievement behavior and has inspired students and colleagues to pursue unexplored analytical approaches. These methods have been applied at the broader macrosociological, political, and historical levels, as well as at the microstructural levels of interaction (Ogbu, 1987a, 1987b; Suarez-Orozco, 1987, in press).

Spindler and Spindler (1982), who have consistently viewed education as a phenomenon of cultural transmission — implying the inculcation of specific values — have recently called attention to educators' need for *reflective cultural analysis* to take into account unconscious biases and cultural ethnocentrism.

In general, educational researchers have not been able to come up with persuasive explanations of the low literacy and achievement of some minorities, and have presented highly controversial arguments pinpointing cultural factors as culprits. Some attempts have been made to analyze the validity of these arguments and explanations (Goldman & Trueba, 1987; Trueba, 1987a, 1987b, 1987c, 1988a, 1988b, 1988c, 1989a, 1989b; Trueba & Delgado-Gaitan, 1988). While neo-Vygotskians have stressed the intimate relationship between social and psychological phenomena and the importance of assisted performance (see the discussion by Tharp & Gallimore, 1989) for cognitive development, anthropologists have pursued an investigation of the role of culture in determining behaviors maximizing cognitive development and achievement motivation. Some attempts to link macro- and microanalytical approaches in the study of instructional effectiveness with children from different cultural and linguistic backgrounds are interdisciplinary and combine current theories from anthropology, sociology, and psychology with Vygotsky's main theoretical assumptions (Trueba, Moll, Diaz, & Diaz, 1984; Trueba, 1987a, 1987b, 1987c, 1988a, 1988b, 1988c, 1989a).

Both academic success and academic failure are socially constructed phenomena. Failure to learn is a consequence of a given sociocultural system. This failure is also related to communication channels that are within the range of culturally congruent and meaningful exchanges. It is not an individual failure; it is a failure of the sociocultural system that denies a child the opportunity for social intercourse and, thus, cognitive development. As such, academic failure is fully understandable only in its macrohistorical, social, economic, and political context. Failure in learning is not caused by a single social institution, such as the school or the family (Cole & Griffin, 1983; DeVos, 1980, 1983).

A Literacy Study Revisited: The South San Diego Writing Project

The South San Diego Writing Project consisted of ethnographic data collected and analyzed over a period of four years (1980-84) in the San Diego South Bay area along the U.S.-Mexican border (Trueba, 1984, 1987b; Trueba et al., 1984). The intent was to explore more effective ways of teaching Chicano youth how to write in English. The two high schools selected for the study had a 45% Chicano population and the lowest academic scores in the school district.

High school Chicano students were not only socially isolated in the community and minimally exposed to English-speaking peers, but they were economically isolated in barrios where violence and other gang activities were frequent. As we gathered the 12 volunteer teachers who wanted to work in our project, we found out that most of them were commuters and lived a significant distance from the communities in which they taught. All were eager to become effective writing instructors and teachers, but most felt that students were so unprepared and ignorant that the teacher alone was doomed to fail. Only three of the 12 teachers knew Spanish well.

The objectives of the project, which were shared with parents and teachers during an orientation, were (a) to improve the quantity and quality of English compositions, (b) to encourage student participation and cooperation in writing activities, and (c) to analyze in detail student responses to instruction. The specific demographic, socioeconomic, and political characteristics of the barrio, as well as the home language and culture of the students, were generally unknown and viewed as irrelevant by teachers. Given the history of low academic performance of Chicano youth in the local schools, teachers felt that students could not succeed in learning how to write in English. The researchers arranged for parents and teachers to meet and become acquainted with each other's cultures. Teachers were asked to organize their classrooms into small groups, which eventually became cohesive work teams with full control of writing activities; they would research topics, develop surveys, interview informants, and cooperatively write long and complex pieces.

The students amazed their teachers as they discovered that writing was no longer a futile exercise but a meaningful activity and a means of sharing important ideas with specific audiences. Thus Chicano high school students not only sharpened their communicative skills significantly but realized that these skills are a powerful instrument for voicing individual and collective concerns. Teachers would often express their surprise: "I am impressed. Look!" they said as they shared their students' compositions. One teacher wrote in her diary: "This [the unexpected high performance of students] was a very successful lesson for me in many ways. It furthers my belief that if what is taught is important in the mind of the learner, much more will truly be learned" (Trueba et al., 1984, p. 131).

In retrospect, however, I see our analysis as limited to a Vygotskian discussion of cognitive development and its application to a writing curriculum, without attempting to account for the psychosocial factors that created high levels of achievement in students. An investigation of the importance of the peer group, especially for Chicano youth undergoing rapid changes in the home environment, would have required more systematic analyses of the Mexican families, their cultural values, and the behavior congruent with such values.

As writing became easier and more rewarding to students within the peer group, and as teachers learned more about students' home lives, aspirations, and potential through the English compositions, we all focused on technical matters and enthusiastically assumed the role of "experts" on writing. As one teacher observed: "The more controversial and relevant I can make the topic, the more willing the students are to unite and write well . . . , the more complicated the assignment is, the better the responses" (Trueba, 1987b, p. 246). We forgot an important psychological principle advanced by DeVos (1973) in one of his classic works — that to understand the motives behind expressed values

> one must deal with the universal emotions of love, fear, and hate . . . ; culture, from one psychological viewpoint, is a mode of expressing, in all their complexity, these primary emotions, which are aroused by inner biological urges or occur as reactions to specific outer stimuli. (p. 63)

It is precisely in the need of Chicano youth to express their love and fears that one finds their motivation to write. Furthermore, because this need was most appropriately met within the peer group — cooperative teamwork is the culturally preferred mode of academic activity for many Mexican-heritage youth — writing groups offered Chicano youth a unique opportunity both to express their collective feelings and to reinforce a cultural value acquired in the home. An important positive side effect had to be considered, however. High academic performance in an English writing class was a vehicle for restoring the credibility Chicanos lacked among other students, and, further, for gaining political representation in the school.

The theoretical importance of using linkages between macro- and microethnographic data leads us to rethink the neo-Vygotskian analysis in light of the work by DeVos. The result is a more penetrating analysis of the role of culture in both achievement motivation and cognitive development of minority youth. DeVos's strategy of going from the broader sociological, psychological, and cultural context to the specific local behaviors and performance observed would have been perfectly appropriate and highly productive in this project. For example, was it more important for these students to communicate their intimate thoughts or to gain status? Was the level of literacy affected by the rewards as perceived by the teacher or as perceived by the students?

Linking macro- and microanalytical levels also has important policy implications. In this research project, for example, there are a number of questions raised about the presumed "limited," but in truth unknown, student potential, about the conditions for active student participation-cultural congruence, and, most important, about the significant role that culture played in the academic achievement of students. Policymakers should reflect on the need to train teachers who can adopt a more flexible and culturally sensitive instructional approach rather than emphasize the role of teachers as masters of discipline and rigorous gatekeepers of mainstream curricula. If one incorporates DeVos's notion of culture as the means of expressing human feelings of love, hate, fear, and desire, culture can also be viewed as the most powerful force behind academic activities, if such activities permit expression and integration of cultural identity in the school setting.

In contrast to the difficulties faced by Mexican immigrant and Chicano migrant families, DeVos (1973, pp. 204-206) describes the relatively smooth transition of Japanese peasants to city life. City employers served as mentors for the young people by helping them find wives and/or child care for their families. The Japanese found culturally appropriate mechanisms to extend kin ties to city persons with whom they came in contact, thus adapting their behavior selectively and gradually to industrial environments without major disruptions. As DeVos (1973) points out:

> In Japan, family and pseudo-kinship ties kept a firm hold on most individuals both socially and motivationally as they gradually shifted into newer forms of commercial and industrial economic life. (p. 207)

Mexican and Mexican American families often find themselves isolated from mainstream society, yet must face drastic changes in a new world whose language and culture are not understandable to them. Children growing up in these families are subject to high levels of anxiety related to their status as illegal aliens in extreme poverty and their inability to communicate with mainstream society. The dramatic change from failure to success in acquiring English literacy must be explained in terms of the sociocultural meaning that writing in English had for Mexican youth. It was indeed a discovery of a powerful instrument that permitted them to express their feelings publicly and to become recognized as "good students." Status and satisfaction in communicating through writing were key sources of internal rewards for English literacy acquisition.

Reflecting on Literacy Research
Across Disciplines

Two important principles of qualitative research on literacy must be stated:

(1) Literacy research is a rigorous scientific process intended to interpret observed behavior in literacy settings by linking it to broader sociohistorical, linguistic, cultural, and cognitive contexts.
(2) The significance of literacy research and its implications for practice depend on the validity of researchers' interpretations established through linkages between macro- and microanalytical levels of data collected, as well as on cross-cultural comparisons.

Based on these two pivotal principles, we should know where and how *not* to explore the role of culture in literacy:

(1) not only in the study of isolated, fragmented literacy events;
(2) nor in literacy events with exclusive focus on the technical aspects of reading and writing;
(3) nor in the performance of culturally different children in teacher-controlled activities that are meaningless to these children;
(4) nor in the narrow context of cognitive processes assessed by standardized instruments normed in mainstream populations.

Where and how should we explore the role of culture in literacy? In both formal and informal learning settings where children handle cultural/linguistic symbolic systems, face to face or through text. The immediate as well as the broader contexts of literacy activities in specific learning settings are essential in understanding the organization of behavior and the type of student participation in literacy activities. The analysis of literacy activities and patterns of student participation should lead us a view of to the "cultural embeddedness" of literacy phenomena. Teachers' knowledge of students' home languages and cultures can be highly useful in their understanding any gaps between the home and school cultural environments and thus in organizing classroom work in order to maximize students' full and meaningful participation in literacy activities. Immigrant children's generation of their own text materials based on prearrival experiences has been shown in recent studies to be very productive (Trueba, 1989b). The analysis of literacy activities in the home, where inquiry strategies, logical inferencing, and cultural appropriateness occur naturally, is also important (see studies by Delgado-Gaitan, 1987, 1989). This analysis can provide insights into possible linkages between self-empowerment efforts on the part of minority parents and their increasingly supportive role of children's literacy development at home.

Can literacy research become a powerful tool in the implementation of educational reform? Yes, provided it reflects genuine concern for the welfare of minority children. In the ultimate analysis, educators' understanding and tolerance of cultural differences are the direct result of two important moral ingredients:

(1) compassion for linguistic minority children, who are not responsible for their academic predicament and their struggles in adjusting to a new cultural and linguistic environment; and

(2) commitment to the principles of educational equity, particularly to that of respect for the home languages and cultures of linguistic minority children.

It is precisely here, in the crossroads of sound pedagogical principles and a humane approach to the education of *all* children, that a better understanding of American democracy and of American culture can be found.

References

Au, K. H., & Jordan, C. (1981). Teaching reading to Hawaiian children: Finding a culturally appropriate solution. In H. Trueba, G. Guthrie, & K. Au (Eds.), *Culture and the bilingual classroom: Studies in classroom ethnography* (pp. 139-152). Rowley, MA: Newbury House.

Cole, M., & D'Andrade, R. (1982). The influence of schooling on concept formation: Some preliminary conclusions. *Quarterly Newsletter of the Laboratory of Comparative Human Cognition, 4*(2), 19-26.

Cole, M., & Griffin, P. (1983). A socio-historical approach to re-mediation. *Quarterly Newsletter of the Laboratory of Comparative Human Cognition, 5*(4), 69-74.

Cook-Gumperz, J. (Ed.). (1986). *The social construction of literacy.* Cambridge: Cambridge University Press.

Delgado-Gaitan, C. (1987). Parent perceptions of school: Supportive environments for children. In H. Trueba (Ed.), *Success or failure? Learning and the language minority student* (pp. 131-155). Rowley, MA: Newbury House.

Delgado-Gaitan, C. (1989). *Literacy for empowerment: Role of Mexican parents in their children's education.* Unpublished manuscript, University of California, Santa Barbara, Graduate School of Education.

DeVos, G. (1973). Japan's outcasts: The problem of the Burakumin. In B. Whitaker (Ed.), *The fourth world: Victims of group oppression* (pp. 307-327). New York: Schocken.

DeVos, G. (1980). Ethnic adaptation and minority status. *Journal of Cross-Cultural Psychology, 11*, 101-124.

DeVos, G. (1982). Adaptive strategies in U.S. minorities. In E. Jones & S. J. Korchin (Eds.), *Minority mental health* (pp. 74-117). New York: Praeger.

DeVos, G. (1983). Ethnic identity and minority status: Some psycho-cultural considerations. In A. Jacobson-Widding (Ed.), *Identity: Personal and socio-cultural* (pp. 135-158). Uppsala, Sweden: Almquist & Wiksell Tryckeri AB.

DeVos, G., & Wagatsuma, H. (1966). *Japan's invisible race: Caste in culture and personality*. Berkeley: University of California Press.

Frake, C. O. (1964). A structural description of Subanum "religious behavior." In W. H. Goodenough (Ed.), *Explorations in cultural anthropology*. New York: McGraw-Hill.

Freire, P. (1973). *Pedagogy of the oppressed*. New York: Seabury.

Goldman, S., & Trueba, H. (Eds.). (1987). *Becoming literate in English as a second language: Advances in research and theory*. Norwood, NJ: Ablex.

Goodenough, W. H. (1976). Multiculturalism as the normal human experience. *Anthropology and Education Quarterly, 7*(4), 4-7.

Gumperz, J. (Ed.). (1982). *Language and social identity*. Cambridge: Cambridge University Press.

Gumperz, J. (1986). Interactional socio-linguistics in the study of schooling. In J. Cook-Gumperz (Ed.), *The social construction of literacy* (pp. 45-68). Cambridge: Cambridge University Press.

Gumperz, J., & Hymes, D. (1972). *Directions in socio-linguistics: The ethnography of communication*. New York: Holt, Rinehart & Winston.

Ogbu, J. (1987a). Variability in minority responses to schooling: Nonimmigrants vs. immigrants. In G. Spindler & L. Spindler (Eds.), *Interpretive ethnography of education: At home and abroad* (pp. 255-278). Hillsdale, NJ: Lawrence Erlbaum.

Ogbu, J. (1987b). Variability in minority school performance: A problem in search of an explanation. *Anthropology and Education Quarterly, 18*(4), 312-334.

Spindler, G., & Spindler, L. (1982). Roger Harker and Schönhausen: From the familiar to the strange and back again. In G. Spindler (Ed.), *Doing the ethnography of schooling* (pp. 20-47). New York: Holt, Rinehart & Winston.

Spindler, G., & Spindler, L. (1987a). Teaching and learning how to do the ethnography of education. In G. Spindler & L. Spindler (Eds.), *The interpretive ethnography of education: At home and abroad* (pp. 17-33). Hillsdale, NJ: Lawrence Erlbaum.

Spindler, G., & Spindler, L. (1987b). Cultural dialogue and schooling in Schoenhausen and Roseville: A comparative analysis. *Anthropology and Education Quarterly, 18*(1), 3-16.

Suarez-Orozco, M. (1987). Towards a psychosocial understanding of Hispanic adaptation to American schooling. In H. Trueba (Ed.), *Success or failure: Linguistic minority children at home and in school* (pp. 156-168). New York: Harper & Row.

Suarez-Orozco, M. (in press). *In pursuit of a dream: New Hispanic immigrants in American schools*. Stanford, CA: Stanford University Press.

Tharp, R., & Gallimore, R. (1989). *Rousing minds to life: Teaching, learning and schooling in social context*. Cambridge: Cambridge University Press.

Trueba, H. (1984). The forms, functions and values of literacy: Reading for survival in a barrio as a student. *Journal of the National Association for Bilingual Education, 9*(1), 21-38.

Trueba, H. (1987a). Ethnography of schooling. In H. Trueba (Ed.), *Success or failure: Linguistic minority children at home and in school* (pp. 1-13). New York: Harper & Row.

Trueba, H. (1987b). Organizing classroom instruction in specific sociocultural contexts: Teaching Mexican youth to write in English. In S. Goldman & H. Trueba (Eds.), *Becoming literate in English as a second language: Advances in research and theory* (pp. 235-252). Norwood, NJ: Ablex.

Trueba, H. (1987c). *Success or failure? Learning and the language minority student.* New York: Newbury/Harper & Row.

Trueba, H. (1988a). Culturally-based explanations of minority students' academic achievement. *Anthropology and Education Quarterly, 19*(3), 270-287.

Trueba, H. (1988b). English literacy acquisition: From cultural trauma to learning disabilities in minority students. *Journal of Linguistics and Education, 1*, 125-152.

Trueba, H. (1988c). Peer socialization among minority students: A high school dropout prevention program. In H. Trueba & C. Delgado-Gaitan (Eds.), *School and society: Learning content through culture* (pp. 201-217). New York: Praeger.

Trueba, H. (1989a). *Raising silent voices: Educating the linguistic minorities for the 21st century.* New York: Harper & Row.

Trueba, H. (1989b). *Report on the multicultural bilingual special education program of California State University, Bakersfield.* Unpublished manuscript, University of California, Santa Barbara, Office for Research on Educational Equity.

Trueba, H., & Delgado-Gaitan, C. (Eds.). (1988). *School and society: Learning content through culture.* New York: Praeger.

Trueba, H., Moll, L., Diaz, S., & Diaz, R. (1984). *Improving the functional writing of bilingual secondary school students* (Contract No. 400-81-0023). Washington, DC: National Institute of Education. (ERIC Clearinghouse on Languages and Linguistics No. ED 240, 862)

Trueba, H., Spindler, G., & Spindler, L. (Eds.). (in press). *Anthropological perspectives on dropping out.* London: Falmer.

Vygotsky, L. S. (1962). *Thought and language.* Cambridge: MIT Press.

Vygotsky, L. S. (1978). *Mind in society: The development of higher psychological processes* (M. Cole, V. John-Teiner, S. Scribner, & E. Souberman, Eds.). Cambridge, MA: Harvard University Press.

Wertsch, J. (1985). *Vygotsky and the social formation of the mind.* Cambridge, MA: Harvard University Press.

Wertsch, J. (1987). Collective memory: Issues from a sociohistorical perspective. *Quarterly Newsletter of the Laboratory of Comparative Human Cognition, 9*(1), 19-22.

9

Classroom Language Use and Educational Equity: Toward Interactive Pedagogy

CHRISTIAN FALTIS

University of Nevada, Reno

A major purpose of schooling is to socialize students in the areas of knowledge and behavior needed for successful adulthood. In the context of public schools in the United States, equitable access to favorable conditions of learning strongly depends on the extent to which teachers and students share a common language, and on whether students are provided opportunities in class to communicate purposefully in that common language. These two requirements place large numbers of school-age children who have limited English proficiency (LEP) in jeopardy of being denied access to favorable conditions of learning for three main reasons. First, less than 10% of the total LEP student population receives any kind of instruction through their native languages (Stein, 1986); the remaining 90% plus are schooled in English-only classrooms, making the first requirement of a common language difficult, but not impossible, to obtain.

Second, LEP students often are placed into less than favorable learning conditions because teachers with inadequate teacher preparation are more likely to teach students assigned to lower ability groups than they are to teach students assigned to higher ability groups (Good & Marshall, 1984). For example, Sanchez and Walker de Felix (1986) found that teachers who were assigned to teach LEP immigrant students in Texas were poorly prepared to deal with these students' language and special instructional needs. They also learned that teachers with low teaching evaluations were regularly shifted to ESL (English as a second language) classrooms.

A related finding is the belief in many elementary schools that anyone can teach low-ability groups, especially LEP students (Murphy, 1987). This belief is best conveyed by the fact that students in low-ability groups often receive a good deal of their instruction from teacher aides (Brookover, Brady, & Warfield, 1981). I have personally observed ESL classrooms that were taught almost entirely by teacher aides. While these kinds of actions and attitudes are truly reprehensible, they can be changed through increased monitoring by principals and through teacher awareness workshops.

The third reason that LEP students may find themselves placed into less than favorable conditions for learning is that there is less teacher-student and student-student interaction in classrooms with high concentrations of minority students (Good & Marshall, 1984; Goodlad, 1984). This finding holds true for bilingual as well as English-only classrooms (see Commins, 1989; Ramirez & Merino, in press). The most prevalent form of instruction in these classrooms is one in which the teacher talks simultaneously to all students. This manner of teaching is commonly referred to as "whole-class instruction," and it is typically supplemented with worksheet activities and other forms of ersatz individualized seatwork (Goodlad, 1984).

In whole-class instruction, the discourse structure is generally predictable and characterized by known-answer questions requiring short-answer display responses (Mehan, 1979). Structurally, access to this kind of discourse is completely reserved for the teacher, who initiates talk with and evaluates talk by students. When the teacher is talking to the class as a whole, social interaction by students is limited both quantitatively and qualitatively. The students' primary role under these circumstances is to receive and recall factual information about which they will be tested later in the lesson. Thus not only is there a complete dependence on the teacher for the transmission and development of knowledge, but the purpose of learning is reduced to the rote acquisition of facts. Teaching limited to this strategy is woefully inadequate to ensure the success of language minority students because it lacks the essential conditions needed for both language acquisition and concept learning.

Creating Effective Learning

This chapter will focus primarily on the third reason language minority students are at educational risk: the problem of studentless classroom language use. A framework for effective classroom discourse will be presented, one that is more equitable for language minority students not only because it promotes favorable conditions of language learning across the curriculum, but because it leads to increased language acquisition as well. A major premise throughout this chapter is that teachers can create the appropriate conditions for effective learning and thus make a difference in student outcomes. Teachers who learn to engage students in interactional activities that draw upon their existing abilities, and that enable them to negotiate meaning in order to communicate ideas, will help their students learn, regardless of what the language of the school is (see Moll, 1988). The key to effective learning is better prepared teachers who advocate for their students (Cazden, 1986), since, as Trueba (1988) states so well, the "academic success or failure of children is not a personal attribute of any child, nor a collective characteristic of any ethnic group, but a social phenomenon linked to historical and social conditions" (p. 282).

The construction of an appropriate learning environment for language minority children rests upon the ability of the teacher (a) to integrate the cultural ways of learning most familiar to the students with those used in the school (see Weisner, Gallimore, & Jordan, 1988), and (b) to provide multiple opportunities for students to use language meaningfully as they acquire knowledge and learn behaviors (Edelsky, Draper, & Smith, 1983; Hudelson, 1984). This chapter will focus on the second condition for favorable learning, including second language acquisition (see Trueba, this volume, for a discussion of the first condition).

One of the most significant findings from research concerned with instructional features that characterize effective learning for LEP students is the integration of English language development with regular in-class instruction (Enright, 1984; Tikunoff, 1983a). Tikunoff (1983b) explains the meaning of integrative teaching in the following passage:

> This integrative approach [involves] developing English-language acquisition during on-going instruction in the regular classroom. . . . Students learn the language of instruction when engaged in classroom instructional

tasks using that language. Thus, if one intended outcome of bilingual instruction is to develop LEP students' English proficiency . . . then such proficiency is best developed in relation to learning the language of instruction while learning to participate competently in instructional activity. (quoted in Milk, 1985, p. 660)

The integration of content and learning by itself, however, is not enough to ensure successful language development and effective learning. The classroom must be organized to enable learners to engage in the kinds of verbal interaction with their teacher and their peers that not only will stimulate second language acquisition, but will lead to conceptual development as well (Milk, 1985). In other words, the teacher must provide opportunities for students to hear and use language in numerous settings, for a variety of purposes, and in connection with an assortment of problems. This means that learners must be actively interacting with the teacher and peers within a classroom environment that makes every provision for real language use (Enright & McCloskey, 1988).

A Vygotskian Perspective on Effective Classroom Language Use

The value of social interaction among children and between children and the teacher for individual learning was first explored by Lev Semenovich Vygotsky (1886-1934) some 60 years ago. Vygotsky posited that the learning process for children depends upon the presence of four interrelated conditions:

(1) the presence of an adult or a more capable peer
(2) the occurrence of social interaction between the learner and the adult/ more capable peer
(3) that interaction be carried out in a common language
(4) that the adult/more capable peer operate within the learner's zone of proximal development

From a Vygotskian perspective, individual learning can occur only if these four social conditions for verbal interaction are met (Faltis & DeVillar, in press). At the heart of Vygotsky's learning theory is the idea that children's thinking processes reflect the organizational properties of the social life from which they are derived. Thus a child who has participated in collaborative problem-solving tasks will use the method of task completion arrived at collectively when attempting to solve a similar problem individually.

From a Vygotskian viewpoint, the goal of learning within the classroom is to transform students into independent thinkers through a process that necessarily begins with social interaction mediated by a common language. For Vygotsky, learning necessarily involves a two-phase process that first requires a learner to receive assistance, mainly through talking with significant others, to complete a particular task. By talking through a problem with someone who understands its nature and solution, the learner ultimately internalizes the ability to solve similar problems individually.

To be effective for learning, social interaction with learners must fall within what Vygotsky calls the "zone of proximal development." Vygotsky (1978) characterizes the zone of proximal development as the distance between a child's "actual developmental level as determined by independent problem solving" and the higher level of "potential development as determined through problem solving under adult guidance or in collaboration with more capable peers" (p. 86). He argues that the child can operate "only within certain limits that are strictly fixed by the state of the child's development and intellectual possibilities" (cited in Wertsch, 1985, p. 70). If the interaction is structured so that the learner can be a successful participant from the start, then the adult/more capable peer is working within the learner's zone of proximal development. Thus the goal of social interaction within the zone is to sustain interaction so that there is always something new to be learned and attempted, including taking over the more capable conversant's role of knower (Cazden, 1988).

Within the context of a classroom, the Vygotskian perspective maintains that if social interaction is to have learning consequences, the language used during the interaction must be suitably tuned to the student's zone of proximal development. Classroom talk that is tuned to the student's zone of proximal development and is done for purposes of helping students gain conceptual understanding must achieve two objectives: First, it must enable the student to participate actively in the task from the outset; second, it must provide interactional support that is both adjustable and temporary (Cazden, 1988). Providing the support needed for sustained interaction within the zone is most effectively accomplished through instructional "scaffolds" (Palincsar, 1986). Bruner (1983) has characterized scaffolds as verbal clues that help learners with conceptual understanding. An important feature of scaffolds is that need for them diminishes in direct proportion to the learner's growth in competence.

Classroom interaction between a teacher and a learner is structurally sustained to the extent that it completes the sequential organization of initiation-reply-evaluation commonly found in instructional settings (Mehan, 1979). Of the three components, only evaluation is ordinarily controlled by the teacher; both the learner and the teacher can initiate and reply. However, as the more capable participant, the teacher alone can use initiations and evaluations of replies as scaffolds for learning. Through initiations, the teacher can have the learner selectively attend to key aspects of the task, and, in the process, can prepare the learner for the solution by asking leading questions and explaining unknown terms. From a Vygotskian perspective, the teacher's goal at this point is twofold: (a) to cast a net over the student's zone of proximal development, a net wide enough to draw on prior knowledge yet fine enough not to exceed what the learner is capable of learning with adult help; and (b) to encourage the learner to ask and answer questions pertinent to the solution of the task.

Based on what the learner contributes verbally, the teacher can annex what the learner appears to understand up to that point, and use it as a means to direct the interaction toward *reconceptualization* or *situation redefinition*, which Wertsch (1984, p. 11) defines as the acceptance of a qualitatively different understanding of the task at hand. Reconceptualization, therefore, becomes the new goal once an initiation-reply pair has been made. Support for the new goal comes primarily through the teacher evaluation, which takes the form of *calibration*, the deliberate but temporary adjustment of information provided to the student during the pursuit of new knowledge (R. DeVillar, personal communication).

To see how teacher scaffolding can support learner reconceptualization, let us examine a piece of interaction taken from a study by Palinscar (1986) designed to improve reading comprehension skills of low-ability first-grade students through reciprocal teaching. In this method, the teacher and students take turns leading a dialogue centered on pertinent features of the text. The first example relates to what occurred on Day 4. The teacher is trying to help a small group of students perform four different strategies: summarizing, questioning, predicting, and clarifying to help understand the text.

(1) T: Today we're going to have a new story about a new animal. We will still be doing the same things. We will try to summarize, we'll ask

questions, we'll try to predict, and we'll also try to clarify any words that you may not understand. . . . The title of today's story is "Cats Do Talk." Any predictions about what you think this story is going to tell us?

(2) S3: That cats can talk.

(3) T: Exactly, I think that it is going to talk about that. How do you think that they talk, Raul?

(4) S3: They move their tails.

(5) T: Any other predictions? Let's see if Raul's predictions are right.

(6) S6: When they want to go out, they scratch on the door. Or, when they want to come in, they scratch on the door.

TEXT: Cats have many ways of "talking." They may not speak words as people do, but cats use sounds and movements to show their feelings. Here are some ways cats communicate.

(7) T: How do cats show their feelings?

(8) S4: They talk. They make a sound.

(9) T: Did the paragraph tell us about any other way they can talk to us?

(10) S1: They come up to you.

(11) T: So, through their movements they can show whether they need something.

(12) S2: They come up to your arm.

(13) T: What do you think they are trying to tell you when they come up to your arm?

(14) S2: That they are your friend.

(15) T: Very good. If I were to summarize, I would say that this is telling us that cats do talk through using movements and sounds. There is a word here that I'm not quite sure if I quite understand. There was a long word "communicate." [repeats sentence] What does that sentence mean?

(16) S1: Um, talk.

(17) T: There are some ways that they talk. All right, so, the talking and the movements let us know something, don't they? So communication is not just talking; it's a way to let us know something. Anna, do you want to try to be the teacher for this next one? I want you to listen and think of a question that you can ask the group.

In this dialogue, the teacher accounts for the majority of the talk. She carefully guides the dialogue by explicitly modeling the strategies she wants the children to learn. She provides extensive support to the students, who at this point are still having difficulty with performing the strategies on their own. For example, when the student's answer falls short, as in line 16, the teacher calibrates by providing an extended definition in the next line, one that incorporates the student's response, but clarifies the meaning inside the student's zone of proximal development.

Let us now examine how the teacher interacted with the same group of first graders 15 days later.

TEXT: Behind the front legs, there are two odor glands. They look like two extra eyes. To protect itself, a daddy longlegs can give off a smelly liquid from these glands. Birds, toads, and large insects don't like it at all. It makes them feel too sick or too weak to try to catch the daddy longlegs.

(1) S6: [question] What does the daddy longlegs do when something comes around it? Jody?

(2) S2: Use that odor and . . . [not audible]

(3) S3: Yeah, Cindy.

(4) S2: When an animal comes along, he puts out his odor and they get too sick to catch him.

(5) S6: Yeah, Manuel.

(6) S4: Or too weak.

(7) S3: They feel too weak and too sick.

(8) S6: Everybody gave me good answers.

(9) T: Very good.

(10) S6: [summary] I will summarize. When an animal comes around it, it gives out its bad smell, and they get weak and too old to catch it . . . [student-to-student dialogue continues for 11 more lines]

TEXT: Daddy longlegs are related to spiders.

(22) S6: [clarification] What does related mean?

(23) T: What do you think, Bobby?

(24) S6: Sort of like, they're the same kind of animal, sort of like. Like, tigers are related to cats.

(25) T: Very good. They may not be in the same family, but they are similar.

TEXT: Daddy longlegs are related to spiders, but they are not true spiders. Daddy longlegs don't spin webs to trap insects for food the way spiders do. Daddy longlegs go out hunting for their food. Daddy longlegs never bite people and they are never poisonous.

(26) S1: [question] Are the spiders ever poisonous or not? Manuel?

(27) S4: They aren't.

(28) S2: I did have a different question.

(29) T: Okay.

(30) S2: [question and clarification] If the spiders didn't spin a web for their food, how did they get their food?

(31) S5: Oh, that's a terrific question.
(32) T: It sure is, isn't it? [dialogue continues for 30 more lines]

Contrasting this dialogue with the one on Day 4, we can see that the children sustain interaction among themselves fairly independently of the teacher. The examples illustrate how the proportion of the responsibility for task completion shifted from a joint effort, with the teacher providing the appropriate scaffolds, to an individual effort where the students came to reconceptualize socially based knowledge. Without the help of the teacher, the students demonstrated a new understanding of how to perform certain comprehension-fostering and comprehension-monitoring strategies. From a Vygotskian perspective, they exemplify the role verbal interaction plays in the development of learning.

So far, the discussion has focused primarily on the benefits of social interaction between teachers and students. However, there is evidence to suggest that interaction among peers of generally equal understanding, but with differing skill preparation, is also a favorable condition for learning. Vygotsky intimates the importance of talk among peers in his definition of the zone of proximal development (see above), referring specifically to the role "more capable peers" may have in developing new conceptual understanding. In this context, a more capable peer is a student who, similar to the teacher, possesses certain skill preparation (including language proficiency) that is particularly appropriate to assisting a fellow student in the completion of a task that is within that student's zone of proximal development. Weisner et al. (1988), for example, found that among the classroom learning activities that are successful with Native Hawaiian children are child-generated interactions that rely on peer assistance for task completion. They also found that the Native Hawaiian peer-assisted interaction system (the KEEP system), with some minor cultural adjustments, worked equally well for Navajo children in northeastern Arizona.

Garcia's (in press) recent study of language use in effective Hispanic classrooms also supports the value of social interaction among peers. He found that in high-achieving classrooms there was a significant amount of student-dominated interaction. In contrast with traditional classrooms, where the teacher plans as well as controls the amount of talk allowed, Garcia discovered an interactional strategy that is represented in Figure 9.1. In the figure, the solid lines signify that students are commenting on what other students are saying. The broken lines indicate that while the teacher initiates and closes an interaction, students are given the opportunity to comment on the topic during the

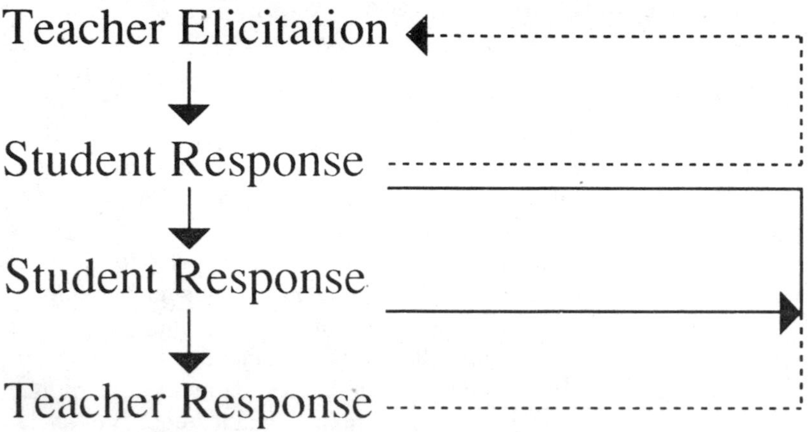

Teacher Elicitation ◄- -┐
                 ↓   ┊
Student Response -┘
                 ↓
Student Response ─────────────────────────────────►
                 ↓   ┊
Teacher Response -┘

Figure 9.1

sequence, similar to the way first-grade students did in Day 19 of the Palinscar example above.

Reporting on the same Hispanic project, Moll (1988) comments that in every classroom "the teacher emphasized the students' active use of language to obtain or express meaning" (p. 467). Underlying the general purpose of teaching in all the classrooms he studied was an effort to create classroom contexts in which the students learned to use, try out, and manipulate language for real purposes.

Classroom Language Use
and Second Language Acquisition

While social interaction between the teacher and students and among students can promote conceptual learning, there is another strong justification for including it as a teaching strategy. Social interaction generates several of the most important ingredients needed to promote second language acquisition. For LEP students, in particular, social interaction in the classroom has the potential to lead not only to cognitive growth, but to language acquisition as well.

Before proceeding to a discussion of how social interaction contributes to effective second language acquisition, let us briefly examine what needs to be present for learners to develop proficiency in a second language. After reviewing some 35 studies, Long (1981) concludes that because modified verbal input and modified verbal interaction were present in all cases of successful second language acquisition, they must be among the necessary and sufficient conditions for acquisition to occur. Long's definition of modified input is comparable to Krashen's (1982, 1985) more widely recognized notion of "comprehensive input," language addressed to the learner that has in some way been adjusted to accommodate for the learner's needs. Generally speaking, adjustment can be in the form of simplified speech that has been slowed down and more clearly enunciated, or it can be speech that has been highly contextualized through the use of visual support and/or physical gestures (Allen, 1986). In both cases, the goal is to provide input that is slightly beyond the learner's current level of competence.

Enright and McCloskey (1988) suggest that teachers can provide the greatest amount of comprehensible language input to groups of mixed-language students by adapting their "teacher talk" through four strategies: (a) body movements — gestures, bodily motions, and facial expressions; (b) vocal sounds — volume, intonation, and manner of delivery; (c) discourse patterns — repeating, recycling, rephrasing, and framing; and (d) materials and the physical environment — visual aids and realia for all five senses.

Comprehensible language input, as Krashen (1985) characterizes it, shares a point of commonality with the role Vygotsky's zone of proximal development plays in learning: Advancement is possible to the extent that language input is made comprehensible to the learner. There is some evidence that language input that is too far beyond learners' current level of ability has no effect on their development. Pienemann (1984), for example, studied 10 Italian children, ages 7-9, who were at stage 2 or stage 3 in German as a second language. After receiving two weeks of language instruction at stage 4, only those children who were at stage 3 progressed to stage 4; stage 2 children did not develop further. Pienemann interpreted the results as evidence that learners can profit only from instruction that is within their range of readiness, an interpretation much in line with both Vygotskian and Krashenian theories of learning.

While comprehensible input is clearly a favorable learning condition because it *promotes* acquisition, it is equally clear that *mastery* of a second language is possible only when students have opportunities to use the second language for communicative purposes, and to do so under conditions that do not create high levels of anxiety. Swain (1985) was among the first to question the sufficiency of comprehensible input as *the* causal variable for second language acquisition. She found that language majority students enrolled in Canadian second language immersion programs enjoyed maximal second lai.guage input that was largely comprehensible, yet none of the students reached what might be considered near-native proficiency levels. Swain suggests that the reason was directly related to the fact that students had no opportunities for verbal interaction with native peers, *opportunities that would have created a compelling need to negotiate for meaning in order to communicate effectively.* Thus, despite numerous years of immersion schooling that exposed students to considerable amounts of comprehensible input, because students did not use the second language to communicate information, to express feelings, to argue opinions, and to explore ideas, they never developed nativelike proficiency. The message is straightforward. In Wong-Fillmore's (1985) words, "In order to learn a new language, learners have to be in a position to engage in interactions with speakers in a variety of social situations, since this is what allows them to figure out what is being said, how the language is structured, and how it is used socially and communicatively by its speakers" (p. 26).

One of the chief advantages of social interaction for language learners is that it offers them the occasion to hear greater amounts of modified language input than they would if their only source were the teacher in a whole-class context (as has been the case in French immersion programs). Moreover, as McGroarty (in press) suggests, input generated from peer interaction provides a natural context for greater redundancy in communication as students exchange information among themselves. Redundancy improves levels of comprehension because speakers naturally tend to repeat words and rephrase ideas as they work to convey meanings.

A second benefit for LEP students arising from classroom interaction is that it provides greater practice opportunities. Recall that in whole-class settings teachers do most of the talking, meaning that while LEP students may be receiving some exposure to comprehensible input, they are nonetheless passive participants in learning. When students are talking and working together, there are substantially more occasions for using language to express meanings. In a meta-analysis of research on the effects of peer involvement on second language development, Gaies (1985) found that practice opportunities increased greatly in classrooms using peer grouping strategies. More recently, August (1987) found that providing LEP students fairly structured opportunities for successful initiation and meaningful interaction with native English speakers in small group settings promoted second language acquisition. Research by DeVillar (in press) and Edfelt (1989) provides additional evidence that social interaction in small groups increases the second language production of students within heterogeneous classrooms. Their work concentrated on the second language use of mixed dyads while working at the computer.

Conclusions

Schools can become equitable environments for learning when the role of social interaction is recognized and used to reinforce the learning process. For the learning process to be favorable for all students, it is first necessary to change the predominant organization of classroom language use. When the teacher directs instruction to the whole class, equitable access to favorable learning for all students is highly unlikely because students are denied one of the most important conditions for learning: verbal interaction. It is increasingly clear that large amounts of classroom interaction account for the greatest gains in both language acquisition and concept development. In this chapter, we have seen how teacher adaptations in the quality and quantity of social interactions with students can lead to reconceptualization and, ultimately, to student ownership of language.

Without the opportunity to interact freely with their teachers and their peers, students will rarely be challenged to solve problems on their own. From a Vygotskian perspective, learning without verbal interaction cannot rise above the level of rote transfer of facts from the teacher to the students. In a similar vein, Long (1981) has argued for years that social interaction involving the negotiation of meaning is a necessary condition for second language acquisition. Both perspectives point to the importance of peer interaction and classroom interaction (in general) not only for conceptual development, but for second language acquisition as well. Therefore, if educational equity for all students (which translates to "students from myriad language and cultural backgrounds") is to be striven for, there must be a concerted effort at all levels to orient prospective teachers and reorient practicing teachers to what might be referred to as *interactive pedagogy*, a manner of teaching and learning based upon the principles of Vygotsky, Krashen, and Long, as well as upon the practices found in the works of Edelsky, Enright, and Moll.

122   EDUCATIONAL ENVIRONMENTS THAT PROMOTE EQUITY

References

Allen, V. G. (1986). Developing contexts to support second language acquisition. *Language Arts, 63*(1), 61-66.

August, D. (1987). Effects of peer tutoring on the second language acquisition of Mexican American children in elementary school. *TESOL Quarterly, 21*(4), 717-736.

Brookover, W. B., Brady, N. V., & Warfield, M. (1981). *Educational policies and equitable education: A report of studies of two desegregated school systems.* East Lansing: Michigan State University, College of Urban Development, Center for Urban Affairs.

Bruner, J. (1983). *Child's talk.* New York: Norton.

Cazden, C. (1986). ESL teachers as language advocates for children. In P. Rigg & D. S. Enright (Eds.), *Children and ESL: Integrating perspectives* (pp. 9-21). Washington, DC: Teachers of English to Speakers of Other Languages.

Cazden, C. (1988). *Classroom discourse: The language of teaching and learning.* Portsmouth, NH: Heinemann.

Commins, N. L. (1989). Language and affect: Bilingual students at home and at school. *Language Arts, 66*(1), 29-43.

DeVillar, R. A. (in press). Second language use within the non-traditional classroom: Computers, cooperative learning, and bilingualism. In R. Jacobson & C. Faltis (Eds.), *Language distribution issues in bilingual schooling.* Clevedon, England: Multilingual Matters.

Edelsky, C., Draper, K., & Smith, K. (1983). Hookin' 'em at the start of school in a "whole language" classroom. *Anthropology and Education Quarterly, 14*(4), 257-281.

Edfelt, N. (1989). *Computer assisted second language acquisition: The oral discourse of children at the computer in a cooperative learning context.* Unpublished doctoral dissertation, Stanford University.

Enright, D. S. (1984). The organization of interaction in elementary classrooms. In J. Handscombe, R. A. Orem, & B. P. Taylor (Eds.), *On TESOL '83: The question of control* (pp. 23-38). Washington, DC: Teachers of English to Speakers of Other Languages.

Enright, D. S., & McCloskey, M. L. (1988). *Integrating English: Developing English language and literacy in the multilingual classroom.* Reading, MA: Addison-Wesley.

Faltis, C., & DeVillar, R.A. (in press). *Computers, cooperation, and culture in the classroom.* Albany: State University of New York Press.

Gaies, S. J. (1985). *Peer involvement in language learning.* Orlando, FL: Harcourt Brace Jovanovich.

Garcia, E. (in press). Instructional discourse in "effective" Hispanic classrooms. In R. Jacobson & C. Faltis (Eds.), *Language distribution issues in bilingual schooling.* Clevedon, England: Multilingual Matters.

Good, T. L., & Marshall, S. (1984). Do students learn more in heterogeneous or homogeneous groups? In P. L. Peterson, L. C. Wilkinson, & M. Hallinan (Eds.), *The social context of instruction: Group organization and group processes* (pp. 15-38). Orlando, FL: Academic Press.

Goodlad, J. (1984). *A place called school: Prospects for the future.* New York: McGraw-Hill.

Hudelson, S. (1984). Kan yuret an rayt en Ingles: Children become literate in English as a second language. *TESOL Quarterly, 18*(2), 221-238.

Krashen, S. (1982). *Principles and practices in second language acquisition.* Oxford: Pergamon.

Krashen, S. (1985). *The input hypothesis: Issues and implications.* London: Longman.

Long, M. H. (1981). Input, interaction, and second language acquisition. In H. Wintz (Ed.), *Native language and foreign language acquisition* (Annals of the New York Academy of Sciences No. 379, pp. 259-278). New York: Academy of Sciences.

McGroarty, M. (in press). Cooperative learning and second language acquisition. In California State Department of Education (Ed.), *Assessing the curriculum through cooperative learning.* Sacramento: California State Department of Education.

Mehan, H. (1979). *Learning lessons.* Cambridge, MA: Harvard University Press.

Milk, R. D. (1985). The changing role of ESL in bilingual education. *TESOL Quarterly, 37*(4), 657-672.

Moll, L. (1988). Some key issues in teaching Latino students. *Language Arts, 65*(5), 465-742.

Murphy, J. (1987). Equity as student opportunity to learn. *Theory into Practice, 27*(2), 145-151.

Palinscar, A. (1986). The role of dialogue in providing scaffolded instruction. *Educational Psychologist, 21*(1-2), 73-98.

Pienemann, M. (1984). Psychological constraints on the teachability of languages. *Studies in Second Language Acquisition, 6,* 186-214.

Ramirez, J. D., & Merino, B. (in press). Classroom talk in English immersion, early-exit and late-exit transitional bilingual education programs. In R. Jacobson & C. Faltis (Eds.), *Language distribution issues in bilingual schooling.* Clevedon, England: Multilingual Matters.

Sanchez, K. S., & Walker de Felix, J. (1986). Second language teachers' abilities: Some equity concerns. *Journal of Educational Equity and Leadership, 6*(4), 313-321.

Stein, S. C. (1986). *Sink or swim: The politics of bilingual education.* New York: Praeger.

Swain, M. (1985). Communicative competence: Some roles of comprehensible input and comprehensible output in its development. In S. M. Gass & C. Madden (Eds.), *Input in second language acquisition* (pp. 235-253). Rowley, MA: Newbury House.

Tikunoff, W. (1983a). Five significant bilingual instructional features. In W. Tikunoff (Ed.), *Compatibility of the SBIF features with other research on instruction for LEP students* (pp. 5-18). San Francisco: Far West Laboratory.

Tikunoff, W. (1983b). *Utility of the SBIF features for instruction of LEP students.* San Francisco: Far West Laboratory.

Trueba, H. T. (1988). Culturally-based explanations of minority students' academic achievement. *Anthropology and Education Quarterly, 19*(4), 270-287.

Vygotsky, L. S. (1978). *Mind in society: The development of higher psychological processes* (M. Cole, V. John-Teiner, S. Scribner, & E. Souberman, Eds.). Cambridge, MA: Harvard University Press.

Weisner, T. S., Gallimore, R., & Jordan, C. (1988). Unpackaging cultural effects on classroom learning: Native Hawaiian peer assistance and child-generated activity. *Anthropology and Education Quarterly, 19*(4), 327-353.

Wertsch, J. V. (1984). The zone of proximal development: Some conceptual issues. In B. Rogoff & J. V. Wertsch (Eds.), *Children's learning in the "zone of proximal development"* (pp. 7-18). San Francisco: Jossey-Bass.

Wertsch, J. V. (1985). *Vygotsky and the social formation of the mind.* Cambridge, MA: Harvard University Press.

Wong-Fillmore, L. (1985). When does teacher talk work as input? In S. M. Gass & C. Madden (Eds.), *Input in second language acquisition* (pp. 235-253). Rowley, MA: Newbury House.

PART III

INSTRUCTION THAT ENHANCES EQUITY

10

Introduction:
Classroom Instruction
That Enhances Equity

HERSHOLT C. WAXMAN

University of Houston

One area that has important implications for the educational improve-ment of disadvantaged students is that of classroom instruction. Recent research has begun to examine the critical role that teachers have on influencing student outcomes. This research assumes that the improve-ment of student learning and attitudes toward learning can emerge through examination of the ways that classroom instruction advantages and disadvantages certain types of students.

This section addresses four key areas where classroom instruction can promote educational equity. First, Margaret Wang discusses how some instructional programs promote educational equity. Second, Adam Gamoran summarizes research on how ability grouping and curriculum tracking influence equity. Third, Yolanda N. Padron and Stephanie L. Knight discuss the importance of cultural considerations within the classroom environment. Finally, Jane A. Stallings and Jane McCarthy discuss the equity implications from teacher effectiveness research. A brief description of each of the four chapters follows.

127

Instructional Programs and Equity

In her chapter on programs that promote educational equity, Margaret Wang raises the important point that in order to ensure equity in schooling, some children need to be treated differentially. Consequently, she argues that it is the responsibility of schools to structure educational programs so that they take into account the individual differences of students. She subsequently reviews four widely adopted instructional approaches that have been found to be effective in achieving educational equity for individual students.

The cooperative learning approach – and an example, the Learning Together Model – is the first instructional program discussed. Its four critical elements are (a) positive interdependence, (b) face-to-face interaction among students, (c) individual accountability for mastering the assigned material, and (d) appropriate use of interpersonal and small group skills. These elements are described, as well as some of the cognitive and affective outcomes associated with the use of this approach.

The teacher collaboration approach – and an example, the Teacher Assistance Team (TAT) model – is the second program discussed. In this model, three regular education teachers chosen by the entire teaching staff work together to identify student needs as well as to plan, implement, and evaluate interventions. The advantages of this program for students, teachers, and administrators are also discussed.

The curriculum design and modification approach – and an example, the Adaptive Learning Environments Model (ALEM) – is the third program discussed. The ALEM includes the following specific programming features: (a) individualized progress plans, (b) diagnostic-prescriptive monitoring system, (c) adaptive program delivery system, (d) data-based staff development program, (e) school and classroom organizational supports, and (f) family involvement. Descriptions of these features and how they accommodate individual needs are also highlighted.

The classroom organization approach – and an example, the Comer Process Model – is the final program discussed. The four key components of this program are (a) a governance and management body, (b) a mental health program, (c) a parent program, and (d) a teaching and curriculum program. These components are discussed in relation to how they enhance the learning of each individual student.

The four programs discussed in Wang's chapter illustrate the importance of how specific programs can enhance the education of individual students who do not do well in traditional direct-instruction classrooms. The challenge to redistribute school resources so that *all* students can be provided with the best opportunities to learn is also addressed.

Instructional Organization and Equity

In his chapter on instructional organization and educational equity, Adam Gamoran focuses on curriculum tracking or ability grouping, that is, the assignment of students to instructional settings based on interests or abilities. He initially discusses some confusion with the term *equity* because of the value preference often associated with it.

In his review of the research on ability grouping in elementary schools, Gamoran reports some of the evidence supporting how ability grouping generally increases the inequality of results. However, he also summarizes studies that indicate that ability grouping increases the academic achievement of students at all levels.

The review of research at the secondary level suggests that grouping and tracking also increase the achievement gap between high and low achievers. The results at the secondary level, however, do not indicate that tracking or grouping increases the achievement of students at all levels. The findings at this level suggest that tracking generally denies equal access to the types of experiences that lead to high achievement.

In the final sections of the chapter, Gamoran discusses additional ways of arranging classes, such as individualized instruction and cooperative grouping. Overall, this chapter provides a great deal of evidence to suggest that the way classes are organized has important implications for educational equity.

Linguistic and Cultural Influences on Classrooms Instruction

In their chapter on linguistic and cultural influences on classroom instruction, Yolanda N. Padron and Stephanie L. Knight focus on three general areas. They first describe Vygotsky's sociohistorical theory, which emphasizes how learning is always mediated through others. They define the "zone of proximal development," which is the difference between what the child can do alone and what the child can do with the help of another person. The implications for classroom instruction from this theoretical framework are then discussed.

The next area discussed in the chapter is the compatibility of culture and instruction. Examples of effective educational programs that consider students' culture, such as the Kamehameha Early Education Program and programs with Native American students, are described. The benefits of bilingual education programs are also summarized in this section.

The third area discussed is the development of higher-order thinking skills for minority students. Studies on cognitive strategy use in reading and reading strategy training programs are summarized. This section particularly emphasizes studies conducted with Hispanic bilingual students.

The final section of this chapter focuses on Tharp's psychocultural variables and constraints: (a) the social organization of the culture, (b) sociolinguistic differences, (c) cognition, and (d) motivation. The two constants that must be provided to all students are language development and contextualized instruction. The implications of these variables for classroom instruction are also discussed.

Teacher Effectiveness Research and Equity

In their chapter on teacher effectiveness research and equity issues, Jane A. Stallings and Jane McCarthy discuss several areas where the research findings have specific implications for educational equity. They first discuss the use of time in classrooms and how it is positively correlated with students' academic achievement. They next discuss the issue of providing the most efficient and effective format for delivering instruction. They describe advantages and disadvantages of particular delivery models such as individualized instruction and cooperative learning. They also raise the issue that sex-related differences are often overlooked by some methods and instructional programs.

In the next section, Stallings and McCarthy discuss how the use of varied activities was one of the most important findings to emerge from the teaching effectiveness research at the secondary level. They argue that, in terms of equity, it is important for teachers to understand that not all students learn best in the same way. Next, the issue of culturally fair and gender-fair curriculum materials is raised. They discuss the importance of matching materials to students and making sure that the textbooks students use are at a level they can read.

The section on interactive instruction describes the process teachers should follow in order to be effective. Reviewing previous materials, stating clear objectives, checking for understanding, calling on all students, asking higher-level questions, positive reinforcement, and oral reading are some of the important concepts discussed.

The following section on cultural differences in active and passive learning highlights the importance of providing all students with active rather than passive roles in the classroom. Factors that influence passivity are discussed, as well as suggestions of how teachers can improve their instruction in this area.

The final two sections of this chapter deal with teacher expectations and classroom management. The implications of these and all the previously mentioned instructional behaviors are discussed in terms of specific suggestions for effective teaching. The authors maintain that strategies and materials that meet the needs of disadvantaged students are often the same strategies that are most effective with all students.

11

Programs That
Promote Educational Equity

MARGARET WANG

Temple University

The United States has a long history of commitment to the goal of building an educated citizenry. With each decade we have increased the proportion of the population in school. We have extended both the diversity of children from various sociocultural and economic backgrounds in our schools and the kinds of educational programs we offer. Indeed, by stressing the value of education and seeing it as a way to social and economic equality, we have made great progress in ensuring equal access to a free public education for all children in this country. This can be celebrated.

However, the progress we celebrate falls far short of our educational vision of providing equal opportunity for schooling success for all the students that schools are challenged to serve today. The statistics clearly point to a trend of increasing numbers of students who drop out of school or graduate from our schools underserved educationally. In fact, this trend has already become a hard fact for many schools in large urban areas (National Center for Educational Statistics, 1988). The statistics on the number of students who experience school failure are alarming.

Despite our commitment to educational equality, the failure to provide for the schooling success of all students in our educational system will become even more alarming in the coming decade if we do not systematically address the issue of equity in terms of educational outcomes. We provide opportunities for students requiring greater-than-usual educational support through well-intentioned "special" programs (e.g., special education, Chapter 1, and other compensatory and remedial programs). However, implementation of these programs for the most part has not measured up to the outcome standards that are considered to be critical indicators of educational equity. Measures to alleviate educational inequality have become an even greater problem in schools (Wang, Reynolds, & Walberg, 1988).

Schools today are facing the challenge of how to teach the diverse children in our educational system successfully, using all forms of knowledge on how best to proceed with instruction. The purpose of this chapter is to synthesize this knowledge base briefly and to discuss its implications for designing and implementing school programs that will achieve the dual goal of educational equity — equal opportunity *and* outcomes. First, educational equity is discussed in the context of the right to schooling success for all students. The research base and current practice are then synthesized. The third section presents brief descriptions of the features and implementation requirements of programs that have potential for achieving educational equity. The chapter concludes with a discussion of the implications for widespread school implementation of such programs.

Educational Equity: Rights to Schooling Success

Opportunity for education has long been a goal of the civil rights movement in this country. The Supreme Court's 1974 decision in *Brown v. Board of Education* made equal access to public education the law of the land. Since then, we have done well by our commitment to provide public education for school-age children and youth. However, if real progress in attaining the goal of educational equity is to be made, we must focus our attention on whether equal opportunities for education lead to equitable outcomes. Providing opportunities for education without being accountable for ensuring educational outcomes simply perpetuates inequity in a more subtle form. Fundamental to this conception is the principle that standards of educational outcomes must be upheld for every child.

Quality education is now the central civil rights challenge facing us today. Schools cannot simply provide educational opportunities for students and be satisfied with just creating special programs to address the equity issue. To assure that equity in schooling success is achieved, some children need to be treated differentially, an action that might be construed as inequitable from certain vantage points. The fact is, there is an expanding number of students who are not achieving well despite efforts to create "increasing opportunities" to learn. Many students have serious learning problems and have difficulty in achieving learning success; they need better help than they are now receiving.

There does not seem to be much argument about the provision of extraordinary resources and efforts to those requiring greater-than-usual educational and related service support. The proliferation of second system programs, such as special education, Chapter 1, and migrant education, are examples of how the concept of providing equity through extra (i.e., inequitable distribution of) resources and efforts has been put into operation. The past two decades of research and innovative program development efforts suggest that it is possible to provide equal access to quality educational opportunities that lead to equality in educational benefits for all students. The issue is not *what* to do, but the commitment to find ways to implement what we already know about making schools more productive for every child.

The Research Base and Current Practice: Strengths and Barriers

Individual Differences and Learning

Students differ in interests, learning styles, and the amount of time needed for learning. These and other related learner differences require different approaches and amounts of instructional support. Some students require more direct instruction with the teacher, while others do better with very little intervention or direct teaching. Although these and related characteristics of learner differences have long been accepted as a given, advances in theories and research during the past two decades have provided substantial grounds for fundamental conceptual changes in the types of information about individual students and their learning that are examined and used for instructional planning. Among the significant developments is an increased recognition that differences in certain personal and learning characteristics are alterable (Bloom,

1976). Some prime examples of variables that are no longer considered to be static are family characteristics, such as parental expectations and family involvement (Walberg, 1984), cognition and processes of learning (Chipman, Segal, & Glaser, 1985), and student motivation and the roles students play in their own learning (Wang & Palincsar, 1989).

Advances in research on learning and social and cognitive awareness have much to contribute to our understanding of how to improve learning. These advances have also resulted in a shift away from describing students based solely on grossly defined outcomes or measures of status. It is becoming more common to describe learner differences in the manner in which information is processed, mental mechanisms and rules that students bring to the learning situation, the motivation and affective response tendencies involved in the acquisition and retention of knowledge, and the knowledge competence of individual students (Wang & Lindvall, 1984). The recognition of the alterability of these learner characteristics points to the wisdom of studying ways to modify the psychological processes and cognitive operations used by individual students (Bransford, Vye, Delclos, Burns, & Hasselbring, 1985; Feuerstein, Jensen, Hoffman, & Rand, 1985; Palincsar & Brown, 1984), as well as learning environments and instructional strategies, to accommodate learner differences (Wang & Walberg, 1985).

The growing research base and theoretical advances have led to an increasing recognition that it is the responsibility of the schools to structure educational programs so that they take account of these alterable differences to assure educational outcomes. Schools are responsible for ensuring educational outcomes for every student, using the standard of mastering the "common curriculum" of elementary and secondary education in this country (Fenstermacher & Goodlad, 1983). If all students are to complete a "basic" education or common curriculum successfully, today's schools must undergo major conceptual and structural changes. We must abolish the current practice of "compensating" for learners' differences by lowering standards, or, in other words, by making school success easier for selected students through establishing differential standards for schooling success.

Effective schooling defined in the context of equity of outcomes requires a shift in our mind-set from a "fixed" system for implementing the common curriculum to a flexible system that will allow all students to acquire the common curriculum. At the same time, we need to recognize that some students require more time and extraordinary instructional support to achieve mastery of the common curriculum and others require less time and little direct instruction; this latter group of students should have the flexibility to complete the common curriculum for basic education in fewer than 12 years.

Schools' Responses to Learner Differences

Despite the advances in theories and research on individual differences in learning and effective teaching (Wittrock, 1986), the knowledge base has had very little impact on how schools respond to individual differences in practice. There are serious problems in how individual differences are characterized and the way information is generated and used for instructional decision making. In many cases, provisions designed to respond to student differences in learning have been counterproductive in promoting student learning (Brandt, 1989).

Students differ as individuals, not as groups. Very exceptionally talented students are about as heterogeneous across the range of learning characteristics as those having learning difficulties or considered to be low achieving or at risk of school failure. Programs designed to accommodate learner differences based on the assumption of group differences rather than individual differences tend to take different approaches and can result in very different outcomes. In current practice, learning differences among students are typically handled by classifying or labeling the perceived differences in terms of macro-level characteristics (i.e., children at risk, low-achieving children from poor families, children with learning disabilities, or socially/emotionally disturbed children). Then the "identified" or "certified" students with these spuriously defined labels are placed "homogeneously" in narrowly framed categorical programs or "special" educational arrangements.

This practice of grouping students with perceived similar instructional needs (yet often instructionally meaningless) has been a commonly accepted programmatic strategy for achieving educational equity. In other words, the strategy of placing students with similar classifications in specially designed programs is considered an educational intervention designed with the implicit and explicit objectives of ensuring educational equity. However, it has not worked well for an increasingly large proportion of children and youth in our nation's schools. In fact, research suggests that these solutions have often limited, rather than broadened, the targeted students' opportunities for achieving educational equity, in terms of both access to knowledge and equity in educational outcomes.

There is substantial evidence to suggest that students may receive *less* instruction when schools provide them with specially designed programs to meet their special learning needs. For example, students provided with remedial reading programs (such as Chapter 1 or resource room programs in special education) often receive less actual reading instruction (Allington & Johnson, 1986; Haynes & Jenkins, 1986). Classification and tracking practices schools now use to respond to differences in the learning characteristics and needs of students have not been shown to confer advantages to students. In fact, in many instances, they have led to further inequity in educational outcomes for students requiring greater-than-usual educational support (Brandt, 1989; Heller, Holtzman, & Messick, 1982; Jenkins, Pious, & Peterson, 1988; Williams, Richmond, & Mason, 1986). In too many cases, the practice of grouping (or tracking) students for instruction based on certain perceived group differences involves the delivery of radically different and not always appropriate content to some students; there is a tendency to neglect fundamental content seriously (Oakes, 1985).

Schools themselves often contribute to children's learning problems. There is evidence of the so-called Matthew effect (Stanovitch, 1984). Students who show limited progress in early phases of instruction in basic subjects, such as reading, tend to show progressive retardation over succeeding years. It has been estimated that in the middle elementary grades, the lowest-achieving students may be reading only one-tenth as many words per day in school as students in a highly skilled reading group (Reynolds, 1989).

Another version of the Matthew effect occurs when teachers interact differently with students who have special learning needs — for example, by giving less feedback on questions to them than to other students, calling on them less often, or waiting less time for them to answer (Cooper, 1983). It has been demonstrated that urban youth are engaged less often in academic interaction with teachers than are students in suburban schools (Greenwood, Wharton, & Delquadri, 1984). Similarly, less time is spent on regular reading instruction in schools with high rates of poverty than in other schools (National Assessment of Educational Progress, 1987). Such differences in school programs that work to the disadvantage of selected groups of students cannot be justified or permitted to continue if we aim to achieve educational equity for all of our students.

Spurious Classification and Barriers to Educational Equity

Several recent research syntheses have revealed serious scientific and practical flaws in the current classification system for placing students in specially designed programs to receive their "entitled" services. Most procedures are unreliable and irrelevant to instructional decision making. For example, about 80% of all schoolchildren can be classified as learning disabled by one or more of the procedures used by schools (Ysseldyke et al., 1983). These approaches assume an underlying taxonomy that is not supported by any consensus of research or theory. For example, the concept of mental retardation has been stretched to include the so-called educable along with the most severely retarded; many thousands of children are labeled mentally retarded based on tests that have little reliability or validity for decisions about instruction or school placement. Similarly, the label of mental illness has been extended to cover some relatively common behavioral problems. The same child may be classified as "handicapped" by one test or diagnostician and not by another. Even a single diagnostician, working from the same case record on two separate occasions, can offer two different diagnoses and classifications (Reschly, 1988; Ysseldyke, 1987). Furthermore, the differences in learning characteristics between children in several of the categories are often minimal or nonexistent. For example, students placed in Chapter 1 programs often make slow progress in reading, as do many students placed in special programs for learning disabilities. The reading abilities of these groups overlap completely, and no clear qualitative differences indicate a need for different services (Jenkins, 1987).

During the past decade, pressures from many fronts have led to the classification of a growing number of children as handicapped. Most children referred by teachers for diagnosis are put into a special category and given a special education placement. Teachers have often referred children at least partly because of behavioral problems rather than learning problems. These children may not receive suitable treatment and might be harmfully stereotyped or given a pseudoscientific excuse for their poor learning progress. Children are often treated differently simply because they have been labeled. Teachers and parents may have unjustifiably lower expectations of children classified as retarded or learning disabled. The children themselves may lose confidence in their own abilities when they have been categorized and removed from regular classes.

Economics, program availability, race, and other factors having no valid implications for instruction have also entered into classification decisions. Black and poor children are particularly vulnerable in being classified under the current system (Heller et al., 1982; National Coalition of Advocates for Students, 1988). School districts arbitrarily change the classifications of children — for example, from mildly retarded to learning disabled — when one label becomes more stigmatized or less renumerative than another. Once students are segregated, they are unlikely to return to regular classrooms. For example, according to a recent report issued by the Council of the Great City Schools, the proportion of special education students enrolled in major urban schools who were returned to general education placement by the end of the school year ranged from 0 to 8.8% (Buttram & Kershner, 1988).

It is scientifically and morally indefensible, and practically useless, to continue the current practice of using extremely time-consuming, costly, and instructionally irrelevant classification procedures to distinguish among students with low IQs (educable mentally retarded), those with ability-achievement discrepancies (learning disabled), those who come from economically and/or language disadvantaged backgrounds (at risk of school failure), and those otherwise considered slow learners (so-called gray-area students). These classification procedures do not provide the information needed for instructional planning. In fact, they tend to result in curricular and organizational variations that selectively limit access to knowledge and equity in outcomes.

Instructional Approaches and Programs
Effective in Achieving Educational Equity

There are a wide range of alternative educational approaches that have been identified in the literature as feasible for school implementation and effective in achieving educational equity for individual students. Four of the most commonly referenced and widely adopted approaches are briefly discussed in this section: (a) cooperative learning, (b) teacher collaboration, (c) curriculum design and modification, and (d) classroom organization. The critical design features of pro-

Table 11.1 Selected List of Programs Designed Based on the Four Instructional Approaches

Instructional Approach	Model Programs
Cooperative learning	Classwide peer tutoring (Delquadri & Greenwood) Learning Together (Johnson & Johnson) Team-assisted individualization (Slavin)
Teacher collaboration	Instructional consultation (Rosenfield) Teacher Assistance Teams (Chalfant)
Curriculum design and modification	Curriculum-based assessment (Deno) Adaptive Learning Environments (Wang) Direct instruction (Becker et al.) Cognitive strategy training (Deschler) Reciprocal teaching (Brown & Palincsar)
School organization	Comer Process (Comer) Effective schools (Ramp)

grams using these approaches have been culled from the research base on effective teaching and school effectiveness, and from the practical experiences and insights of practitioners engaging in efforts to improve instruction and learning in schools. While the focus of discussion will be on the unique aspects of each of the four approaches, it is important to note that all of the approaches include common elements, and many of them are similar to one another.

To provide a concrete illustration of the design features of specific programs, I present a brief description of a specific widely used program that applies each approach. In addition, Table 11.1 provides a selected list of widely known programs that were designed based on each of the four instructional approaches.

Cooperative Learning Approach

The cooperative learning approach is gaining increasing recognition as an innovative educational approach with both a substantial data base and practical guidelines for its implementation as an effective means of improving the social and academic attainment of students (Johnson & Johnson, 1975; Johnson, Johnson, & Maruyama, 1983; Slavin, Leavey, & Madden, 1982). The basic premise of this approach is that the competitive peer dynamics of the traditional school environment are counterproductive in maintaining student motivation and achievement in academics, especially for students at either end of the normal distribution. Cooperative learning approaches attempt to alter the social dynamics of peer groups to foster peer support for positive achievement outcomes. This approach does not require altering the content or method of instructional delivery. The change lies in the way in which students study the assigned material.

Four critical elements of cooperative learning are generally incorporated in the various cooperative learning models. As noted by Johnson and Johnson (1975), they are as follows:

- *Positive interdependence:* In order for a learning situation to be cooperative, students must perceive that they are positively interdependent with other members of their learning group. This may be achieved through mutual goals (goal interdependence); division of labor (task interdependence); division of materials, resources, or information among group members (resource interdependence); assignment of roles to students (role interdependence); and/or giving joint rewards (reward interdependence).
- *Face-to-face interaction among students:* There is no magic in positive interdependence in and of itself; it is the interaction among students promoted by positive interdependence that promotes learning and social growth.
- *Individual accountability for mastering the assigned material:* The purpose of a learning situation is to maximize the achievement of each individual student. Feedback mechanisms for determining the level of mastery of each student are necessary for students to provide appropriate support and assistance to one another.
- *Appropriate use of interpersonal and small group skills:* Placing socially unskilled students in a learning group and telling them to be cooperative obviously will not be successful. Students must be taught the social skills needed for high-quality collaboration, and they must be motivated to use those skills.

Cooperative learning has been used as a strategy for improving student learning in a range of subject matters and in varied settings. It has been incorporated in the teaching of math to elementary school children (Slavin et al., 1982), the teaching of higher-order cognitive processes such as in problem-solving and reasoning strategies (Skon, Johnson, & Johnson, 1981), the teaching of inquiry in science (Johnson, 1976) and in social studies (Wheeler & Ryan, 1973), and the teaching of high school reading (Rutter, Maughan, Mortimore, & Ouston, 1979).

An overall consistently positive result has been noted in various studies on the efficacy of the cooperative learning approach as an intervention strategy to improve student learning. The approach has been shown to result in a generally consistent increase in student achievement and to produce noncognitive outcomes such as improved self-esteem and attitude toward school and schoolwork (Jones, 1974), improved racial relations (Gartner, Kohler, & Reissman, 1971), and acceptance of mainstreamed handicapped students (Johnson et al., 1983).

An example of a program using the cooperative learning approach is the Learning Together Model (Johnson & Johnson, 1975). This model emphasizes the effectiveness of peer cooperation and a cooperative versus a competitive learning environment within the classroom. Competition and individual action do have their place in the classroom; the Learning Together Model stipulates that students need to learn to function in all three settings. The emphasis is on avoiding inappropriate competition in the classroom, and on teaching students when competition is the appropriate behavior.

One goal of this model is that students learn to participate freely in the learning process without comparing their abilities to those of their peers. Heterogeneous groups have been shown to increase the achievement of high-achieving students as well as that of less successful students, and to teach social skills and democratic values. Further, the cooperative environment encourages students who are less knowledgeable to exert themselves so they can share in the satisfaction of group efforts.

This model emphasizes how goals can be structured to promote valued behaviors among students, and how teachers can promote cooperative behaviors by describing their expectations clearly. Teachers increase the degree of program implementation by consciously laying the necessary groundwork for students to work collaboratively. One step is to discuss openly with students the idea of working together, and to help them identify skills that they might need when they begin their collaborative efforts. The classroom teacher facilitates successful cooperative learning by helping students develop skills in communication, building and maintaining a trusting climate, self-monitoring of personal behavior, and positive competition skills.

The specific expected outcomes of the model include high interaction among peers, effective communication, high utilization of resources of other students, high sharing and helping, high emotional involvement of all students, high coordination of efforts and division of labor where possible, high risk taking and divergent thinking, and no comparison of self versus others. In addition, this model stresses affective as well as cognitive outcomes. Affective goals and outcomes are emphasized at every step of planning, implementation, and assessment.

Teacher Collaboration Approach

Teacher collaboration is an approach designed to provide support services to students with special needs and their teachers in regular education settings (Lilly, 1971; Pugach & Johnson, 1988). This approach provides a consultation/training framework for reducing inappropriate placements in special programs through the collaboration and sharing of knowledge and skills of all professionals who work with the students.

The teacher collaboration approach stipulates the use of consulting or child-study teams made up of general and special education teachers and, in some cases, parents or other special service providers. These support personnel primarily provide indirect services to students with special needs as consultants to the regular education teacher. Their work has several goals: to assist regular education teachers in meeting the unique needs of individual students; to provide prereferral intervention and screening for special education services; to facilitate communication among teachers within a building; to generate constructive problem-solving attitudes among teachers; and to increase teachers' skills in working with students with diverse needs.

The teacher collaborative team focuses on individual students. Each child's learning difficulties are evaluated by the team, and individualized interventions are proposed to meet that child's unique needs. Under the teacher collaboration approach, curriculum modifications are aligned with the instructional needs of the student as evaluated by the child-study team or consulting teachers. Continuous monitoring, assessment, and feedback occur as part of the step-by-step implementation and evaluation process of the chosen intervention. Administrative and instructional support of teachers is assured as teachers and other support and service personnel may be on the consulting team and thus part of a collaborative effort to serve all students.

One example of a program using the teacher collaboration approach is the Teacher Assistance Team (TAT) model developed by James C. Chalfant. This model is a problem-solving system within a particular school, where teachers work together to identify student needs and to plan, implement, and evaluate appropriate interventions. The goals of this model are to help teachers meet the diverse needs of all students, to provide support to teachers in the mainstreaming process, and to provide an efficient prereferral service to special education. In addition to these goals, the TAT also serves to facilitate communication among teachers, to generate constructive problem-solving attitudes, and to increase teachers' skills in working with all students.

Under TAT, the team is made up of three regular education teachers elected by the teaching staff, who possess the following skills or characteristics: supportive personalities, excellent communication skills, excellent teaching skills, and willingness to offer help to colleagues. A team leader is generally selected from among the three team members to take responsibility for the functioning of the team and the planning of meetings, referrals, and follow-up procedures. In large schools, two teams may be needed to handle referrals.

Referrals may be made by any teacher or parent, or even by the student. The referring teacher must submit a referral form to the team that includes (a) a description of the desired classroom performance, (b) a list of the student's strengths and weaknesses, (c) a description of what the teacher has already tried to resolve the problem, and (d) any relevant background information and test results.

After the referral form has been presented to the team, the team leader reviews the referral form, schedules a meeting, and assigns a team member to observe the child briefly in the classroom. The team members are responsible for reading the referral and analyzing the problem before the scheduled meeting. In some cases, the referring teacher, the parent, and special service providers may attend meetings; however, it is not recommended that principals or special education teachers serve on the team, as teachers may be less apt to speak freely and offer solutions in the presence of such "experts."

During the meeting, the team must come to a consensus about the identification of the student's problem, discuss and negotiate one or two objectives to work on first, brainstorm alternatives for intervention, have the referring teacher select a few approaches to try, refine the chosen approaches, and, finally, provide a follow-up plan. The referring teacher is now responsible for initiating the interventions and measuring progress. This information is recorded on the Instructional Recommendations Form developed by the team.

Informal progress checks are done by visiting the classroom and talking with the teacher. A formal follow-up meeting is scheduled within 2-6 weeks of the initial meeting. At this meeting, progress is discussed and additional plans are made. The process continues until the referring teacher and parent are satisfied that the student's problem is resolved.

The TAT model offers advantages to administrators in using staff more efficiently, improving staff communication, and saving time and money by reducing referrals to special education. TAT has an impact on special education by providing an efficient prereferral screening for special education, and by providing support to mainstreamed students. Parents and other students benefit as TAT offers alternatives for slow learners and those gray-area students not eligible for special education, includes parents in the planning of interventions, and allows students to receive immediate intervention.

Curriculum Design and Modification Approach

The curriculum design and modification approach focuses on adapting the curriculum to meet the instructional support needs of individual students. This approach typically involves specification of the curriculum objectives and sequence of instructional and learning objectives, and a detailed description of what a child already knows and does not know. It is precise about the cognitive and social characteristics necessary to perform a given learning task or to acquire new skills in a given instructional domain. A major salient characteristic of the curriculum design and modification approach is that attention is directed to program modification rather than to characteristics of the child, a method that may only lead to categorization. This approach includes a systematic mechanism for sending signals showing that instruction requires modification because it is not working for some students.

The following is a sample list of design features that are frequently cited as focal points in curriculum design and modification efforts for improving program effectiveness.

- Curriculum is designed with a built-in mechanism to link instruction systematically to assessments of current level of performance.

- Curriculum-based assessment approaches are used to evaluate student learning outcomes and to provide teachers with instructionally relevant information for instructional planning and for making placement decisions.
- Curriculum provides frequent checkpoints for monitoring student progress and instructional planning, and for providing feedback.
- Curriculum focuses on the mastery of the subject-matter content and critical basic skills required for efficient processing of information and successful performance.
- Curriculum provides for direct instruction as well as for opportunities for students to explore and solve problems independently.
- Curriculum includes a continuum of alternative paths and a variety of learning activities.
- Curriculum has built-in flexibility in terms of pacing for individual students and the amount of time teachers spend on providing direct instruction to individual students when needed.
- Curriculum materials and an instructional management system convey the expectation that students take self-responsibility for the management of their own learning progress and behaviors.
- Curriculum is designed with built-in opportunities for students to work cooperatively in groups.

An example of a program using the curriculum design and modification approach is the Adaptive Learning Environments Model (ALEM), developed by Margaret C. Wang (1980). The ALEM is a research-based program that has been widely adopted by schools aiming to serve individual students with diverse learning needs effectively in regular classes. The overall goal of the ALEM is to establish and maintain school environments that accommodate individual needs and characteristics, thereby ensuring learning success for all students. To this end, the ALEM design includes programming, management, and technical support for school administrators and instructional staff. The ALEM design includes the specific programming features described below.

Individualized progress plans. In ALEM classrooms, curriculum materials are modified when necessary for the development and implementation of individualized progress plans for each student. These plans generally consist of two complementary curriculum components. The first is a highly structured, prescriptive learning component for fostering basic skills mastery in academic subject areas. The second is an exploratory learning component designed to foster students' ability to plan, make curricular decisions, apply problem-solving skills in social and academic learning situations, and manage their own learning behavior.

Diagnostic-prescriptive monitoring system. The adaptive instruction process under the ALEM begins with the diagnosis of each student's entering level of skills and knowledge in the basic subject-matter areas. The program's diagnostic-prescriptive monitoring system uses criterion-referenced assessments (e.g., curriculum-based assessment procedures built into the various basic skills curricula) to ensure that appropriate educational tasks are individually assigned and lead to successful learning. This system calls for ongoing monitoring of each student's progress through record-keeping procedures that incorporate paper-and-pencil or microcomputer formats.

Adaptive program delivery system. The ALEM's approach to an effective program delivery system is to complement and supplement the existing resources and staff expertise of particular schools through redeployment and training. School personnel are supported to adjust ALEM implementation to their own improvement goals. Based on a systematically designed needs assessment process, a site-specific implementation plan is developed. The plan includes, for example, a specially tailored awareness program for all relevant stakeholders (e.g., teachers, parents, school boards), curriculum revisions (if needed), plans for restructuring and redeploying school resources and personnel, and a time line for program implementation.

Data-Based Staff Development Program. Preimplementation and ongoing support for the introduction and maintenance of the various ALEM components are provided through the Data-Based Staff Development Program (Wang & Gennari, 1983). The training sequence for school personnel has three levels. The first, basic training, provides an overview of the ALEM and working knowledge of the program's implementation requirements. The second level, individualized training, is keyed to particular functions of each staff role. The third level, in-service training, consists of an interactive and iterative process of program assessment, feedback, planning, and staff development.

School and classroom organizational supports. Adapting instruction to the needs of individual students requires flexibility in school and classroom organizational patterns. At the school level, the ALEM encourages staffing patterns that include instructional teaming to support effective program implementation. Under the ALEM, the roles of instructional personnel are redefined to achieve an interface between general and specialized educational and related services. The role of special education teachers, for example, includes consultation with general education teachers as well as the provision of direct instructional services for students with special needs in regular classes.

Principals play an integral role in creating a supportive organizational climate for implementation of the ALEM. As instructional leaders, principals work actively with teachers in identifying and solving classroom problems. They participate in in-service activities and conduct both formal and informal staff development sessions. They observe classrooms and provide feedback to teachers, working closely with them to identify instructional goals and the means to achieve them. Because adaptive instruction programs require flexible scheduling, restructuring of relationships among teachers, and ongoing training support, all of these instructional leadership functions take on increased importance.

Family involvement. Learning occurs at home as well as in school. Given the limited amount of time in the school day, even students in the most effectively implemented educational programs can benefit from instructional reinforcement at home. Thus the ALEM supports an active program of family involvement to increase communication and cooperation between school and home. Parents are encouraged to participate in designing and refining their children's educational plans and to provide home instruction in consultation with teachers. In addition, parents may work as volunteers in ALEM classrooms.

School Organization Approach

Several salient characteristics are common among model programs identified with the school organization approach. Such models tend to base their program design on a broad-based framework that recognizes multifaceted influences on learning within the classrooms and schools, homes, and cultures of the community of adults and peers. Therefore, school improvement efforts are viewed as an evolving process that includes all stakeholders whose work affects the student's learning in and out of school, directly or indirectly over time.

School organization models use an interactive paradigm that assumes that individual students possess unique profiles of instructionally relevant characteristics (e.g., family characteristics such as parental expectations, English as a second language, attitudes toward learning and academic competence) that interact with particular elements in the classroom learning environment (e.g., design of the instructional program, staffing pattern, class size, the reward system) to elicit certain classroom processes (e.g., amount of interaction with teacher on management versus instructional matters). These processes are seen as directly related to an individual student's learning outcomes.

These models also emphasize the importance of creating school environments and implementation support systems that will enhance the learning of each individual student. Teachers know more than they actually put to use in the classroom, given the current structure of school programs and the level of classroom organization support. A systematically restructured classroom/school learning environment is viewed as essential for capitalizing on the knowledge base and the technical know-how that already exists among the school staff. Model programs using the classroom organization approach utilize a broad-based systems approach to improve schooling practice. They emphasize the development of coordinated instructional programming through a school-based planning and teaming approach to support program implementation.

The Comer Process Model, developed by Dr. James P. Comer of the Yale Child Study Center Mental Health Team, is one example of a program using the school organization approach. There are four key components in the Comer Process Model. The first is school governance. A "governance and management body" is formed to establish a comprehensive building plan designed to create a desirable school climate, improved academic performance, and staff development opportunities based on building-level objectives and goals. This group or committee is composed of two or three teachers (representing two grade levels), two or three parents (representing the PTA and other constituencies, such as minorities or socioeconomic groups), one support staff member (social worker, psychologist or the like), and the principal. Using the principle of shared power and decision making, the committee is the vehicle of change in the school, planning and directing implementation and evaluating all project interventions. Specifically, the committee reviews and develops school policies and procedures, selects new school staff, and plans and monitors a variety of projects, including special services for children, training activities, and curriculum projects (Comer, 1985).

The second key component is the mental health program. A mental health team is established to deal with behavioral problems and to offer staff workshops, faculty presentations, and informal conferences. The team meets with teachers to assist them with particular students or general behavior management problems. The team discusses case-relevant social-emotional issues and behavioral principles, helping teachers to formulate specific management plans. Interventions involve both child-change strategies and changes in the school environment or operation. The mental health program also includes the establishment of a crisis program as a means of intervening before or at the moment of major upsets in a student's behavior.

The third key component in the Comer Process Model is the parent program. Parent participation in all aspects of school life is seen as a critical element in improving school climate and school-community relationships. There are three levels of parent participation. The first and highest level is direct participation in school governance and other program committees. The second level is involvement in the "parent assistant program" (working as teacher aides and tutors) and in managing special fund-raising and extracurricular activities. The third level of parent participation is attendance at school functions or training activities and interaction through student conferences or parent outreach activities. In all these levels, especially the first two, school staff and mental health team personnel help parents to develop planning, organizational, and management skills. The presence of parents in the schools increases the schools' accountability and responsiveness to the values and needs of the community. Parents' involvement in governance enhances their commitment to the overall project and their understanding of school operations.

The fourth key component is the teaching and curriculum program. Improvement in teaching and curriculum is a major goal of the model. In grade-level meetings, occasionally assisted by a curriculum consultant, teachers clarify goals for students, develop materials, share instructional methods, and make evaluation more systematic. Demonstration teaching and follow-up consultation are used to help teachers integrate instruction in the basic academic skills with instruction in creative arts, such as art, music, and dance. Teachers develop curriculum units that integrate social and academic skills training in a variety of concrete learning experiences. Planned instruction in social skills is considered especially important for low-income minority children, who might not otherwise acquire these skills.

Conclusion:
Implications for Implementation

Achieving the goal of equity in educational outcomes will require a major shift in our mind-set on how educational equity is defined. The way we think about differences among students, how we view the purpose of elementary and secondary education, and the way we choose to organize schools are all fundamental to this conceptual shift. If schooling success is recognized as possible for everyone through instructional accommodation, the major task of the schools is the creation of learning environments that uphold a standard of equity in educational outcomes for all students. The focus should be on identifying practices that deny equal access to schooling success and practices that promote it.

The instructional approaches and examples of specific programs discussed in this chapter are illustrations of programs aiming to maximize the chances of schooling success for students who are not well served under the conventional group-paced approach to instructional delivery. School implementation of innovative programs of the type discussed here, together with other research-based innovative programs and practices (Graden, Zins, & Curtis, 1988; Wang & Walberg, 1985; Wittrock, 1986), have yielded a rich knowledge base on how schools can implement highly complex and sophisticated instructional procedures to meet the learning needs of their diverse student populations.

A premise underlying the design of all these programs is that schooling success can be nurtured through effective educational intervention. These approaches all incorporate advances in theories and research on learning and instruction. Rather than attempting to identify a general underlying deficit in students requiring greater-than-usual instructional support, these programs focus on curriculum adaptations to ensure student mastery of curriculum content. Provision of equality of opportunity for educational success can be characterized, therefore, in terms of the use of school time, the quality of instruction, the content of the instruction, and instructional grouping practices.

Whether student diversity is addressed through the adoption of innovative instructional approaches or through some organizational restructuring approach, one principle should remain paramount: All students can achieve the educational goals of basic education if properly supported. If one student cannot learn a given set of program objectives for whatever reason, then he or she should be given the additional time and instructional support needed.

Admittedly, the implementation of programs that promote educational equity and accountability is complicated by many programmatic, administrative, attitudinal, and fiscal roadblocks that will likely continue to plague school districts. However, the past two decades of experience with successful implementation of innovative approaches to instructional accommodation have shown that many of the barriers can be removed. There is no lack of knowledge about what to do or how to do it. The central issue in implementing the vision of educational equity as discussed in this chapter is how to tie together resources (e.g., teacher expertise, curricular accommodations, administrative and organizational support for program implementation) and outcomes in ways that simultaneously achieve equity goals and accountability. Achieving educational equity will require using the best of what we currently know about effective instruction and schooling effectiveness. The challenge is to distribute school resources in such a way that extra resources can be devoted to facilitate the development of students who have the most difficulty, while providing *all* students with the best possible opportunities to succeed in learning.

References

Allington, R. L., & Johnston, P. (1986). The coordination among regular classroom reading programs and targeted support programs. In B. I. Williams, P. A. Richmond, & B. J. Mason (Eds.), *Designs for compensatory education: Conference proceedings and papers* (Vol. 6, pp. 3-40). Washington, DC: Research and Evaluation Associates.

Bloom, B. S. (1976). *Human characteristics and school learning.* New York: McGraw-Hill.

Brandt, R. S. (Ed.). (1989). Dealing with diversity: Ability, gender, and style differences [Special Issue]. *Educational Leadership, 46*(6).

Bransford, J. D., Vye, N. J., Delclos, V. R., Burns, M. S., & Hasselbring, T. S. (1985). *Improving the quality of assessment and instruction: Roles for dynamic assessment* (Learning Technology Center Technical Report Series). Nashville, TN: George Peabody College of Vanderbilt University.

Buttram, J. L., & Kershner, K. (1988). *Special education in America's cities: A descriptive study.* Washington DC: Council of the Great City Schools.

Comer, J. P. (1985, September). *The school development program: A nine step guide to school improvement.* New Haven, CT: Yale Child Study Center.

Chipman, S. G., Segal, J. W., & Glaser, R. (Eds.). (1985). *Thinking and learning skills: Vol. 2. Research and open questions.* Hillsdale, NJ: Lawrence Erlbaum.

Cooper, H. M. (1983). Communication of teacher expectations to students. In J. M. Levine & M. C. Wang (Eds.), *Teacher and student perceptions: Implications for learning* (pp. 193-211). Hillsdale, NJ: Lawrence Erlbaum.

Fenstermacher, G. D., & Goodlad, J. I. (Eds.). (1983). *Individual differences and the common curriculum.* Chicago: University of Chicago Press.

Feuerstein, R., Jensen, M., Hoffman, M. B., & Rand, Y. (1985). Instrumental enrichment, an intervention program for structural cognitive modifiability: Theory and practice. In J. J. Segal, S. F. Chipman, & R. Glaser (Eds.), *Thinking and learning skills: Vol. 1. Relating instruction to research* (pp. 43-82). Hillsdale, NJ: Lawrence Erlbaum.

Gartner, A., Kohler, M., & Reissman, F. (1971). *Children teach children: Learning by teaching.* New York: Harper & Row.

Graden, J. L., Zins, J. E., & Curtis, M. J. (1988). *Alternative educational delivery systems: Enhancing instructional options for all students.* Washington DC: National Association of School Psychologists.

Greenwood, C. R., Wharton, D., & Delquadri, J. C. (1984). Tutoring methods: Increasing opportunity to respond and achieve. *Association for Direct Instruction News, 3*(3), 4-7, 23.

Haynes, M. C., & Jenkins, J. R. (1986). Reading instruction in special education resource rooms. *American Educational Research Journal, 23*(23), 161-190.

Heller, K., Holtzman, W., & Messick, S. (Eds.). (1982). *Placing children in special education: A strategy for equity.* Washington, DC: National Academy of Sciences Press.

Jenkins, J. R. (1987). Similarities in the achievement levels of learning disabled and remedial students. *Counterpoint, 7*(3), 16.

Jenkins, J. R., Pious, C., & Peterson, D. (1988). Categorical programs for remedial and handicapped students: Issues of validity. *Exceptional Children, 55*(2), 147-158.

Johnson, D. W., & Johnson, R. T. (1975). *Learning together and alone: Cooperation, competition, and individualization.* Englewood Cliffs, NJ: Prentice-Hall.

Johnson, D. W., Johnson, R. T., & Maruyama, G. (1983). Interdependence and interpersonal attraction among heterogeneous and homogeneous individuals: A theoretical formulation and a meta-analysis of the research. *Review of Educational Research, 53,* 5-54.

Johnson, R. (1976). The relationship between cooperation and inquiry in science classrooms. *Journal of Research in Science and Technology, 10,* 55-63.

Jones, W. C. (1974). *Some effects of tutoring experiences on tutoring and tutored children.* Unpublished doctoral dissertation, University of Georgia. (University Microfilms No. 74-04, 825)

Lilly, M. S. (1971). A training-based model for special education. *Exceptional Children, 37,* 745-749.

National Assessment of Educational Progress. (1987). *Learning by doing: A manual for teaching and assessing higher-order thinking skills in science and mathematics* (Report No. 17-HO5-80). Princeton, NJ: Educational Testing Service.

National Center for Educational Statistics. (1988). *State higher education profiles.* Washington, DC: U.S. Department of Education.

National Coalition of Advocates for Students. (1988). *100 largest school districts: A special analysis of 1986 elementary and secondary school civil rights survey data.* Boston: Author.

Oakes, J. (1985)). *Keeping track: How schools structure inequality.* New Haven, CT: Yale University Press.

Palincsar, A., & Brown, A. (1984). Reciprocal teaching of comprehension-fostering and comprehension-monitoring activities. *Cognition and Instruction, 1,* 117-175.

Pugach, M., & Johnson, L. J. (1988, Spring). Peer collaboration. *Teaching Exceptional Children,* pp. 75-77.

Reschly, D. J. (1988). Special education reforms: School psychology revolution. *School Psychology Review, 17*(3), 459-475.

Reynolds, M. C. (Ed.). (1989). *Knowledge base for the beginning teacher.* Oxford: Pergamon.

Rutter, M., Maughan, B., Mortimore, P., & Ouston, J. (1979). *Fifteen thousand hours: Secondary schools and their effects on children.* Cambridge, MA: Harvard University Press.

Skon, L., Johnson, D. W., & Johnson, R. (1981). Cooperative peer interaction versus individual competition and individualistic efforts: Effects on the acquisition of cognitive reasoning strategies. *Journal of Educational Psychology, 73,* 83-92.

Slavin, R. E., Leavey, M., & Madden, N. A. (1982, March). *Effects of student teams and individualized instruction on student mathematics achievement, attitudes, and behaviors.* Paper presented at the annual meeting of the American Educational Research Association, New York.

Stanovitch, K. E. (1984). The interactive-compensatory model of reading: A confluence of developmental, experimental, and educational psychology. *Remedial and Special Education, 5*(3), 11-19.

Walberg, H. J. (1984). Families as partners in educational productivity. *Phi Delta Kappan, 65*(6), 397-400.

Wang, M. C. (1980). Adaptive instruction: Building on diversity. *Theory into Practice, 19*(2), 122-127.

Wang, M. C., & Gennari, P. (1983). Analysis of the design, implementation, and effects of a data-based staff development program. *Teacher Education and Special Education, 6*(4), 211-226.

Wang, M. C., & Lindvall, C. M. (1984). Individual differences and school learning environments. In E. W. Gordon (Ed.), *Review of research in education* (pp. 161-225). Washington, DC: American Educational Research Association.

Wang, M. C., & Palincsar, A. S. (1989). Teaching students to assume an active role in their learning. In M. C. Reynolds (Ed.), *Knowledge base for the beginning teacher* (pp. 71-84). Oxford: Pergamon.

Wang, M. C., Reynolds, M. C., & Walberg, H. J. (1988). Integrating the children of the second system. *Phi Delta Kappan, 70*(30), 248-251.

Wang, M. C., & Walberg, H. J. (Eds.). (1985). *Adapting instruction to individual differences.* Berkeley, CA: McCutchan.

Wheeler, R., & Ryan, F. (1973). Effects of cooperative and competitive environments on the attitudes and achievement of elementary school students engaged in social studies inquiry activities. *Journal of Educational Psychology, 65,* 402-407.

Williams, B. I., Richmond, P. A., & Mason, B. J. (1986). *Designs for compensatory education: Conference proceedings and papers.* Washington, DC: Research and Evaluation Associates.

Wittrock, M. C. (1986). Students' thought processes. In M. C. Wittrock (Ed.), *Handbook of research on teaching* (3rd ed., pp. 297-314). New York: Macmillan.

Ysseldyke, J. E. (1987). Classification of handicapped students. In M. C. Wang, M. C. Reynolds, & H. J. Walberg (Eds.), *Handbook of special education: Research and practice: Vol. 1. Learner characteristics and adaptive education* (pp. 253-271). Oxford: Pergamon.

Ysseldyke, J. E., Thurlow, M., Graden, J., Wesson, C., Deno, S., & Algozzine, B. (1983). Generalizations from five years of research on assessment and decision making. *Exceptional Educational Quarterly, 4*(1), 75-93.

12

Instructional Organizational Practices That Affect Equity

ADAM GAMORAN

University of Wisconsin — Madison

If there is one thing we have learned from research on school effects, it is that differences within schools have more influence on educational outcomes than do differences between schools (e.g., Coleman et al., 1966; Jencks et al., 1972; for reviews, see Averch, Carroll, Donaldson, Kiesling, & Pincus, 1972; Hanushek, 1986). Student achievement, to take the prime example, varies much more within schools than between schools; consequently, we are more likely to discover the causes of variation in achievement if we examine differences within schools. Although a substantial portion of the within-school variation in achievement has been attributed to background differences among students, a growing literature suggests that differences in the experiences students have in schools also play an important role (e.g., Barr & Dreeben, 1983; Dreeben & Gamoran, 1986; Gamoran, 1986, 1987; Heyns, 1974; Oakes, 1985).

These findings have great importance for anyone interested in educational equity. They indicate that questions of equity need to be

Author's Note: This chapter was prepared at the National Center on Effective Secondary Schools, Wisconsin Center for Education Research, University of Wisconsin — Madison, which is supported in part by a grant from the Office of Educational Research and Improvement (Grant No. G-008690007). Any opinions, conclusions, or recommendations expressed in this chapter are those of the author and do not necessarily reflect the views of this agency or the U.S. Department of Education.

addressed by examining differences in what happens to students inside schools. How are students arranged for instruction? How is the organization of instruction related to instructional processes? What are the connections among instructional organization, teaching practices, and student outcomes? These questions are fundamental to the study of equity in school systems because they pertain to the level of analysis at which student inequality is most evident: within schools.

This chapter explores the implications for educational equity of a key feature of the arrangement of pupils for instruction: the assignment of students to instructional settings according to their perceived interests and abilities, a practice known as curriculum tracking or ability grouping. Writers on ability grouping, especially those critical of it, have often been concerned with equity. The present study attempts to organize these concerns by placing them in the context of a more general discussion of the meaning of educational equity. It then assesses the impact of ability grouping on equity, both as it is currently practiced and as it may potentially be implemented. This assessment is furthered by comparing ability grouping to other forms of instructional organization. Finally, the chapter presents some considerations for educators who must choose among competing values offered by different ways of arranging students.

Equity as a Value in Education

Equity in education, or "equality of educational opportunity," is a concept with multiple meanings. For the first two-thirds of this century, it referred to equal *access* to education. In the late 1960s, however, if became clear that equality of access mattered little when students' experiences outside school limited their capacity to profit from such access. What mattered instead was equality of *results* (Coleman, 1968; Coleman et al., 1966).

The frame of reference for defining equity is not self-evident. Whose results are supposed to be equalized? According to one view, equality of results exists when *all* students obtain similar outcomes (see Gutmann, 1987).[1] According to this perspective, the goal of equity requires that education be used to overcome *any* preexisting differences among students (not just differences tied to common bases of social inequality such as gender, race, and socioeconomic status). As Gutmann (1987) and Strike (1988) point out, this view ultimately leads to a situation in which all resources are devoted to the least able students, at least until they reach the same level of achievement as their more able peers. This notion seems defensible only if one accepts the underlying assumption that all persons are capable of and have the right to similar attainment, and that differences in ability, effort, or any other characteristic among persons does not provide reason to differentiate opportunities or expectations. Because of this assumption, the position must be viewed as extreme, and it is certainly not a majority view in the United States.

More commonly, *equality of results* refers to equality across subgroups of society, such as males and females, Blacks and Whites, and rich and poor (e.g., see Coleman, 1968). The assumption standing behind this view is that educational results should be unrelated to characteristics that are in principle irrelevant for education, such as sex, race, and economic standing (Strike, 1988). In contrast to the previous view, this approach accepts the validity of native ability and effort for influencing outcomes. Thus, according to this view, educational results may vary according to certain characteristics — those deemed, in Strike's (1988) term, "morally relevant" to the educational process — but not according to "morally irrelevant" ones.

It should be clear, however, that as soon as one permits unequal results within certain collections of students — for example, among students of equivalent backgrounds who differ in intelligence or effort — it becomes necessary to reintroduce the concept of equality of *access*. A notion of equity requires that even if unequal results are allowable under certain conditions, all students have a right to equal access to effective educational resources. Thus the conception of equity for this chapter has two components, depending on the frame of reference: It implies equality of results across population subgroups, and it calls for equality of access (or "opportunity," in the earlier sense of the word) with respect to the population as a whole.

Equity is of course only one of many goals or values in education. Even if we restrict our focus to achievement outcomes, other goals include raising average scores, increasing the attainment of the highest-achieving students, and improving the efficiency of schooling (obtaining the highest level of outcome per resource input). It is unlikely that any decision about how to allocate educational resources will satisfy all of these.

Writers on ability grouping have tended to differ in the attention they pay to these competing values. Often, critics of grouping emphasize inequality of results, both among population subgroups and in the general population (e.g., Oakes, 1985; Rosenbaum, 1976). Proponents, in contrast, point out that ability grouping is supposed to increase achievement on the average, or for the highest-achieving students; and while they may be committed to equality of access, they have little concern for equality of results (e.g., Conant, 1967; Coxe, 1936). Even if these authors were to agree about the impact ability grouping has, they might still disagree about its appropriateness, because they are concerned with divergent ends.

In reviewing the effects of grouping and tracking, I will call attention to both sorts of goals: the effects of grouping on the levels of outcomes, which may be termed "educational productivity," and the effects on the dispersion of outcomes, or "educational inequality" (Gamoran & Mare, 1989). The two types of results are connected: If ability grouping has no effects on productivity, then it can have no effects on inequality. Moreover, the direction of differences in levels of results for subgroups determines the dispersion of outcomes across such groups. For example, if grouping raises achievement for students from wealthy backgrounds (who have higher achievement to begin with), but lowers it for children of poor backgrounds, then it must also increase inequality between advantaged and disadvantaged students.

My own goal in describing the effects of instructional arrangements and discussing their implications for equity is not to argue for or against a particular value, but to show what values are served by current and theoretically possible practices; I hope to provide evidence that will help educators make informed choices, given their own value preferences. Some choices may be easy — if one form of organization produced the highest means and the lowest variance, and with the greatest efficiency, it would be a unanimous choice. Unfortunately, the real world is more complex than that, and emphasis on one goal may limit the attainment of another.

The Effects of Ability Grouping and Curriculum Tracking

Despite their widespread use, for at least two decades grouping and tracking have been under attack as being unnecessarily inegalitarian (e.g., Esposito, 1973; Findley & Bryan, 1971; Heathers, 1969; Oakes, 1985; Rist, 1970; Rosenbaum, 1976, 1980a; Schafer & Olexa, 1971).[2] A review of the studies upon which this critical stance is based shows that it is well founded in certain ways, but that it does not hold unambiguously. The ambiguity stems from the fact that whether a given finding is judged as equitable sometimes depends on the definition of equity that is applied. Furthermore, different forms of ability grouping and different levels of the school system reveal different implications for equity.

Ability Grouping in Elementary Schools

At the elementary school level, there is convincing evidence that ability grouping increases inequality of results in the general population. That is, pupils who begin the school year with different achievement levels end up even farther apart at the end of the year, partly as a result of ability grouping. Studies describing this result have been reviewed by Esposito (1973), Good and Marshall (1984), and Slavin (1987). Perhaps the most direct evidence on this issue comes from Hallinan and Sørensen (1983; Sørensen & Hallinan, 1986), who show that during the course of a school year, the variance in reading and math achievement increases most in classes containing homogeneous ability groups. This occurs because even after controlling for ability and background differences, students in high groups gain more than their low-group counterparts (Gamoran, 1986; Sørensen & Hallinan, 1986).

This finding may or may not indicate inequity, depending on one's definition. In the most extreme version, it would be considered inequitable purely because it involves unequal outcomes. Viewed by less severe standards, however, the finding does not provide enough information to judge it by. What happens to the mean outcomes of students in different groups? Does the gap widen because high-group students are pushed forward, or because low-group students are held back, or some combination? Second, what are the mechanisms that lead to the unequal results? Do high-group students have access to better resources, such as more interesting texts and more instructional time? Or do high-group students profit more from the resources to which they are exposed?

With regard to mean outcomes, several reviews have concluded that ability grouping sometimes raises achievement for high-group students, but that it has little impact for students in average groups and may be detrimental to achievement for low-group students (Esposito, 1973; Findley & Bryan, 1971; Good & Marshall, 1984; Heathers, 1969). Recently, however, Slavin (1987) has challenged this view, arguing that earlier reviews distorted the evidence by failing to consider different forms of ability grouping separately. Using "best-evidence synthesis," a technique that combines quantitative meta-analysis with traditional narrative review, Slavin (1987) shows that whereas assignment to ability-grouped classes for the entire school day has no overall consistent effect on achievement, two other forms of grouping — within-class grouping and regrouping for specific subjects (especially when students are regrouped across grades) — lead to higher achievement on the average. Moreover, the studies reviewed by Slavin indicate that the achievement advantage generally occurs at all group levels — in average and low groups as well as in high.

Of the studies that provided separate results for the different group levels, some showed the highest gains in low groups. More often, however, while students in all groups gained, high-group students recorded the highest gains. This finding is consistent with studies comparing achievement in high and low groups that observed a widening gap between the two over the course of the year (Gamoran, 1986; Sørensen & Hallinan, 1986). If this is true — and it has not been accepted without controversy (Hiebert, 1987) — then it indicates that although ability grouping in elementary schools leads to greater inequality of achievement, it also produces higher average achievement for students at all ability levels.[3] Educational decision makers are thus faced with a choice between competing values: equality of achievement or higher levels of achievement.

The discussion of equity above led to the conclusion that if inequality of results occurs in the general population, if should be considered inequitable if it derives from unequal access to valued resources. In light of the higher gains for high-group students, it is important to examine equality of access for students in different groups. Unfortunately, the evidence is somewhat equivocal. One of the clearest findings on this topic is that in grouping for reading, the faster gains of high-group students result from greater coverage of the curricular material (Barr & Dreeben, 1983; Gamoran, 1986; Rowan & Miracle, 1983). What these studies do not show, however, is whether the faster pace of instruction in high groups is appropriate or not. Presumably, low groups cover less material in order to allow students to master what they do cover; it is not known whether the slower pace is at students' capacity or below it. Thus it is not clear whether the unequal access to content coverage should be considered inequitable.

Other studies show mixed findings on the quality of teaching in varied ability groups. In reading, low groups are characterized by more interruptions and fewer opportunities to read and discuss stories (Eder, 1981; for a review see Hiebert, 1987). At the extreme, Rist (1970) describes a class in which the low group was practically ignored by the teacher. However, another case study found more praise given to low-group students, and that the smaller size of low groups allowed more time per student with the teacher (Weinstein, 1976).

Rist's (1970) case suggests bias against poor children in assignment to ability groups. However, this finding appears to be atypical. Studies examining multiple classrooms have failed to uncover significant effects of race or socioeconomic status on ability-group assignment after taking prior achievement into account (Gamoran, 1989; Haller, 1984; Haller & Davis, 1980; Sørensen & Hallinan, 1984). Still, group assignment is correlated with background variables because of the association between background and test scores. Despite equality of access to groups, then, ability grouping may increase inequality between advantaged and disadvantaged students because high-group students gain at a faster rate. On this issue, too, one is faced with a value choice, because the higher achievement from ability grouping may also produce greater inequality of results among population subgroups.

Grouping and Tracking in Secondary Schools

Research at the secondary level suggests that, as in elementary schools, grouping and tracking tend to increase the dispersion of achievement by widening the gap between high and low achievers. Although this point has been debated (Alexander & Cook, 1982; Jencks & Brown, 1975), recent studies with large national data sets show that students in high groups and college-preparatory programs gain more than their non-college-bound peers (Gamoran, 1987; Gamoran & Mare, 1989; Kerckhoff, 1986; Shavit & Featherman, 1988; Vanfossen, Jones, & Spade, 1987; for a review, see Gamoran & Berends, 1987). In contrast to the evidence for elementary schools, however, these studies give no indication that gains occur at all ability levels in comparison to heterogeneous grouping. In a study of British schools, Kerckhoff (1986) compared achievement in different "streams" of stratified schools to one another and to achievement of similar students in undifferentiated schools. His findings showed, first, that high- and low-group students tended to move further apart over time, as noted above; and second, that high-group students learned more, and low-group students less, than similar students in heterogeneous settings. In other words, grouping appeared beneficial to students in high groups, roughly neutral to middle-group students, and detrimental to the achievement of students in the lower ranks. Consistent with Kerckhoff's findings, a simulation conducted by Gamoran and Mare (1989) with U.S. data suggests that students assigned to non-college-preparatory programs would have had higher achievement had they enrolled in the academic track.

Unlike at the elementary level, these unequal results in the general population cannot be defended with the argument that they occur in the context of raising achievement at all ability levels. Gains in high tracks are offset by low-track losses, and overall average achievement is barely higher, if at all (Kerckhoff, 1986; Kulik & Kulik, 1982). The goal of equity is not served here, although the competing value of high achievement for the most promising students may be accomplished.

Does the inequality of results stem from unequal access? A large number of observational studies suggest that in secondary schools, this may be the case. Students in higher tracks are exposed to more interesting and more complex material at a faster pace; their teachers are more enthusiastic, spend more time preparing for class, and place more emphasis on discussing the meaning of concepts and less on memorization (Ball, 1981; Keddie, 1971; Metz, 1978; Oakes, 1985; Rosenbaum, 1976). Instruction in low-track classes is more likely to be fragmented and skill based, relying on drills and worksheets (Hargreaves, 1967; Metz, 1978; Oakes, 1985; Page, 1987). More critical thinking and more exposure to culturally valued knowledge (e.g., high-status literature) occurs in high-track classes (Ball, 1981; Oakes, 1985). Teachers judged more successful are more likely to be assigned to teach high-track classes (Ball, 1981; Finley, 1984; Lacey, 1970).

Although some instructional differences may be appropriate — for example, students with better reading skills may be able to read more books — the weight of the evidence clearly shows inequities between tracks in the quality of instruction. Although quantitative studies have yet to document the effects of instructional quality on achievement, data strongly suggest that at least part of the reason for inequality of results in the general population is inequality of access across different tracks.

To compare results for population subgroups, it is first necessary to consider the track assignment process. Although placement appears largely meritocratic — that is, based on prior academic performance — student socioeconomic characteristics also influence track assignment (Alexander & Cook, 1982; Alexander & McDill, 1976; Gamoran & Mare, 1989; Heyns, 1974; Rehberg & Rosenthal, 1978). The effect of SES probably occurs through a combination of different aspirations held by students and varied expectations on the part of school staff (Cicourel & Kitsuse, 1963). This effect means that, through track assignment, the achievement advantage of students from high-SES backgrounds increases over time.

At the same time, controlling for SES and prior achievement, Black students are more likely than Whites to enroll in college-preparatory programs (Alexander & Cook, 1982; Alexander, Cook, & McDill, 1978; Gamoran & Mare, 1989; Rosenbaum, 1980b). By examining track assignment and track outcomes simultaneously, Gamoran and Mare (1989) show that, in their study, the favorable assignment pattern for Blacks meant that tracking helped to *compensate* for the initial advantage of Whites over Blacks in mathematics achievement. Because they were more likely to enroll in the academic program (net of background and prior achievement), Blacks' achievement became closer to that of Whites than it would have in the absence of tracking.[4]

Gamoran and Mare (1989) found the same results for a comparison of males and females. That is, females were more likely to be assigned to the college track, so on the average their math achievement deficit became smaller than it would have in the absence of tracking. This finding is less secure than the one for race differences, however, because, whereas several studies have shown a net advantage for Blacks in the track assignment process, this was the first one to find a significant advantage for females (compare, e.g., Alexander & Cook, 1982; Alexander & Eckland, 1975; Rosenbaum, 1980b).

These equity-producing aspects of tracking must be seen in light of the overall effects, which clearly operate in an inequitable fashion. Although average achievement may not be harmed by tracking — and the average achievement of Blacks appears to benefit — these averages are maintained through an overall inequality of results in the general population, which probably derives from inequality in the distribution of instructional quality between tracks.

Limitations on Equity: Comparisons Among Forms of Instructional Organization

The evidence reviewed here suggests that grouping and tracking, as they are currently practiced, contribute to an increase in the variance of student achievement. This finding is particularly troublesome at the secondary level, because high school tracking does not appear to raise achievement much in the population as a whole, nor does it provide equal access to the types of experiences that are likely to contribute to high achievement. Does this circumstance follow inevitably from the differentiation of students in schools? Or can the conditions of grouping and tracking be manipulated in order to remove or mitigate the resulting inequities?

One way of addressing this question is to consider why the impact of grouping on inequality is most severe at the secondary level. At least two conditions seem implicated. First, the forms of grouping appear to differ across levels of the school system. The prototypical form at the high school level is tracking, a system in which students are divided into distinct programs that dictate most or all of their courses. The form of elementary school grouping that is most like tracking — ability-based class assignment for the entire day — is the one type that clearly did *not* result in achievement gains in Slavin's (1987) review. Slavin offers two reasons for the poor performance of this type of grouping, which may also apply to tracking in high schools: (a) Because students are divided for all subjects at once, the classes are not really homogeneous for any one subject, thus minimizing whatever advantages accrue to ability grouping; and (b) because the divisions have such wide scope, they are especially salient, which probably magnifies grouping's negative psychological consequences for students in low groups. If more flexible grouping systems were adopted in high schools, the achievement gap between tracks might be lessened. This possibility is consistent with Gamoran's (1988) finding that high schools with more mobility in their tracking systems exhibit smaller achievement differences between tracks. Moreover, evidence from interviews suggests that high schools are moving toward less extensive tracking systems, at least formally (Moore & Davenport, 1988; Oakes, 1985).

A second reason for the large degree of inequality in high school tracking may be that the difficulties of providing high-quality instruction to low-track classes are greater at the secondary level. In elementary schools, students are relatively pliant, more willing to follow the teacher's lead. In middle and high schools, students take a more active role in resisting teachers' demands. If we think of instruction not as what teachers do to students, but as what teachers and students do together (Nystrand & Gamoran, 1988), then students' unwillingness to perform may limit the quality of the instruction they receive. Observational evidence suggests that low-track students discourage teachers from challenging them. They prefer structured written work, finding it more comfortable and more private than brisk oral discussions (Metz, 1978). Yet this kind of worksheet-based instruction is exactly the fragmented, simplified work that is said to heighten inequality of results. A similar point is made by Willis (1977) in reference to class reproduction (rather than tracking): Working-class adolescents actively participate in creating their own inequalities of opportunities. Thus, although it may be theoretically possible to provide instruction of equal quality to students in all track levels, this strategy may be difficult to implement.

Ability grouping appears to increase inequality greatly when it is used to provide challenging instruction to high groups but slow-paced, fragmented work to low groups. Its impact on inequality may be considerably smaller when it is used to provide appropriate instruction to the various levels, as may occur in elementary schools. Thus the impact of ability grouping on equity depends to a significant extent on how grouping is implemented. Much the same can be said for heterogeneous grouping. There are many ways of organizing a mixed-ability class, and the different arrangements vary in their implications for equity.

For instance, one can imagine using heterogeneous grouping to reduce variance in achievement with a tightly regulated curriculum in which new concepts are not introduced until all students have fully mastered the previous ones. In such a system, the class would be taught as a whole, and the most capable students would not be allowed to proceed until all are ready. This example seems extreme, but it may not be far from current practice. A comparison of the math curriculum in the United States with that of other countries shows that American classes spend far more time on review than others, so that knowledge introduced each year constitutes a minimal advance over the previous year (McKnight et al., 1987). This "spiral curriculum" is said to account, in part, for the dismal math performance of American children in international comparisons.

More generally, some writers suggest that teachers typically attend to a "steering group" of students at about the thirtieth percentile of the class (Barr & Dreeben, 1977; Dahllof, 1971). The teacher introduces new concepts when students at this level are prepared to move on. Burns's (1987) study of eighth-grade mathematics instruction suggests that teachers did teach to a steering group; moreover, this technique had a "leveling effect" — students whose initial performance was high failed to gain as much as similar students in a comparison group who paced their own instruction. Whole-class, mixed-ability grouping does appear to produce greater equality of results, but lower achievement overall, particularly for students at the top of the achievement distribution. This conclusion is, of course, the converse of the findings for ability grouping discussed above.[5]

Individualized instruction is another way of using mixed-ability classroom organization. In theory, it allows each student to maximize his or her achievement by pacing instruction to each one's level. Used successfully, this approach would likely result in a high degree of inequality of results, given the diversity of academic and socioeconomic backgrounds with which students arrive at school. Indeed, it is probably only because individualized instruction is used less widely that its potential for unequal results has received less attention than that applied to ability grouping. In any case, reviews have concluded that individualized instruction is no more effective than whole-class instruction in raising achievement, probably because of classroom and curriculum management difficulties (Bangert, Kulik, & Kulik, 1982; Miller, 1976; Schoen, 1976).

Besides whole-class and individualized instruction, cooperative learning is a third way of arranging heterogeneous classes. This technique has several variants, but most involve placing students in small, mixed-ability groups within the class and then assigning schoolwork as group tasks rather than (or in addition to) individual tasks (see Slavin, 1983). Frequently, cooperative learning also involves competition among the groups. Like ability grouping, cooperative learning at the elementary level has been found to contribute to higher achievement when compared to whole-class instruction in heterogeneous classes (reviews include Johnson, Johnson, & Maruyama, 1983; Sharan et al., 1984; Slavin, 1980). Presumably, this outcome occurs along with less inequality of results than that derived from ability grouping (Slavin, 1977). This question has received less attention, and it is not known whether cooperative learning in heterogeneous classes raises achievement over that produced by homogeneous grouping.

Less research has been done on the effects of cooperative learning at the secondary level. Studies in junior high schools suggest that there, too, cooperative learning is more successful than traditional whole-class instruction at raising achievement (Newmann & Thompson, 1987). Yet of six studies conducted in grades 10-12, only two showed positive effects (Newmann & Thompson, 1987). Still, given the weak overall performance of ability grouping at the secondary level, and the high degree of resulting inequality, it seems clear that cooperative learning is worth further exploration (Oakes, 1985).

A critical question for cooperative learning at the secondary level is whether it can maintain the high level of achievement among the strongest students that curriculum tracking allows. Another issue is whether it can accommodate the subject matter differentiation that occurs in tracking. Cooperative learning is a classroom-based system, but by the time students begin high school, their skill and knowledge levels may be so disparate that, at least in some subjects, it may not be possible to teach all of them within the curriculum of a single course. In math, for example, it is not clear how cooperative learning would handle a cohort of ninth graders whose level of readiness ranges from arithmetic to geometry.

Conclusions

This chapter presents clear evidence to show that the way classes are organized for instruction has implications for educational equity. The relation is not a simple one, however, because it is not only how the students are arranged but the experiences they have in class that make a difference. Indeed, a single type of instructional organization — for example, within-class ability grouping — can have different sorts of impacts on equity, depending on the quality of instruction provided to the various subgroups.

Ability grouping in particular seems to affect equity. At the elementary school level, it leads to greater inequality of results, but may occur in concert with higher achievement at all ranks. Furthermore, at this level, there is no evidence of assignment bias related to students' social or economic characteristics. By contrast, grouping and tracking in secondary schools appear to produce higher achievement in academic tracks but lower achievement in other programs when compared to alternative instructional arrangements. Overall mean achievement is roughly similar, but inequality is greatly increased. Moreover, the inequality of results is likely linked to inequality of access, in that the quality of instruction in low-track classes appears to suffer. The only equitable aspect of grouping at the secondary schools is the finding that Blacks (and, in one study, females) were more likely than their counterparts to be assigned to the college track; this made Black-White inequality of results smaller than it would have been in the absence of tracking.

The limits and possibilities of ability grouping are not yet known. It seems likely that there are ways of improving the quality of instruction in low groups that would produce more equitable results without sacrificing performance in the high groups. However, improvement of instruction is no simple matter, particularly at the secondary level. Heterogeneous arrangements likewise demand further exploration, but they also provide no guarantee of equitable results unless one is willing to sacrifice achievement at the highest levels.

Educational decision makers pondering alternative forms of instructional organization are thus confronted with choices among alternative models and competing goals. Although knowledge is incomplete, it is possible to describe some tentative conclusions about current practice. In comparison to traditional whole-class instruction in heterogeneous classes, ability grouping produces higher average achievement but more inequality. This finding is particularly problematic at the secondary level, because the inequality of results very likely stems in part from inequality of access to effective instruction. Improvement of the quality of low-track instruction would both raise average achievement and reduce inequality of results, but whether this goal can be accomplished has yet to be demonstrated.

Grouping and tracking are particularly successful at producing high achievement for the strongest students. It is not known whether cooperative learning, another form of organization that produces higher achievement than whole-class instruction, can match ability grouping for the achievement of highly able students. Further, while cooperative learning has clearly been successful in elementary schools, its success at the secondary level is less secure. Yet it is in secondary schools that ability grouping seems to have the most severe consequences for inequality. Future research might evaluate the likelihood of effective instruction in low-track classes along with the prospects for maintaining high achievement for the strongest students with the use of cooperative learning in heterogeneous classes.

Notes

1. Bloom (1976, 1987) seems to support this position. His scheme calls for devoting a much greater proportion of resources (in the form of teaching time) to the least able students. Likewise, Jencks et al. (1972) appear to hold this view for income inequality.

2. Although a few critical voices were heard earlier (e.g., Raup, 1936), the criticism did not cumulate until the 1960s.

3. It is important to emphasize that this claim has been made only for elementary school ability grouping, and only for certain forms: within-class grouping and regrouping for specified subjects, especially when grade levels are mixed (the "Joplin plan").

4. The comparison to the "absence of tracking" by Gamoran and Mare (1989) was to a simulated situation in which all students were assigned to a single program, the effects of which were either like those of the academic track or like those of the nonacademic track. The Black-White achievement gap turns out to be smaller under current tracking systems than it would be under either of the simulated alternatives.

5. Japanese elementary education is often touted as an example of undifferentiated instruction that produces high levels of achievement. Japanese elementary schools have no ability grouping, and their teachers use whole-class instruction. It appears that the steering group used by Japanese teachers is near the top of the class rather than at the bottom. This does appear to produce high achievement, but it also leads to a high degree of inequality of results (at least relative to the level of diversity at the beginning of school). Japanese secondary education is highly stratified among schools, and students differ widely in their skills by the onset of secondary education (Rohlen, 1983). Based on this information, one can speculate that the Japanese system of "teaching to the top" in heterogeneous classes produces higher achievement but more inequality than American heterogeneous classes in which instruction is geared lower.

References

Alexander, K. L., & Cook, M. A. (1982). Curricula and coursework: A surprise ending to a familiar story. *American Sociological Review, 47*, 626-640.

Alexander, K. L., Cook, M. A., & McDill, E. L. (1978). Curriculum tracking and educational stratification. *American Sociological Review, 43*, 47-66.

Alexander, K. L., & McDill, E. L. (1976). Selection and allocation within schools: Some causes and consequences of curriculum placement. *American Sociological Review, 41*, 963-980.

Averch, H., Carroll, S. J., Donaldson, T. S., Kiesling, H. J., & Pincus, J. (1972). *How effective is schooling?* Santa Monica, CA: RAND Corporation.

Ball, S. J. (1981). *Beachside comprehensive: A case-study of secondary schooling.* Cambridge: Cambridge University Press.

Bangert, R., Kulik, J., & Kulik, C. L. (1982). Individual systems of instruction in secondary schools. *Review of Educational Research, 53*, 143-158.

Barr, R., & Dreeben, R. (1977). Instruction in classrooms. In L. S. Shulman (Ed.), *Review of research in education* (Vol. 5, pp. 89-162). Itasca, IL: Peacock.

Barr, R., & Dreeben, R. (1983). *How schools work.* Chicago: University of Chicago Press.

Bloom, B. S. (1976) *Human characteristics and school learning.* New York: McGraw-Hill.

Bloom, B. S. (1987). A response to Slavin's mastery learning reconsidered. *Review of Educational Research, 57*, 507-508.

Burns, R. B. (1987). Steering groups, leveling effects, and instructional pace. *American Journal of Education, 96*, 24-55.

Cicourel, A. V., & Kitsuse, J. I. (1963). *The educational decision-makers.* Indianapolis: Bobbs-Merrill.

Coleman, J. S. (1968). The concept of equality of educational opportunity. *Harvard Education Review, 38*, 7-22.

Coleman, J. S., Campbell, E., Hobson, C., McPartland, J., Mood, A., Weinfield, F., & York, R. (1966). *Equality of educational opportunity.* Washington, DC: Government Printing Office.

Conant, J. V. (1967). *The comprehensive high school in America.* New York: McGraw-Hill.

Coxe, W. W. (1936). Social problems and pupil grouping. In G. M. Whipple (Ed.), *National Society for the Study of Education yearbook: Vol. 35, part I. The grouping of pupils* (pp. 14-30). Bloomington, IL: Public School Publishing.

Dahllof, U. (1971). *Ability grouping, content validity, and curriculum process analysis.* New York: Teachers College Press.

Dreeben, R., & Gamoran, A. (1986). Race, instruction and learning. *American Sociological Review, 51,* 660-669.

Eder, D. (1981). Ability grouping as a self-fulfilling prophecy: A microanalysis of teacher-student interaction. *Sociology of Education, 54,* 151-161.

Esposito, D. (1973). Homogeneous and heterogeneous ability grouping: Principal findings and implications for evaluating and designing more effective educational environments. *Review of Educational Research, 43,* 163-179.

Findley, W., & Bryan, M. (1971). *Ability grouping: 1970.* Athens, GA: Center for Educational Improvement.

Finley, M. K. (1984). Teachers and tracking in a comprehensive high school. *Sociology of Education, 57,* 233-243.

Gamoran, A. (1986). Instructional and institutional effects of ability grouping. *Sociology of Education, 59,* 185-198.

Gamoran, A. (1987). The stratification of high school learning opportunities. *Sociology of Education, 60,* 135-155.

Gamoran, A. (1988). *A multi-level analysis of the effects of tracking.* Paper presented at the annual meeting of the American Sociological Association, Atlanta, GA.

Gamoran, A. (1989). Rank, performance, and mobility in elementary school grouping. *Sociological Quarterly, 30,* 109-123.

Gamoran, A., & Berends, M. (1987). The effects of stratification in secondary schools: Synthesis of survey and ethnographic research. *Review of Educational Research, 57,* 415-435.

Gamoran, A., & Mare, R. D. (1989). Secondary school tracking and educational inequality: Compensation, reinforcement, or neutrality? *American Journal of Sociology, 94,* 1146-1183.

Good, T., & Marshall, S. (1984). Do students learn more in heterogeneous or homogeneous groups? In P. L. Peterson, L. C. Wilkinson, & M. T. Hallinan (Eds.), *The social context of instruction* (pp. 15-38). Orlando, FL: Academic Press.

Gutmann, A. (1987). *Democratic education.* Princeton, NJ: Princeton University Press.

Haller, E. J. (1984). Pupil race and elementary school ability grouping: Are teachers biased against black children? *American Educational Research Journal, 22,* 465-483.

Haller, E. J., & Davis, S. (1980). Does socioeconomic status bias the assignment of elementary school students to reading groups? *American Educational Research Journal, 17,* 409-418.

Hallinan, M. T., & Sørensen, A. B. (1983). The formation and stability of instructional groups. *American Sociological Review, 48,* 838-851.

Hanushek, E. (1986). The economics of schooling: Production and efficiency in the public schools. *Journal of Economic Literature, 24,* 1141-1177.

Hargreaves, D. H. (1967). *Social relations in a secondary school.* London: C. Tinling.

Heathers, G. (1969). Grouping. In R. L. Ebel (Ed.), *Encyclopedia of educational research* (4th ed., pp. 559-570). New York: Macmillan.

Heyns, B. (1974). Social selection and stratification within schools. *American Journal of Sociology, 79,* 1434-1451.

Hiebert, E. H. (1987). The context of instruction and student learning: An examination of Slavin's assumptions. *Review of Educational Research, 57*, 337-340.

Jencks, C. L., & Brown, M. (1975). The effects of high schools on their students. *Harvard Educational Review, 45*, 273-324.

Jencks, C. L., Smith, M., Acland, H., Bane, M. J., Cohen, D., Gintis, H., Heyns, B., & Michaelson, S. (1972). *Inequality: A reassessment of the effects of family and schooling in America.* New York: Basic Books.

Johnson, D. W., Johnson, R. T., & Maruyama, G. (1983). Interdependence and interpersonal attraction among heterogeneous and homogeneous individuals: A theoretical formulation and a meta-analysis of the research. *Review of Educational Research, 53*, 5-54.

Keddie, N. (1971). Classroom knowledge. In M.F.D. Young (Ed.), *Knowledge and control* (pp. 133-160). London: Collier-Macmillan.

Kerckhoff, A. C. (1986). Effects of ability grouping in British secondary schools. *American Sociological Review, 51*, 842-858.

Kulik, C. L., & Kulik, J. (1982). Effects of ability grouping on secondary school students: A meta-analysis of evaluation findings. *American Educational Research Journal, 19*, 415-428.

Lacey, C. (1970). *Hightown grammar.* Manchester, England: Manchester University Press.

McKnight, C. C., Crosswhite, F. J., Dossey, J. A., Kifer, E., Swafford, J. O., Travers, K. J., & Cooney, T. J. (1987). *The underachieving curriculum: Assessing U.S. school mathematics from an international perspective.* Champaign, IL: Stipes.

Metz, M. H. (1978). *Classrooms and corridors: The crisis of authority in desegregated secondary schools.* Berkeley: University of California Press.

Miller, R. (1976). Individualized instruction in mathematics: A review of research. *Mathematics Teacher, 69*, 345-351.

Moore, D., & Davenport, S. (1988). *The new improved sorting machine.* Madison, WI: National Center on Effective Secondary Schools.

Newmann, F. M., & Thompson, J. A. (1987). *Effects of cooperative learning on achievement in secondary schools.* Madison: Wisconsin Center for Education Research.

Nystrand, M., & Gamoran, A. (1988). *A study of instruction as discourse.* Paper presented at the annual meeting of the American Educational Research Association.

Oakes, J. (1985). *Keeping track: How schools structure inequality.* New Haven, CT: Yale University Press.

Page, R. N. (1987). Lower-track classes at a college-preparatory school: A caricature of educational encounters. In G. and L. Spindler (Eds.), *Interpretive ethnography of education at home and abroad* (pp. 447-472). Hillsdale, NJ: Lawrence Erlbaum.

Raup, R. B. (1936). Some philosophical aspects of grouping. In G. M. Whipple (Ed.), *National Society for the Study of Education yearbook: Vol. 35, part I. The grouping of pupils* (pp. 48-67). Bloomington, IL: Public School Publishing.

Rehberg, R. A., & Rosenthal, E. R. (1978). *Class and merit in the American high school.* New York: Longman.

Rist, R. (1970). Student social class and teacher expectations: The self-fulfilling prophecy in ghetto education. *Harvard Educational Review, 40*, 411-451.

Rohlen, T. P. (1983). *Japan's high schools.* Berkeley: University of California Press.

Rosenbaum, J. E. (1976). *Making inequality.* New York: John Wiley.

Rosenbaum, J. E. (1980a). Social implications of educational grouping. In L. S. Shulman (Ed.), *Review of research in education* (Vol. 8, pp. 361-401). Itasca, IL: Peacock.

Rosenbaum, J. E. (1980b). Track misperceptions and frustrated college plans: An analysis of the effects of tracks and track perceptions in the National Longitudinal Survey. *Sociology of Education, 53,* 74-88.

Rowan, B., & Miracle, A. W., Jr. (1983). Systems of ability grouping and the stratification of achievement in elementary schools. *Sociology of Education, 56,* 133-144.

Schafer, W. E., & Olexa, C. (1971). *Tracking and opportunity.* Scranton, PA: Chandler.

Schoen, H. (1976). Self-paced mathematics instruction: How effective has it been? *Arithmetic Teacher, 23,* 90-96.

Sharan, S., Kussel, P., Hertz-Lazerowitz, R., Bejarano, Y., Raviv, S., & Sharan, Y. (1984). *Cooperative learning in the classroom: Research in desegregated schools.* Hillsdale, NJ: Lawrence Erlbaum.

Shavit, Y., & Featherman, D. L. (1988). Schooling, tracking, and teenage intelligence. *Sociology of Education, 61,* 42-51.

Slavin, R. E. (1977). *Student learning team techniques: Narrowing the gap between the races* (Report No. 228). Baltimore: Center for the Social Organization of Schools.

Slavin, R. E. (1980). Cooperative learning. *Review of Educational Research, 50,* 315-342.

Slavin, R. E. (1983). *Cooperative learning.* New York: Longman.

Slavin, R. E. (1987). Ability grouping and student achievement in elementary schools: A best-evidence synthesis. *Review of Educational Research, 57,* 293-336.

Sørensen, A. B., & Hallinan, M. T. (1984). Race effects on the assignment to ability groups. In P. L. Peterson, L. C. Wilkerson, & M. T. Hallinan (Eds.), *The social context of instruction* (pp. 85-103). Orlando, FL: Academic Press.

Sørensen, A. B., & Hallinan, M. T. (1986). Effects of ability grouping on growth in academic achievement. *American Educational Research Journal, 23,* 519-542.

Strike, K. (1988). The ethics of resource allocation. In D. H. Monk & J. Underwood (Eds.), *Microlevel educational finance: Issues and implications for policy* (pp. 143-180). Cambridge, MA: Ballinger.

Vanfossen, B. E., Jones, J. D., & Spade, J. Z. (1987). Curriculum tracking and status maintenance. *Sociology of Education, 60,* 104-122.

Weinstein, R. S. (1976). Reading group membership in first grade: Teacher behaviors and pupil experience over time. *Journal of Educational Psychology, 68,* 103-116.

Willis, P. L. (1977). *Learning to labour: How working class kids get working class jobs.* Driffield, England: Nafferton.

13

Linguistic and Cultural Influences on Classroom Instruction

YOLANDA N. PADRON

University of Houston, Clear Lake

STEPHANIE L. KNIGHT

Texas A&M University

Differences in cultural background have been related to student differences in achievement (Cohen, 1981). Although the question of cultural influences on cognition has been studied in anthropology, philology, and psychology (see Cole & Scribner, 1977, for review), the results of these studies have provided little information to guide educators in dealing with culturally diverse students in our schools. Most of the recent cross-cultural research in cognitive psychology has been conducted in laboratory settings using contrived cognitive tasks that are not representative of the wide range of classrooms. These studies, however, do reaffirm, even if they do little to explain, the influence of culture on learning. In addition, when we examine minority students who have experienced success in the classroom, we often find one common underlying factor: Cultural differences have been taken into consideration in the development of their learning environment. An examination of minority students who have been successful within the existing educational environment reveals that the consideration of cultural differences has enhanced their achievement. There is evidence that when the school environment is compatible with students' culture, students exhibit higher achievement and increased satisfaction with school (Tharp, 1989).

In order to improve the educational status of minorities, students' total classroom experience may have to be taken into consideration. In particular, examining the match between cultural background and classroom learning and interaction for minority students may determine whether these students stay in school or eventually drop out. Since maintaining a classroom environment that is compatible with students' cultural backgrounds can be achieved with relatively few additional resources, manipulation of this factor appears to be a promising area of study.

Given the relationship between cultural background and student achievement, three general areas have been identified for examination in this chapter. First, a theory of learning and instruction for minority students will be examined using a Vygotskian perspective. Then, cultural components that should be considered in planning and implementing instruction for minorities will be discussed. Finally, the chapter will extend the consideration of learning for minority students to higher-order skills and outcomes in terms of the Vygotskian theory described in the first section. Within this context, research dealing with the use of cognitive strategies for reading comprehension will be discussed in relation to minority populations. Implications for cognitive reading strategy instruction for Hispanic bilingual students will be addressed, and ways that cultural considerations can be included will be suggested.

Learning and Instruction:
A Vygotskian Perspective

A perspective that can be used to examine learning and instruction for Hispanic bilingual students is that of Vygotsky's (1962, 1978) sociohistorical theory. Vygotsky emphasizes that learning is always mediated through others — parents, peers, teachers, and so on. The mediators provide both the substance and tools for problem solving by aiding in the organization and interpretation of the child's environment and by demonstrating the cognitive processes used to manipulate information gained from experience (Day, Cordon, & Kerwin, 1989). Therefore, the knowledge and intellectual skills that children acquire are directly related to how they interact with others in specific problem-solving situations. Thus Vygotsky's theory points to the importance of instruction in the enhancement of cognitive development and the essential role of the teacher as a mediator of both what and how knowledge is acquired and used.

Vygotsky (1978) defines the "zone of proximal development" as the distance between actual developmental level as determined by individual problem solving and the level of potential development as determined through problem solving under adult guidance. In other words, the zone of proximal development is the difference between what the child can do alone and what the child can do with the guidance of an adult or advanced peer. Two basic assumptions that underlie the theory of the zone of proximal development are that (a) language and communicative competence are critical for the development of higher psychological abilities, and (b) this development is possible if students participate in an environment that is culturally meaningful (Trueba, 1989).

Given this theoretical framework, two implications for classroom instruction can be derived. First, instruction will be most effective for individual students when it is aimed at the student's zone of proximal development. Next, in order for instruction to be effective for linguistic and ethnic minorities in the classroom, teachers must be sensitive to learning difficulties that may be related to language and cultural differences between the home and school. Language and culture influences on learning, however, may be difficult to examine separately because they are closely connected (McGroarty & Galvan, 1985). Furthermore, language has been argued to be the tool used for thought, and psychologists have had difficulty distinguishing between the two (Stigler & Baranes, 1989). Therefore, it is necessary to consider both language and cultural background in relation to the learning and instruction of minority groups in classroom situations.

Compatibility of Culture and Instruction

According to Tharp (1987, 1989), improvements in basic skills acquisition, social skills, and problem-solving abilities occur when the native culture patterns are matched with instruction. Since individuals from different cultural groups perceive experiences differently, students' cultures may affect their preferred modes of learning (Escobedo & Huggans, 1983). The Kamehameha Early Education Program (KEEP), for example, has developed a language arts program for children of

Hawaiian ancestry. In this program, patterns of the culture pertaining to social organization, sociolinguistic patterns, cognitive patterns, and motivation have been incorporated in the instruction. For example, more informal patterns of group interaction have been adopted in the classroom setting because these patterns are more compatible with Hawaiian story-telling traditions. Traditional classroom turn-taking practices are relaxed during reading lessons to allow students to interrupt when they want to contribute to the discussion (Charbonneau & John-Steiner, 1988).

Programs with Native American students have also provided successful results when the instructional environment includes activities and teacher-student interactions that are compatible with students' cultural backgrounds (John-Steiner & Osterreich, 1975; cited in Tharp, 1979). For example, to teach mathematical representation to Native American children, a program was developed to take advantage of their strong visual-spatial skills and their tendency to learn best by doing and observing (Charbonneau & John-Steiner, 1988). Other considerations that must also be taken into account in designing instruction for Native American students include (a) poor performance in the traditional classroom situation that emphasizes the direct questioning technique and (b) preference for the use of methods involving peer interaction rather than interaction with adults (Charbonneau & John-Steiner, 1988).

Like Native Americans, Hispanics tend to prefer cooperative rather than competitive learning situations that mirror the cooperative attitudes characteristic of work patterns in their homes and communities (Charbonneau & John-Steiner, 1988). De Avila (1988) describes a study that used peer cooperation to enable students to acquire mathematical concepts successfully. Students had access to materials both in their homes and in second languages and were able to use their teacher as a resource as well. The program was successful because Hispanic students not only seem to learn more in a cooperative environment working with peers, but also enjoy working individually with the teacher.

There is some evidence, however, that culture-related preferences are either not known or not considered in classrooms. For example, in a study conducted by Knight (in press), 150 Hispanic elementary students' perceptions of their classroom environment in relation to their use of cognitive strategies during reading comprehensions were examined. Results indicated that Hispanic bilingual students did not perceive the type of cooperative classroom environment that was previously described as compatible with Hispanic home and community culture. Students, for example, perceived that large group instruction was used most of the time and mentioned little teacher-encouraged peer cooperation or individual instruction.

Benefits of Bilingual Education

As described above, according to Vygotsky, language and communicative competence are prerequisites of development of students' higher psychological abilities. Furthermore, language and culture are so inextricably intertwined that it is often difficult to consider one without the other. For these reasons, programs that develop native language competence must also be considered when examining the influence of culture on learning. In fact, it has been found that several programs that are bilingual/bicultural have resulted in students staying in school more years, learning the mainstream language, and competing in the greater society more effectively (Alfonsin, 1984).

Although there have been some mixed results pertaining to the effectiveness of bilingual education programs, several studies have found that programs incorporating the students' language and culture are beneficial (Ramirez, 1985). Troike (1978), for example, examined several studies and found that bilingual programs were beneficial for the student populations they serve. Other studies examining bilingual/bicultural programs have found that participation in the such programs has resulted in improved literacy skills, improved attendance, and a more positive self-concept for students ("San Diego Demonstration Project," 1982; "Study of Bilingual Education," 1982). A more recent meta-analysis of research in bilingual education has also found that participation in bilingual education programs has consistently resulted in higher English test scores in reading, language skills, math, and total achievement (Willig, 1985). There seems to be some evidence, therefore, that educational methods that address cultural and linguistic needs of students are the effective methods for preparing students to compete in mainstream society. Nonetheless, students that are not part of the mainstream culture are not doing well in schools (Tharp, 1989). An area of research that may provide some explanations for the lack of success in reading for Hispanic bilingual students is that of student perceptions. This research assumes that there may be incompatibility between what the teacher teaches and students' perceptions of the instruction.

Developing the Higher-Order
Thinking Skills of Minority Students

Although recently there has been an emphasis on the development
of all students' higher-order thinking skills (Association for Supervision and Curriculum Development, 1985, 1986), there is evidence
that schools have not been successful in teaching these higher-level
thinking skills to all students (National Assessment of Educational
Progress, 1981). Reading research, for example, has found that more
instructional time is spent on assignment giving than on comprehension
instruction (Durkin, 1978-79). In particular, instruction for limited
English proficient students usually concentrates at the lower levels of
the curriculum, focusing more on language than on the development of
higher-order thinking skills (Farr, 1986; Moll, 1986; Padron & Bermudez, 1987). In contrast, educators agree that the higher-order skill of
reading comprehension, as opposed to decoding, is the most important
problem in reading instruction today (Chipman & Segal, 1985).

These concerns have led educators to seek remedies for the apparent
problem of teaching higher-level thinking, particularly to the minority
students who form part of our "at-risk" student population. One of the
remedies involves the identification and development of the cognitive
strategies students use during higher-level thinking activities such as
reading comprehension. Following Vygotsky's theory of the zone of
proximal development, instruction for minority students must move
from low-level instruction to instruction in higher-level thinking skills.
In order to accomplish this transition effectively, instruction must be
conducted at the students' zone of proximal development. The following section reports on several studies that have examined students'
perceptions of the cognitive reading strategies they use to comprehend
text written in English. These studies are a part of current efforts to
identify factors that influence the reading performance of bilingual/
bicultural children.

Reading Cognitive Strategy Research

Several studies have investigated the cognitive strategies students
use to obtain meaning from text (e.g., Brown, Campione, & Day, 1981;
Chou Hare & Smith, 1982; Hansen, 1981a, 1981b). A cognitive strategy
is "a goal-directed sequence of mental operations" (Gagne, 1985, p. 140).

When considered in relation to reading, the goal of the mental operations becomes the comprehension of text, and reading is viewed as a problem-solving process in which the reader applies strategies that relate prior knowledge to the text (Olshavsky, 1976-77).

Good and poor comprehenders of text can be differentiated by their use of cognitive strategies (Garner & Reis, 1981; Hansen & Pearson, 1983). More successful learners, for example, use more elaborative strategies (Weinstein, 1978) that help them link new information to already existing knowledge. The success or failure of these strategies has been related to the type and depth of processing that they encourage. Goetz (1984), for example, in a review of the research on comprehension strategies, suggests that paraphrasing and verbal and imaginal elaborative strategies are successful because they require and ensure deep processing.

Several studies have been conducted examining the cognitive reading strategies that Hispanic bilingual students use (see, e.g., Padron, Knight, & Waxman, 1986; Padron & Waxman, 1988). The quality and quantity of strategies used are influenced by contextual differences, including the characteristics of the student and the task (Knight & Padron, 1986; Padron & Knight, 1986). For example, studies have revealed differences in the type and number of cognitive reading strategies mentioned by bilingual students (Padron, 1985; Padron et al., 1986; Padron & Waxman, 1988). Bilingual elementary students mention significantly fewer strategies than their English-monolingual peers. Furthermore, several within-group differences have been revealed in the type and number of strategies mentioned. These include gender differences (Padron & Knight, 1986) and age and ability differences (Padron, 1985). These findings highlight the importance of considering individual differences within cultural groups. Studying only the differences among cultural groups may mask great individual variations.

Strategies that enable students to link new information to prior knowledge may exhibit age- or culture-related differences. Expert comprehenders, in general, try to relate new material to personal experience (Campione & Armbruster, 1985). Differences in background knowledge of experience due to cultural differences, therefore, may be an important source of variation for strategy use and outcomes (Steffenson, Joug-Dev, & Anderson, 1979). In addition, certain populations, especially young, low-ability, or culturally different students, may not be able to tap into prerequisite prior knowledge without help and may need teacher-directed activity to help them accomplish the linkage. Training programs have been conducted to help students to distinguish between text-based and reader-based knowledge (Raphael, 1982), to draw on personal experiences involving social interactions and relationships (Moss & Oden, 1983), and to predict outcomes based on prereading activities designed to link students' prior knowledge to text (Hansen, 1981a, 1981b).

Although several successful reading strategy training studies have been conducted (see e.g., Palincsar & Brown, 1984, 1985), few studies have specifically examined differences in training outcomes for Hispanic bilingual students. Work with Hispanic populations has suggested that training programs may be an effective means of improving the reading comprehension of culturally different students (Knight & Padron, 1988). In studies where Hispanic bilingual students have been trained in strategy use, results have indicated that students who participated in the training (i.e., reciprocal teaching or the question-answer relationship) did better on a standardized reading achievement test than students who participated in one of the control groups (Padron, 1986). Also, it has been found that bilingual students, after training in using the reciprocal teaching approach, reported using the strong strategies of imaging, self-generated questions, and taking notes significantly more than the control group students (Padron, 1989). In addition, students in the question-answer relationship group also were found to use two strong strategies more often than students in the control groups. On the other hand, students in the control group also reported using two weak strategies significantly more than students in the question-answer relationship group. In summary, results indicate that strategy instruction has beneficial results for elementary bilingual students.

Making Schools More Compatible with Language Minority Students: Some Suggestions

In providing classrooms that are more compatible with students' culture, Tharp's (1989) psychocultural variables and constants should be considered. First, the social organization of the culture should be addressed. For Hispanics, for example, the social organization is based on collaboration, cooperation, extended families, and older children taking care of siblings. Instruction for this group, therefore, may include the need for small groups and peer teaching with a great deal of interaction.

The second aspect to consider pertains to sociolinguistic differences. An example provided by Tharp (1989) is that of wait time. Differences, for example, have been found between the wait time of Anglo teachers and that of Navajo teachers. Navajo teachers have longer wait time following a student response before speaking again than Anglo teachers. Anglo teachers may inadvertently deny minority students who are accustomed to a longer wait time the opportunity to participate in classroom discussions, particularly if the student has limited ability in the language and requires more time to decipher the message and to monitor the output.

The third variable to be considered deals with cognition. According to Tharp (1989), schools presume that students bring to school a certain pattern of cognitive functioning. This pattern generally includes being verbal and using analytic thought. Those students whose cognitive patterns are congruent with the school's culture are more likely to succeed in school than students whose cognitive functioning patterns differ (Casanova, 1987). For Hispanic students, the cognitive patterning appears to be different from the mainstream pattern described by Tharp (1989). Hispanic students, for the most part, are poor at analytical problem solving (Bennett, 1986).

In terms of motivation, the mainstream classroom seems to be directed at individual and independent achievement. Hispanic students, on the other hand, are sensitive to social environment, favor a "spectator approach" to learning, and are extrinsically motivated and responsive to social reinforcement (Bennett, 1986). Also, they are highly motivated when working individually with the teacher (Bennett, 1986).

In addition, Tharp (1989) discusses two constants that must be provided to all students: language development and contextualized instruction. Students then should be provided with an educational environment where they are able to learn the language. Furthermore, this educational environment should provide instruction that makes use of students' experiences.

Discussion

This chapter has presented evidence of the importance of cultural considerations within the classroom environment. Since students' learning and behavior are influenced by their cultural perspectives, good teaching must consider cultural differences (Garcia, 1982). In discussing cultural differences, however, some caution must be taken. First, differences among groups must not mask great individual variations, since little is known about these cultural differences. Second, considering Vygotsky's work, minority students' lack of success in school may be due to the failure of the educational system to provide these students with opportunities to engage in activities that fall within their zone of proximal development (Trueba, 1989). Perhaps the reason Hispanic bilingual students who have been studied mention the use of only a few cognitive reading strategies is that they are not receiving this type of instruction. It is evident that Hispanic bilingual students are able to learn the use of cognitive strategies through strategy instruction. Therefore, instruction must focus on those higher-level skills necessary for success in mainstream society.

Finally, although studies that have examined cognitive strategy instruction indicate evidence of success for Hispanic students, more studies are needed that incorporate appropriate cultural considerations, as discussed in the previous sections. To conclude, teachers who are to prepare the next generation to cooperate in a pluralistic society must be aware of the cultural differences all around them, must understand the influence of culture on educational achievement, and must implement a variety of strategies for teaching all students within the mainstream of the classroom (Howard, 1988).

References

Alfonsin, R. (1984). Mensaje a los pueblos indios. *Pueblo Indio, 3*(4), 15.

Association for Supervision and Curriculum Development. (1985, December). Education organizations firm up a five-part plan to improve student reasoning. *ASCD Update, 27*(8), 1, 7.

Association for Supervision and Curriculum Development. (1986, January). Nation needs intentional thinking instruction: Here's why – here's how, say associations. *ASCD Update, 27*(1), 1, 6.

Bennett, C. (1986). *Comprehensive multicultural education: Theory and practice.* Boston: Allyn & Bacon.

Brown, A., Campione, J., & Day, J. (1981). Learning to learn: On training students to learn from texts. *Educational Researcher, 10*, 14-21.

Campione, J., & Armbruster, B. (1985). Acquiring information from texts: Analysis of four approaches. In J. Segal, S. Chipman, & R. Glaser (Eds.), *Thinking and learning skills: Vol. 1. Relating instruction to research* (pp. 317-359). Hillsdale, NJ: Lawrence Erlbaum.

Casanova, U. (1987). Ethnic and cultural differences. In V. Richardson-Koehler (Ed.), *Educators' handbook: A research perspective* (pp. 370-393). New York: Longman.

Charbonneau, M. P., & John-Steiner, V. (1988). Patterns of experience and the language of mathematics. In R. R. Cocking & J. P. Mestre (Eds.), *Linguistic and cultural influences on learning mathematics* (pp. 91-100). Hillsdale, NJ: Lawrence Erlbaum.

Chavez, R. C. (1988). Theoretical issues relevant to bilingual multicultural classroom climate research. *Journal of Educational Issues of Language Minority Students, 3,* 5-14.

Chipman, S., & Segal, J. (1985). Higher cognitive goals for education: An introduction. In J. Segal, S. Chipman, & R. Glaser (Eds.), *Thinking and learning skills: Vol. 1. Relating instruction to research* (pp. 1-20). Hillsdale, NJ: Lawrence Erlbaum.

Chou Hare, V., & Smith, D. (1982). Reading to remember: Studies of metacognitive reading skills in elementary school-aged children. *Journal of Educational Research, 75,* 157-164.

Cohen, G. (1981). Culture and educational achievement. *Harvard Educational Review, 51*(2), 270-285.

Cole, M., & Scribner, S. (1977). Cross-cultural studies of memory and cognition. In R. V. Karl, Jr., & J. W. Hagen (Eds.), *Perspectives on the development of memory and cognition* (pp. 252-269). Hillsdale, NJ: Lawrence Erlbaum.

Day, J. D., Cordon, L. A., & Kerwin, M. L. (1989). Informal instruction and development of cognitive skills: A review and critique of research. In C. B. McCormick, G. E. Miller, & M. Pressley (Eds.), *Cognitive strategy research: From basic research to educational applications* (pp. 83-103). New York: Springer-Verlag.

De Avila, E. A. (1988). Bilingualism, cognitive function, and language minority group membership. In C. B. McCormick, G. E. Miller, & M. Pressley (Eds.), *Cognitive strategy research: From basic research to educational applications* (pp. 104-121). New York: Springer-Verlag.

Durkin, D. (1978-79). What classroom observations reveal about reading comprehension instruction. *Reading Research Quarterly, 14*(4), 481-533.

Escobedo, T. H., & Huggans, J. H. (1983). Field-dependence-independence: A theoretical framework for Mexican American cultural variables? In T. H. Escobedo (Ed.), *Early childhood bilingual education: A Hispanic perspective* (pp. 119-135). New York: Teachers College Press.

Farr, M. (1986). Language, culture, and writing: Sociolinguistic foundations of research on writing. In E. R. Rothkopt (Ed.), *Review of research in education* (Vol. 13, pp. 195-223). Washington, DC: American Educational Research Association.

Gagne, E. P. (1985). *The cognitive psychology of school learning.* Boston: Little, Brown.

Garcia, R. L. (1982). *Teaching in a pluralistic society: Concepts, models, strategies.* New York: Harper & Row.

Garner, R., & Reis, R. (1981). Monitoring and resolving comprehension obstacles: An investigation of spontaneous lookbacks among upper grade good and poor comprehenders. *Reading Research Quarterly, 16,* 569-582.

Goetz, E. (1984). The role of spatial strategies in processing and remembering text: A cognitive-information-processing analysis. In C. Holley & D. Dansereau (Eds.), *Spatial learning strategies: Techniques, applications, and related issues* (pp. 47-77). New York: Academic Press.

Hansen, J. (1981a). An inferential comprehension strategy for use with primary grade children. *Reading Teacher, 34*(6), 665-669.

Hansen, J. (1981b). The effects of inference training and practice on young children's reading comprehension. *Reading Research Quarterly, 16,* 391-417.

Hansen, J., & Pearson, P. D. (1983). An instructional study: Improving the inferential comprehension of good and poor fourth-grade readers. *Journal of Educational Psychology, 75*, 821-829.

Howard, R. E. (1988). Broadening the teacher's perspective about language and culture. *Journal of Educational Issues of Language Minority Students, 3*, 21-26.

John-Steiner, V. P., & Osterreich, H. (1975). *Learning styles among Pueblo children: Final report to National Institute of Education.* Albuquerque: University of New Mexico, College of Education.

Knight, S. L. (in press). The relation between the classroom learning environment and students' cognitive reading strategies. In H. C. Waxman & C. Ellet (Eds.), *Study of Learning Environments.*

Knight, S. L., & Padron, Y. N. (1986). Investigating gender differences. *Journal of Educational Equity and Leadership, 6*, 340-341.

Knight, S. L., & Padron, Y. N. (1988). Teaching cognitive reading strategies to at-risk students. In H. C. Waxman, S. L. Knight, & Y. N. Padron (Eds.), *Teaching strategies that promote higher-level thinking skills for at-risk learners* (pp. 8-17). La Marque, TX: Consortium for the Advancement of Professional Excellence.

McGroarty, M., & Galvan, J. L. (1985). Culture as an issue in second language teaching. In M. Celce-Murcia (Ed.), *Beyond basics: Issues and research in TESOL* (pp. 81-95). Rowley, MA: Newbury House.

Moll, L. C. (1986). Writing as communication: Creating strategic learning environments for students. *Theory into Practice, 25*(2), 102-107.

Moss, J., & Oden, S. (1983). Children's story comprehension and social learning. *Reading Teacher, 26*(8), 784-789.

National Assessment of Educational Progress. (1981). *Reading, thinking, and writing.* Denver: Education Commission of the States.

Olshavsky, J. (1976-77). Reading as problem-solving: An investigation of strategies. *Reading Research Quarterly, 12*, 654-674.

Padron, Y. N. (1985). *Utilizing cognitive reading strategies to improve English reading comprehension of Spanish-speaking bilingual students.* Unpublished doctoral dissertation, University of Houston, Houston.

Padron, Y. N. (1986). *The use of cognitive strategy training to improve reading comprehension.* Paper presented at the annual meeting of the Southwest Educational Research Association, Houston.

Padron, Y. N. (1989). *Effect of training on bilingual students' cognitive reading strategies.* Paper presented at the annual meeting of the American Educational Research Association, San Francisco.

Padron, Y. N., & Bermudez, A. B. (1987, April). *Examining Hispanic students' perceptions of writing instruction.* Paper presented at the annual meeting of the American Educational Research Association, Washington, DC.

Padron, Y. N., & Knight, S. L. (1986, January). *A research study on gender differences in the use of cognitive strategies.* Paper presented at the annual meeting of the Southwest Educational Research Association, Houston.

Padron, Y. N., Knight, S., & Waxman, H. C. (1986). Analyzing bilingual and monolingual students' perceptions of their reading strategies. *Reading Teacher, 39*, 430-433.

Padron, Y. N., & Waxman, H. C. (1988). The effect of students' perceptions of their cognitive strategies on reading achievement. *TESOL Quarterly, 22*(1), 146-150.

Palincsar, A. S., & Brown, A. L. (1984). Reciprocal teaching of comprehension-fostering and comprehension-monitoring activities. *Cognition and Instruction, 1*(2), 117-175.

Palincsar, A. S., & Brown, A. L. (1985). Reciprocal teaching: A means to a meaningful end. In J. Osborn, P. Wilson, & R. C. Anderson (Eds.), *Reading education: Foundations for a literate America* (pp. 299-310). Lexington, MA: Lexington.

Ramirez, A. G. (1985). *Bilingualism through schooling: Cross-cultural education for minority students.* Albany: State University of New York Press.

Raphael, T. (1982). Question-answering strategies for children. *Reading Teacher, 36*(2), 186-191.

Raphael, T., Winograd, P., & Pearson, P. D. (1980). Strategies children use when answering questions. In M. L. Kamil & A. J. Moe (Eds.), *Perspectives on reading research and instruction* (pp. 156-163). Washington, DC: National Reading Conference.

San Diego Demonstration Project. (1982, October). *National Clearinghouse for Bilingual Education Forum, 5*(9), 1, 3, 6.

Steffenson, M., Joug-Dev, C., & Anderson, R. (1979). A cross-cultural perspective on reading comprehension. *Reading Research Quarterly, 15*(1), 10-29.

Stigler, J. W., & Baranes, R. (1989). Culture and mathematics learning. *Review of Research in Education, 15,* 253-306.

Study of bilingual education in Colorado. (1982, July/August). *National Clearinghouse for Bilingual Education Forum, 5*(7), 2-3.

Tharp, R. (1987, October). *Culture, cognition and education: A culturogenetic analysis of the wholistic complex.* Paper presented at the Conference of the Institute on Literacy and Learning, University of California, Santa Barbara.

Tharp, R. (1989). Psychocultural variables and constants: Effects on teaching and learning in schools. *American Psychologist, 44,* 1-11.

Troike, R. (1978). *Research evidence for the effectiveness of bilingual education.* Rosslyn, VA: National Clearinghouse for Bilingual Education.

Trueba, H. T. (1989). *Raising silent voices: Educating linguistic minorities for the 21st century.* Rowley, MA: Newbury House.

Vygotsky, L. S. (1962). *Thought and language* (E. Hanfmann & G. Vakar, Trans.). Cambridge: MIT Press.

Vygotsky, L. S. (1978). *Mind in society: The development of higher psychological processes* (M. Cole, V. John-Teiner, S. Scribner, & E. Souberman, Eds.). Cambridge, MA: Harvard University Press.

Weinstein, C. (1978). Elaboration skills as a learning strategy. In H. F. O'Neill (Ed.), *Learning strategies* (pp. 31-55). New York: Academic Press.

Willig, A. C. (1985). A meta-analysis of selected studies on the effectiveness of bilingual education. *Review of Educational Research, 55*(3), 269-317.

14

Teacher Effectiveness Research and Equity Issues

JANE A. STALLINGS
JANE McCARTHY

University of Houston

In the recent stampede toward school reform and excellence, some basic things of value should not be forgotten. Some aspects of schooling and instruction can be researched easily and others cannot. Reformers tend to grab hold of those things that can be researched easily and base school and teacher evaluations solely on those factors. As educators and researchers, it is important for us to take careful steps to ensure that what we value most is included in the agendas of school and instructional reform. A recent review of articles on educational reform by Sadker, Sadker, and Steindam (1989), for example, led them to conclude that there was a "glaring omission of equity concern, particularly the needs of girls in schools, from reform agendas" (p. 44). Their inspection of articles on reform in nine professional journals from January 1983 to January 1987 led them to conclude that only 1% of article content was related to gender equity. Is this lack of concern a function of the disappearance of the gender equity issue from American public schools? It would seem not. In a recent *New York Times* article, Markoff (1989) reported that a study done by Harvard indicated that three of four children enrolled in computer camps were male. The study also found that parents were more willing to spend significantly more money to send their sons to these camps than their daughters. The

186

Computer Literacy Project in San Francisco, as reported in the same article, asserts that different styles of learning — most important, the emphasis on boyhood rule-based games — greatly advantage men when it comes to computer experimentation. Data from the National Assessment of Educational Progress, as reported by La Pointe and Martinez (1988), indicate that "males and females and the members of various racial and ethnic groups do not seem to have equitable access to computers both in school and at home" (p. 61). Gender inequity, then, is alive and well but no longer often studied.

In an effort to identify methods that were effective in teaching basic skills, a great deal of classroom observation research was funded by the federal government during the 1970s. There was a reasonable payoff from this investment in terms of the identification of effective teaching practices. Much of this research, as we shall see, has an equity basis that underlies the findings yet is seldom emphasized when the findings are reported.

The Use of Time in Classrooms

The Beginning Teacher Evaluation Study (BTES), conducted by Fisher et al. (1977), found that available time was not used very effectively in some California classrooms. This study established that although students attended school for 6 hours each day, only 4.75 hours were actually allocated to in-class instruction. Some teachers in the study spent as little as 2 hours per day providing instruction, while others spent as much as 4 hours teaching. It was not surprising that students had higher gain on achievement tests in the classrooms where 4 hours were spent on instruction. Furthermore, in classrooms where students spent 3.5 hours engaged in appropriate learning tasks, more progress was made than in classrooms where students were engaged only 1.5 hours.

Further studies have consistently shown that the use of time in the classroom is correlated with achievement (Evertson & Emmer, 1980; Fisher et al., 1980; Good & Grouws, 1979; Stallings, Cory, Fairweather, & Needels, 1978; Stallings & Kaskowitz, 1974; Stallings & Mohlman, 1981). A recent survey conducted by Louis Harris and Associates for the Metropolitan Life Insurance Company reported that 40% of the teachers surveyed said they taught less than 75% of the time they spent with students; 13% said they taught less than 50%. Teachers also reported that students spent even less time listening to them. A majority of the teachers said that most students did not pay attention most of the time (Daniels, 1988b). These results are disturbing, coming more than a decade after the research on the importance of time utilization began to be published.

Stallings et al. (1978) explored the findings regarding use of time further. They looked at 43 teachers in six school districts. These teachers taught a total of 905 junior or senior high school students in basic reading skills courses. To participate in the study, the school district had to offer remedial and compensatory programs in basic skills at the secondary level. The population in these classes included a disproportionate number of non-English-speaking students, Black students, and low socioeconomic status students.

The study indicated that in classrooms where students achieved high gains in reading scores, teachers were efficient in organizing and managing, provided more interactive instruction, actively monitored seatwork, and had high student on-task ratings. The high gain group teachers used drill and practice only 4% of the time and only after students understood the concepts and vocabulary. The high gain group teachers also engaged their students in oral reading for 21% of the time (Stallings, 1986).

Efficiency in taking roll, making assignments, passing out materials, and controlling behavior allows more time for instruction. In classrooms where teachers are efficient in "getting the show on the road," students are on task more and make greater gains in achievement (Evertson & Emmer, 1980). Stallings and Mohlman (1981) found that effective teachers spent no more than 15% of their time organizing and managing. A study by Martinez (1989), conducted in the classrooms of nine teachers of limited English proficiency students who taught 132 students, measured the achievement of students of teachers trained in the Stallings Time Effectiveness Framework. She found that students of teachers who had received the training scored significantly higher on reading achievement tests than the students of the control group teachers.

Grouping for Instruction and Instructional Delivery

The most efficient and effective format for delivering instruction has recently received much attention from educators and researchers. During the 1960s and 1970s, many theoreticians and educators embraced the notion of individualized instruction, especially for the "slow" or "disadvantaged" learner. Proponents of compensatory education and equity programs, in attempting to provide equity of outcomes for all students, argued that since students entered school with different needs and backgrounds, they must receive individual educational treatment (Shakeshaft, 1986). According to Bereiter (1985), it was considered to be fairer to "assign educational treatments according to a child's demonstrated needs and abilities" rather than assign a child to "an educational treatment group because he or she comes from a family with income below a certain level, has a Hispanic surname, or lives on the wrong side of the railroad tracks" (p. 540).

While the goal may have been a noble one, research on diagnostic/prescriptive teaching and individualized instruction has not found it to be particularly effective in most classrooms. While there is a certain appeal to having students work at their own pace through sequenced, programmed materials and having the teacher work with one student at a time, there are distinct inequities in this approach. Given a 50-minute period and 30 students, a teacher cannot provide instruction and feedback to every student every day. All students cannot get their questions answered and receive the guidance they need. Some students will get a lot of attention and some will get none. Students waste much time waiting for help. Very often the result is that in classrooms where each student is working at a different place in a workbook or on a ditto sheet, *students are off task more often and make less academic gain.* Furthermore, all students gain from a variety of academic activities that allow several modalities to be used.

In a study conducted in 14 elementary schools in 11 California school districts, Stallings and Kaskowitz (1974) found that elementary reading classes where teachers or aides worked with one student at a time had high off-task or disruptive behaviors and lower posttest scores than classrooms where teachers spent most of their time engaged in interactive instruction with large groups. A question-response-feedback instructional technique was found to be most effective in keeping students involved and on task.

Individualized programs often did not take into consideration the fact that the culture of the very children they were striving to help often encouraged cooperative, communal activities and that children from various ethnic and racial groups may not learn best when working alone. Stages of social development were also ignored by individualized instruction. We know that, typically, by the fourth grade the peer

group becomes of utmost importance to most children. Thus individualized programs, as perfectly structured and sequenced as they were,
were doomed to failure in most middle schools and junior high schools,
where the students' needs for social interaction outweighed all other
factors.

Sexual preferences for learning are also overlooked by such programs. A 1982 study by Gilligan (cited in Shakeshaft, 1986) indicates
that competitive learning situations are favored by boys, while connection is preferred by girls. Shakeshaft (1986) asserts that both the curriculum and instructional strategies in public school classrooms mirror
the physical and mental development of males (p. 500).

In the best sense, individualized instruction requires that student
needs be diagnosed and that appropriate instructional strategies and
curricula be prescribed. This does not mean that all students will be
taught on a one-to-one basis, but that different strategies can be used
with different groups of students.

Stallings and Mohlman (1981) found significant differences in the
instructional activities of higher- and lower-achieving junior high
English and mathematics classes. Lower-achieving students' attention
span for seatwork was considerably shorter than that of higher-achieving students. Lower-achieving students needed more instruction and
discussion to stay on task. In Stallings's study of secondary classrooms,
teachers who were effective in helping low-achieving students gain 1.5
to 2 years in reading spent 60% or more of class time in active instruction and allocated only 20% to seatwork activities. High-achieving
students spent 35% or more time in guided seatwork activities. Bereiter
(1985) asserts that children need different degrees of help with learning
and that children who have been labeled as disadvantaged generally
need more than ordinary amounts of help. He believes that direct
instruction holds the most promise for providing these children with the
help they need. When the range of student achievement levels is great,
teachers may find it necessary to group students for some portion of the
instructional time. Some studies have examined the benefits of grouping for instruction.

A review of studies on the effects of ability grouping on secondary
school students by Kulik and Kulik (1982) indicates that students who
were grouped in some classes had a more positive attitude toward
school and themselves. Slavin (1980) suggests grouping students to
encourage cooperation rather than competition. He reports positive
effects upon high- and low-achieving students when in-class teams

work on projects. He also reports high motivation when grades are determined by gain made by each of the group participants.

Slavin's (1987) review of the research on Chapter 1 programs reports that the most effective are comprehensive programs where modifications have been made to existing classroom programs to enable teachers to meet better a wide range of student needs. Cooperative learning, in terms of small mixed-ability learning teams and small skill-specific groups where students work through a sequence of carefully defined objectives, has been found to be effective. The most effective programs are those that assess student progress frequently and modify the groupings or instructional content to meet student needs (Slavin & Madden, 1989). Flexible grouping also allows for cross-cultural communication and interaction in integrated classrooms.

Learning to work with other students on a joint effort is an important life skill. Most work in life requires working with groups of people to accomplish tasks. Many skills are required for a person to work cooperatively with others. These include active listening, speaking clearly, taking turns, respecting others' skills and ideas, arriving at group consensus, and summarizing and reporting. It is especially important that all students have the opportunity to develop these skills in multicultural classrooms. Pull-out programs, where students are removed for individual help for 30 minutes per day, have not produced the desired achievement. In addition, Slavin (1987) states that the Chapter 1 programs that were shown to be most effective were effective for all students, not just for those at risk. Direct instructional strategies and grouping are not incompatible. Both require the active participation and supervision of the teacher.

Varied Activities

One of the most important findings to emerge from studies of teaching basic skills in secondary schools is that effective teachers provide several activities during one class period. Students do not spend the entire period doing worksheets or silent reading or being lectured. Effective teachers plan activities that required students to use several modalities (Stalling & Mohlman, 1981). Less effective teachers spend more time organizing and more time on noninteractive instruction. They tend to jump from instruction to written work. They omit checking for understanding and reteaching.

Recent research on learning styles and whole-brain instruction seems to support these findings. Rothman (1987) contends that since all parts of the brain contribute to the learning and understanding of concepts, each lesson should provide students with opportunities to read about the topic, view visual or graphic representations of it, and also act it out. Research by Stallings and Mohlman (1981) indicates that in classrooms where at least three different instructional strategies are used, students are actively engaged in their lessons more of the time.

In terms of equity, it is important for teachers to realize that not all children learn best in the same way and that all children certainly do not learn best in the way the teacher does. Since teachers tend to teach the way they were taught, they need to make a conscious effort to present instruction in many ways so as to have a better chance of meeting the needs of all students. Learning style research shows that there are many factors that influence the way children learn best. Some may be biological and others may be cultural or developed through experience or interaction with the environment (Dunn, Beaudry, & Klavas, 1989). While some groups are proponents of distinctive racial or cultural learning styles (see Berger, 1988), most research indicates that there are as many within-group differences in learning as there are between-group differences (Dunn et al., 1989). In order to be effective, teachers must use varied activities and strategies appropriate to "the vast range of learning styles and cultures that are found in our multi-ethnic, multiracial society" (First, 1988, p. 218).

The job of a teacher is to arrange learning environments, select materials, and provide activities that will support all children in their attempts to learn. Activities that allow students to use several modalities facilitate the integration of new material and help link the new learning to what is already known.

Appropriate Materials

The issue of culturally fair and gender-fair curriculum materials is still a concern. The research on the use of time in the classroom addresses the concept of academic learning time. Berliner (1987) defines this as "that part of allocated time in which students are engaged with materials or activities related to the outcome measures that are being used and in which students experience a high success rate" (p. 101). Berliner states that in the Fisher et al. (1980) study, allocated learning time consistently accounted for approximately 10% of the variance in student achievement. The materials and activities selected by teachers should provide students with what they need in order to learn what they are supposed to learn (p. 102). Standardized tests are often biased with information familiar only to certain cultural or socio-economic groups. (See Daniels, 1988a, for a discussion of bias in the PSAT.)

When students are given reading readiness worksheets that test them on their ability to identify family roles unlike any they have ever known, there is an inappropriate match between what is taught and what is being tested. (See the section at the end of this chapter headed "An Author's Note.") Inappropriate materials, activities, or tests inhibit efficient and effective learning and the formative and summative evaluation of learning.

Other studies point to the importance of an appropriate match of materials to students. A recent study conducted in an urban high school troubled by the lowest achievement and highest dropout rate of any in its metropolitan area yielded some interesting findings (McCarthy, 1988). The high school, which is composed of one-third Hispanic students and two-thirds Black students, also had the highest absentee rate in the district. One fact that clearly stood out from the wealth of available data was that freshman students at this school were failing courses at an alarming rate and in alarming numbers—the 1987 fall semester grades indicated that there were 819 failures (17%). Ninth-grade students received the highest number of failing grades, 512, or 21%. Only 7% of all freshman grades were As. An examination of course-by-course failures showed that some instructors were giving failing grades to between 90% and 100% of all their freshman students. The effects of this failure were manifesting themselves in many ways, all of which were negative and nonproductive. Apathy in class, high dropout rates between ninth and tenth grades, poor performance on standardized tests, and behavior problems were the most obvious (McCarthy, 1988, p. 70).

An examination of the curriculum materials utilized in these class-rooms indicated that students were unable to read them. Texts with a readability level of tenth or eleventh grade were being used with students who were reading, on average, at the sixth-grade level. Teaching strategies being used were primarily lecture and seatwork. Off-task behavior was extremely high in many classrooms. Students were expected to be passive absorbers of knowledge. The necessity of appropriate materials was an important finding of the study.

As a result of the comprehensive study conducted by 23 university faculty, exciting things are happening at this high school. The school has been designated as a basic skills center and dramatic changes are occurring in both instructional strategies and curriculum materials and offerings. Collaborative planning with feeder middle schools is ongoing, and plans are under way to begin working with feeder elementary schools. Poor test results, failures, and dropout rates have abated. Other urban schools are currently involved in equally exciting programmatic developments that make use of what we know about how students learn best.

Interactive Instruction

As research has indicated, effective teachers spend 50% of their time providing interactive instruction to students. An important first step in interactive instruction is to review previous materials. These might include homework, seatwork from the day before, or a returned test.

The next step is for the teacher to state clear objectives and provide some new information or concept. It is crucial that the new information be linked to previous knowledge and that a conceptual framework be built to incorporate the new knowledge. Teaching is a search for a means to link students' prior knowledge and experience to new information. In culturally diverse classrooms, this presents a challenge for the classroom teacher. This can often be accomplished by giving comparisons or making contrasts, providing examples of what the essential elements of the new concept are as well as what they are not. The information needs to be structured in such a way that it can be stored in students' long-term memories.

After the instruction has been provided, it is essential that teachers check to see whether the students have learned what is expected (Good & Grouws, 1979; Stallings & Kaskowitz, 1974). During a question-and-answer period, it is important that the teacher call on students by name rather than call exclusively on volunteers.

Every time a teacher asks a question, he or she makes a decision regarding whom to call upon. These are important decisions because they determine who will participate and the level of thinking to be stimulated. For the most part, unless they consciously make an effort, teachers call upon volunteers. The effect of this procedure is to limit the access to participation in the class to volunteers. The research on interactions suggests that, to offer equal access to participation in classrooms, teachers should call on students by name rather than call-ing upon volunteers. There is substantial evidence in studies by Good and Brophy (1980) that higher-achieving students are called upon most often, and that this reinforces their higher achievement. Low-achieving students are called upon least often, and this reinforces their low achievement. By making a conscious decision regarding whom to call upon, teachers can distribute appropriate questions to all students. This does not mean asking all low-level, easy questions of low-achieving students. This approach only perpetuates the low image that these students have of themselves and the low image their classmates have of them.

Greta Morine-Dershimer (1983) found that higher-level questions asked of lower-level students by trained teachers elicited higher-level thinking. Lower-achieving students could take part in discussions when they were asked to compare, contrast, hazard a guess, or give an opinion or a feeling. In these classes, when students were asked to check the names on a list of those who made good contributions to the class discussion, low-achieving students' names were checked as well as those of higher-achieving students. Interestingly, the low achievers even checked their own names. They experienced themselves as mak-ing contributions. In classrooms where teachers did not ask low-achiev-ing students higher-level questions, those low achievers were not rated as making contributions to class discussions. This point is important. If teachers do not expect that students can take part in a higher-level discussion, those students are not even given a chance to participate.

Students also need to receive some low-key positive reinforcement for acceptable responses. They need many opportunities to succeed on either written work or oral responses. In such a positive environment, students stay on task more; they experience more feelings of accom-plishment, and learning becomes a pleasurable experience for them.

It is very important that low-achieving students be given the oppor-tunity to answer questions at all levels and not be limited to knowledge-level drill-type questions (Good, 1987). Factual questions are crucial to effective teaching, but all students must have the opportunity to be challenged in order to see if they have truly internalized and are comfortable with the concepts being presented. If some students do not understand the concepts taught, then a small group of those students can be formed and the teacher can reteach the concept by using dif-ferent examples and illustrations.

Another interactive technique, oral reading, was found to be espe-cially effective in the lowest ability group of secondary remedial reading classes (Stallings, Needels, & Stayrook, 1979). This activity allows the teacher to diagnose students' reading ability and provide auditory input and oral expression for students. Remedial students need to hear words and say words as well as read them and write them. Students from dialect groups that are different from that of the school especially need oral language development opportunities in reading class. In New York City, newly arrived immigrant students are placed in a special "Welcome School," where classes are small and each is assigned a "buddy" to orient him or her to American schools. Language classes emphasize oral communication, thus easing student transition into regular schools (Fiske, 1989).

Oral reading also provides opportunities for active involvement with and processing of the skills to be mastered. As Cummins (1986) states, a review of the research on at-risk students shows that they need interactive teaching and learning, a "reciprocal interaction model" the central tenet of which is that speaking and writing are essential for learning (p. 28).

Cultural Differences
in Active and Passive Learning

As discussed above, research tells us that active, interactive teaching/learning processes produce higher achievement in classrooms than do passive, noninteractive teaching/learning processes. Yet there are many societal, cultural, and instructional forces that actually encourage passivity on the part of our students (Harvey, 1986; Sadker & Sadker, 1986; Sadker et al., 1989; Shakeshaft, 1986).

One major influence, of course, is that of television. It has been estimated that by the age of 18, American children will have spent more than 22,000 hours watching television, or more than 20 hours per week of passive viewing (Merrow, 1985). This is a startling statistic, especially for teachers who grew up in the era when television was a new phenomenon. It is difficult for today's students to comprehend the fact that the first commercial radio station went on the air in the United States in 1920 and that it was not until the 1923 live broadcast of President Calvin Coolidge's State of the Union Address that radio became part of the national culture. It is harder still for them to comprehend that television became available to the general public in 1946 and that it did not take off in popularity until the 1947 broadcasts of the World Series and the Joe Louis-Jersey Joe Walcott fight (Davis, 1987). One of the authors can recall her family being the first in the neighborhood to own a television and having a houseful of children come over each afternoon to watch the *Howdy Doody Show.*

How very different is the life-style of today's children, even most disadvantaged children, with constant access to television, from that of their teachers, who grew up reading books and playing games, with television as only an occasional source of entertainment. Does television influence students to be passive in their approach to learning? Is watching television a more passive activity than reading? If so, it is important for teachers to understand this and to make deliberate attempts to implement instructional strategies that encourage interaction.

Cummins (1986) found that at-risk children often are provided with instruction that puts them into a passive role in the classroom, which encourages them to remain dependent learners. Good (1981, 1987) found, in his review of research on teacher expectations, that as many as one-third of all teachers observed responded to low-achieving students in ways that encouraged passivity. Low-achieving students received less frequent praise for success, received briefer and less informative feedback, tended to be seated further away from the teacher, and had less frequent interaction with the teacher. The interaction they did have tended to be criticism. These factors, according to Good (1987; Good & Brophy, 1980), encourage low-achieving students to keep a low profile in the classroom and discourage them from attempting to answer questions or participate; as a result, they fail to remedy their initial learning deficiencies, and in fact compound them.

There are certainly many other factors that influence passivity on the part of students. One that needs to be considered by classroom teachers is the educational systems from which their students come. This is especially important for teachers in schools districts with large numbers of immigrant students. According to studies conducted by First (1988), many of these children come into American schools from school systems that are quite different. They are used to a formal, transmittal type of instruction, with little or no interaction. In order to function appropriately in the American system, which is less formal, much more active and interactive, they need to be oriented to the new system rather than just immersed with no preparation (First, 1988, p. 215). In discussing the needs of Asian immigrants in American schools in an article in the *New York Times,* Fiske (1989) comments, "In dealing with students who have been taught not to challenge authority,

American teachers find it easy to misinterpret a student's silence as comprehension."

Shakeshaft (1986) found that males in the classroom receive both more positive and more negative attention from teachers. Boys are also given more opportunities to interact in the classroom, with the average female being ignored. Harvey (1986) found that minority females receive the least attention in the classroom. He adds that most teachers are seemingly unaware of the inequitable interactions they foster in their classrooms. Sadker and Sadker (1986) report similar findings. They also assert that brief but focused training can reduce or eliminate this inequitable classroom interaction.

Thus interactive teaching strategies are crucial for student achievement. Teachers must carefully structure their lessons so that all students have the opportunity to participate every day in interaction with materials and activities that are appropriate for them. The best way to ensure that this occurs is to provide a rich variety of effective teaching strategies and carefully selected materials and activities and to train students who are unfamiliar with these types of activities to become more actively involved in the instructional process. While the research indicates that achievement is higher when students are actively involved, it is also important that students from different cultural and ethnic backgrounds not be thrown into a new way of doing things without adequate preparation. Suzuki (1979) states that his definition of a truly multicultural education would be one that "provides multiple learning environments that properly match the academic and social needs of students" (p. 47).

Teacher Expectations

What teachers believe about students' ability to learn has a profound effect upon the types of lessons they provide for students. Even on the first day of school teachers have opinions and expectations for some of their students. The opinions are usually based upon society's prejudices and confirmed in school records, family reputations, and previous teachers' reports. As the year progresses, teachers' opinions and expectations may be modified as they observe and experience the students' participation in class, work in groups, performance on tests, and completion of homework and other projects.

If a teacher believes a student cannot learn (or learns very slowly) and rigidly maintains that opinion, the student perceived to be a low performer is likely to have few chances to be involved in some of the more interesting activities that can occur in classrooms. Research indicates that teachers' expectations, rigidly maintained and consistently projected to students, will affect students' self-concepts, levels of aspiration, motivation, classroom conduct, interactions with the teacher, and, of course, achievement.

If a teacher expects students to perform at a low level, the students are likely to perform as expected, thus reinforcing the teacher's expectations. As indicated by research reported by Rosenthal and Jacobson (1968) in *Pygmalion in the Classroom*, positive or negative teacher expectations can project to students and function as a self-fulfilling prophecy. Teachers need to be aware of their classroom behavior and make deliberate plans to behave in ways that encourage and facilitate the learning and achievement of all their students.

Classroom Management:
Creating and Maintaining an
Environment That Facilitates Learning

A supportive environment is more conducive to learning for most people, but it is especially important for students who have a history of failure. Stallings et al. (1978) found that in classrooms where students were provided with a supportive environment, interactive instruction, and varied instructional activities, they stayed on task a greater percentage of time (90-95%) and were absent less often. The same study indicated that in secondary classrooms where teachers posted clear rules for behavior and where rules were consistent throughout the school, there was less misbehavior and absenteeism.

Studies by Evertson and Emmer (1980) found that effective managers made the rules for behavior clear on the first day of school and integrated the procedures into a workable system. They planned the first day for maximum control over students. They began the period by explaining rules and procedures and the reasons for having them. The more effective managers spent considerable time during the first week reminding the students of the rules and allowing them opportunities to practice going-to-school skills.

Evertson and Emmer (1980) also found that effective teachers had planned the classroom ecology ahead of time so that traffic patterns and furniture arrangement facilitated effective and efficient movement and

grouping for instruction. Routines, rules, and procedures were carefully developed to make material collection and dispersal smooth and
nondisruptive. In classrooms with low-income students, it is important
for teachers to understand that those students often cannot afford study
materials and supplies from home that many other students can take for
granted. Teachers who understand the characteristics of their students
and are able to "see things through their eyes" are able to provide
learning environments conducive to learning.

Just as not all students learn best in one way, not all students respond
best to just one method of managing behavior. In some cases, teachers
may want to provide students with more effective tools for managing
their own behavior and becoming responsible for their own actions.
Thus it is important that effective teachers have a large repertoire of
managerial behaviors at their disposal so as to meet the behavioral
needs of their students. The teachers can then utilize these strategies
in ways that maximize student engagement (McCarthy-Goldstein &
Weber, 1981).

Despite the high level of concern with behavior in the classroom and
evidence that links student on-task behavior with student achievement
in basic skills, little empirical evidence had been gathered with regard
to those specific teacher behaviors that are related to the establishment
and maintenance of student on-task behavior prior to the studies conducted by Stallings, Evertson, Fisher, and Berliner in the mid-1970s
(McCarthy-Goldstein & Weber, 1979, 1980, 1981). There are still many
teacher-preparation programs that offer little or no training in classroom management. Effective instruction cannot take place in the classrooms of teachers who are not proficient in classroom teacher
managerial behaviors shown to be correlated with student time on task
(McCarthy-Goldstein & Weber, 1981).

Implications

Research on teaching has indicated that effective teachers are those
who utilize a broad repertoire of instructional and managerial activities
in the classroom in order to meet a wide range of student needs and
abilities. They use time carefully and efficiently. They select learning
activities and materials carefully to be sure they are at an appropriate
level of difficulty and address several learning modalities. They em-

phasize active, interactive instruction and learning, and group students appropriately for instruction.

In brief, effective teachers do the following:

(1) Spend about half (50%) of class time on interactive academic activities: explaining new materials, discussing and reviewing assigned work, question-and-answer sessions, and so on.

(2) Spend about one-third (35%) of class time on actively monitoring silent reading, written work, lab work.

(3) Spend less than 15% of class time on classroom management and organization: passing papers, explaining activities, arranging desks, making lesson transitions, taking roll, making announcements, and so on.

(4) Have a system of behavior rules that are clear, posted in view, and consistently enforced.

(5) Spend very little in-class time socializing with students, visitors, or aides.

(6) Plan daily activities in advance and make them clear to students, for example, by writing the day's schedule on the board.

(7) Plan a variety of academic activities that require students to use three or more modalities during one class period.

(8) State the objectives and purpose of the lesson.

(9) Check for students' understanding.

(10) Give short quizzes and give immediate feedback.

(11) Focus most instruction on the whole class or small groups rather than on individuals.

(12) Distribute opportunities for verbal response equally among students.

(13) Praise student success and effort.

(14) Give a student who answers incorrectly another chance to get it right by rephrasing the question or giving hints.

(15) Have a review of what was learned yesterday and today, and tell what to expect tomorrow.

Effective teachers are able to plan instructional materials, activities, and strategies carefully to meet the needs of their students. As Brophy and Good (1986) state, "Effective instruction involves selecting (from a larger repertoire) and orchestrating those teaching behaviors that are appropriate to the context and to the teacher's goals" (p. 360).

Effective teachers are also able to select and implement classroom management techniques and teacher behaviors from a broad repertoire of potentially effective behaviors. They choose strategies that are appropriate to the context and their social, behavioral, and instructional goals for students. In addition, effective teachers recognize that strategies and materials that meet the needs of culturally diverse or disadvantaged populations are often those strategies that are most effective with all students. All students have the right to receive the most appropriate, efficient, and effective instruction we can provide in order to facilitate maximum achievement, not only in basic skills, but in social and personal domains as well. Research findings linking instructional strategies to student outcomes are abundant. A firm commitment is needed to implement these finding in all classrooms. This requires dissemination of research findings to classroom teachers, opportunities for staff development, and support by building and district supervisors. The goal is a quality education that enables all students to maximize their effectiveness and to experience success.

An Author's Note

The little boy came home from kindergarten with tears in his eyes. In his hands he clenched a paper with a big red F on it. "Mommy, I failed in school today," he said as his chin quivered. "And I don't even know what these things are, anyway!" His mother calmed him down and suggested that they sit down together and look at the paper. It was a typical reading readiness worksheet. At the top it had a picture labeled "Mommy" and a picture labeled "Daddy." The instructions read: "Draw a line from Mommy to the things she uses in the house. Then draw a line from Daddy to the things he uses in the house."

"What are these things, anyway?" asked the child. The items pictured included an iron and an ironing board, which this child, in the world of permanent press and working mother, had never seen. A sewing machine was also pictured. This child's Halloween costume had been stapled together. There was a mending basket in his home, but no one ever went near it. He had drawn a line from the mop and bucket to Daddy. In his family, Daddy washed the floors on Saturday. Upon closer examination, a copyright date was found on the paper—it was 1952. The year was 1974, and the world the child lived in was very different from the one pictured on the worksheet.

The child is now a straight-A student in a prestigious university. Yet he still remembers the day he "failed" in kindergarten. And so does his mother.

References

Bereiter, C. (1985). The changing face of educational disadvantagement. *Phi Delta Kappan, 66*(9), 538-541.

Berger, J. (1988, July 6). Backers push learning style. *New York Times*.

Berliner, D. C. (1987). Simple views of effective teaching and a simple theory of classroom instruction. In C. C. Berliner & B. V. Rosenshine (Eds.), *Talks to teachers*. New York: Random House.

Brophy, J., & Good, T. (1986). Teacher behavior and student achievement. In M. Wittrock (Ed.), *Handbook of research on teaching* (3rd ed., pp. 326-375). New York: Macmillan.

Cummins, J. (1986). Empowering minority students: A framework for intervention. *Harvard Educational Review, 56*(1), 18-26.

Daniels, L. A. (1988a, June 29). Groups charge bias in merit scholarship testing. *New York Times*, p. 25.

Daniels, L. A. (1988b, October 5). More minority teachers may quit. *New York Times*, p. 28

Davis, S. (1987). *Say kids! What time is it? Notes from the peanut gallery*. Boston: Little, Brown.

Dunn, R., Beaudry, J. S., & Klavas, A. (1989). Survey of research on learning styles. *Educational Leadership, 46*(6), 50-58.

Evertson, C. (1982). Differences in instructional activities in higher- and lower-achieving junior high English and math classes. *Elementary School Journal, 82*(4), 186-230.

Evertson, C., & Emmer, E. (1980). *Effective management at the beginning of the school year in junior high classes*. Austin: University of Texas, Research and Development Center for Teacher Education.

First, J. M. (1988). Immigrant students in U.S. public schools: Challenges with solutions. *Phi Delta Kappan, 70*(3), 205-218.

Fisher, C. W., Berliner, D. C., Filby, N. N., Marliave, R., Cahern, L. S., & Dishaw, M. M. (1980). Teaching behaviors, academic learning time and student achievement: An overview. In C. Denham & A. Lieberman (Eds.), *Time to learn*. Washington, DC: Government Printing Office.

Fisher, C. W., Filby, N., Marliave, R., Cahern, L., Dishaw, N., Moore, J., & Berliner, D. (1977). *Beginning teacher evaluation study* (Technical Note IV-16). San Francisco: Far West Laboratory.

Fiske, E. B. (1989, March 8). Lessons: Meeting the needs of Asian-Americans who don't fit the model minority role. *New York Times*, p. 24.

Good, T. L. (1981, February). Teacher expectations and student perceptions: A decade of research. *Educational Leadership*, pp. 415-422.

Good, T. L. (1987). Teacher expectations. In D. C. Berliner & B. V. Rosenshine (Eds.), *Talks to teachers* (pp. 159-200). New York: Random House.

Good, T. L., & Brophy, J. (1980). *Educational psychology: A realistic approach* (2nd ed.). New York: Holt, Rinehart & Winston.

Good, T. L., & Grouws, D. A. (1979). The Missouri Mathematics Effectiveness Project. *Journal of Educational Psychology, 71*, 355-362.

Harvey, G. (1986). Finding reality among the myths: Why what you thought about sex equity in education isn't so. *Phi Delta Kappan, 67*(7), 509-512.

Kulik, C., & Kulik, J. (1982). Effects of ability grouping on secondary school students: A meta-analysis of evaluation findings. *American Educational Research Journal, 19*(3), 415-428.

La Pointe, A. E., & Martinez, M. E. (1988). Aims, equity, and access in computer education. *Phi Delta Kappan, 70*(1), 59-61.

Markoff, J. (1989, February 13). Computing in America: A masculine mystique. *New York Times.*

Martinez, A. (1989). *The effect of the Effective Use of Time Program on the academic achievement of limited English proficient students.* Unpublished doctoral dissertation, University of Houston, Houston.

McCarthy, J. (1988). Curriculum. In W. R. Houston (Ed.), *Wheatley High School Project: Final report.* Houston: Houston Independent School District.

McCarthy-Goldstein, J., & Weber, W. A. (1979). *Managerial behaviors of elementary school teachers and student on-task behavior.* Paper presented at the annual meeting of the American Educational Research Association, San Francisco.

McCarthy-Goldstein, J., & Weber, W. A. (1980). *Teacher managerial behaviors and student on-task behavior in the elementary school: A replication.* Paper presented at the annual meeting of the Association for Teacher Education, Washington, DC.

McCarthy-Goldstein, J., & Weber, W. A. (1981). *Teacher managerial behaviors and student on-task behavior: Three studies.* Paper presented at the annual meeting of the American Educational Research Association, Los Angeles.

Merrow, J. (1985). Children and television: Natural partners. *Phi Delta Kappan, 67*(3), 211-214.

Morine-Dershimer, G. (1983). Instructional strategy and the "creation" of classroom status. *American Educational Research Journal, 20*, 645-661.

Plunkett, V.R.L. (1985). From Title 1 to Chapter 1: The evolution of compensatory education. *Phi Delta Kappan, 66*(9), 533-537.

Rosenthal, R., & Jacobson, L. (1968). *Pygmalion in the classroom: Teacher expectations and pupils' intellectual development.* New York: Holt, Rinehart & Winston.

Rothman, R. (1987, September 16). Brain research fuels drive to alter teaching of the gifted. *Education Week*, p. 8.

Sadker, M., & Sadker, D. (1986). Sexism in the classroom: From grade school to graduate school. *Phi Delta Kappan, 67*(7), 512-515.

Sadker, M., Sadker D., & Steindam, S. (1989). Gender equity and educational reform. *Educational Leadership, 46*(9), 44-47.

Shakeshaft, C. (1986). A gender at risk. *Phi Delta Kappan, 67*(7), 499-503.

Slavin, R. (1980). *Using student team learning* (rev. ed.). Baltimore: Johns Hopkins University, Center for Social Organization of Schools.

Slavin, R. E. (1987). Making Chapter 1 make a difference. *Phi Delta Kappan, 69*(2), 110-119.

Slavin, R. E., & Madden, N. A. (1989). What works for students at risk: A research synthesis. *Educational Leadership, 46*(5), 4-13.

Stallings, J. (1980). Allocated academic learning time revisited, or beyond time on task. *Educational Researcher, 8*(11), 11-16.

Stallings, J. (1986). Effective use of time in secondary reading programs. In J. V. Hoffman (Ed.), *Effective teaching of reading: Research and practice* (pp. 85-106). Newark, DE: International Reading Association.

Stallings, J., Cory, R., Fairweather, J., & Needels, M. (1978). *A study of basic reading skills taught in secondary schools.* Menlo Park, CA: SRI International.

Stallings, J., & Kaskowitz, D. (1974). *Follow through classroom evaluation, 1972-73.* Menlo Park, CA: SRI International.

Stallings, J., & Mohlman, G. (1981). *Principal leadership style, school policy, teacher change and student behavior in eight secondary schools.* Final report prepared for the National Institute of Education, Washington, DC.

Stallings, J. A., Needels, M., & Stayrook, N. (1979). *The teaching of basic reading skills in secondary schools, phase II: Final report.* Menlo Park, CA: SRI International.

Stallings, J. A., & Stipek, D. (1986). Research on early childhood and elementary school teaching programs. In M. Wittrock (Ed.), *Handbook of research on teaching* (pp. 727-753). New York: Macmillan.

Suzuki, B. H. (1979). Multicultural education: What's it all about? *Integrated Education, 17*(1-2), 43-49.

PART IV

EDUCATIONAL PREPARATION
FOR EQUITY

15

Introduction:
The Challenge of Preparing for Equity

H . PRENTICE BAPTISTE, Jr.

University of Houston

The major challenge facing our society and specifically our schools is how to prepare for equity. Perhaps more precisely, how do we meet the challenge of developing valid and reliable programs that will enable educators to provide effective equity programs (Willie, 1989)? These programs must incorporate in a confluent manner the cognitive and affective dimensions of equity. Educators must be taught not only how to recognize issues and situations of inequity in our society and schools, but, more important, what they can do to confront them. Educators must also be willing to internalize philosophical principles that will commit them to action for equity on behalf of all students (Baptiste, 1986).

In dealing with this issue, Charol Shakeshaft points out that equity issues are related to both the content and environmental facets of administrative preparation programs. In her chapter, she takes the position that all administrators and teachers must be taught about the conceptual, philosophical, and societal issues involved in educational equity. She indicates that future administrators must understand the importance of examining enrollment patterns in such elective subjects as science, math, and life-skills courses. Additionally, they must be able to conceptualize and organize curricula that cover the range of human experiences.

Shakeshaft also notes the significance of experiential learning for students in ascertaining the differential treatment of majority and minority students in schools. Discrimination and exclusion have undoubtedly affected communication and interaction patterns among majority and minority members, as well as between females and males. Clearly, the roles of race and gender in supervisory style need to be made known to all administrative students. Shakeshaft highlights the importance of the equity issues infusing all administrative courses, such as those dealing with law, personnel, and finance. She ends her chapter with some insightful guidelines for preparing administrators to deal effectively with equity issues.

In her chapter, Geneva Gay deals with teacher preparation for equity. She points out that teaching is a sociocultural process and thus its effectiveness with culturally different students is due as much to social and cultural competence as to pedagogical capabilities. She argues that the kinesthetic, multimodal, simultaneous sensory stimulation and cultural socialization process of certain youngsters dooms them to failure in passive teacher-controlled classrooms. Furthermore, she discusses three categorical needs that are essential for teachers to understand in order to provide equity for diverse learners, linking many inequitable student outcomes to the use of various instructional grouping models. She challenges administrators and teachers to put aside these old, biased models and to replace them with creative techniques and strategies. Moreover, she asserts that textbooks do not give comparable treatment to the heritages, experiences, perspectives, and contributions of all ethnic, cultural, and social groups in the United States. Rather, they practice intellectual discrimination and educational inequity.

Gay contends that a negative relationship may exist between teacher attitudes and learning in children that could lead to what she terms "disinvitations to learning." She explains how educational equity may be promoted by sensitizing teachers to traits of "learning disinvitations" and developing teacher skills in invitational instruction. Finally, she makes a strong case for the importance of the commitment of teacher education programs to cultural diversity and the willingness to hold themselves and their graduates accountable to the values that underlie equity.

In his chapter, James B. Boyer echoes this sentiment, lamenting that teacher education programs are woefully traditional and leave teacher candidates painfully limited in the areas of ethnic literacy, racial and cultural contributions, and a philosophical respect for human diversity.

He also charges that reform movements in teacher education have failed to address the new demographic picture and age of consumerism.

Additionally, Boyer notes that the overriding assumption in many teacher education programs is that different backgrounds and languages constitute deficits to be corrected rather than strengths to build upon. He maintains that teacher education bears responsibility for creating instructional discrimination, for equity in instruction exists when varied teaching approaches are employed, such that varied learning styles may receive an appropriate reaction or response. To this end, Boyer advocates a "celebration" of teacher education that embraces the affirmation of ethnic differences. He suggests that this will positively affect the dropout problem, which he prefers to relabel as a "cultural departure" problem. Further, he asserts that teacher educators must refuse to participate in any further research that essentially blames the victim. Instead, teacher education must embrace the concept of multicultural education for preparing competent teachers.

In contrast, Carlos E. Cortés's chapter explores the role of education and school in what he refers to as the "societal curriculum." He uses the media as a formidable example of our societal curriculum that often assaults our youngsters with stereotypical and prejudicial images and ideas about various cultural, racial, and ethnic groups. He accepts that students will learn more from society in lifelong experiences, yet he challenges our schools to prepare students to deal effectively and analytically with the process of lifelong learning.

Cortés examines four educational relationships between schooling and society that must exist if equity is to emerge. He further proposes that the societal curriculum operates in four general curriculum sections: immediate, institutional, serendipitous, and media curriculum. He also discusses the significance of motion pictures, media entertainment, and television, and their impact on equity education. He makes the case that our youngsters' exposure to these media causes them to absorb ideas contrary to societal equity. Even so, Cortés suggests that an agenda for action can use mass media — television, motion pictures, and the like — as a force for educating students to be analytical consumers of media equity.

The chapters in Part IV attempt to present ideas for education that provides equity by being sufficient for all students. As Willie (1989) points out, education must have the purpose of being mutually fulfilling. Thus it is my belief that the reader will find enough stimulating ideas in the following chapters for the creation of preparation programs that provide equity for all students.

References

Baptiste, H. P., Jr. (1986). Multicultural education and urban schools from a sociohistorical perspective: Internalizing multiculturalism. *Journal of Educational Equity and
Leadership, 6*(4), 295-312. (Reprinted in J. L. Burdin [Ed.], *School leadership: A
contemporary reader* [pp. 187-203]. Newbury Park, CA: Sage, 1989)

Willie, C. (1989). *Equity and ethics issues in institutionalizing shared responsibility:
Developing school leaders* (Report of the Danforth Foundation Program for the
Preparation of School Principals). St. Louis: Danforth Foundation.

16

Administrative Preparation for Equity

CHAROL SHAKESHAFT

Hofstra University

It will not surprise most people reading this chapter that administrative preparation programs have not incorporated equity into the central core of what an administrator should know. Most programs offer nothing in the preparation sequence that addresses equity issues. In the rare program where equity is included, it is most often presented as an isolated topic in an introductory course in administration, and then usually only to point out the absence of all women and minority males in administrative positions.

Of the few programs that do provide a forum for the discussion of equity issues, the mode of delivery is usually the elective course, and most often it is something called "multicultural education." Fewer programs offer electives on gender and schooling, and, to my knowledge, no program *requires* a comprehensive examination of equity and schooling.

Equity has always been important in the delivery of good schooling. However, it has been only in the past decade that we have come to understand the relationship between equitable practices and achievement in the classroom. Research has helped school people realize not only that equity is a moral obligation of schools, but that student learning and achievement are highly related to equitable practice. The evidence for why administrative programs should acquaint all potential administrators with issues of equity has been presented forcefully in earlier chapters in this book. This chapter, then, will offer some suggestions about how administrative preparation programs might go about incorporating the issues of equity into already-existing preparation programs. Obviously, administrator preparation occurs outside of university preparation programs. Administrative centers and professional organizations play a large role in the continuing education of school administrators. They, too, need to incorporate equity issues into the services offered to administrators. Much of what is prescribed here can be adapted for these training functions. However, this chapter primarily examines preservice preparation programs and the role they play in teaching administrators about equity.

Equity in the preparation of school administrators must center upon both content and the environment in which the content is presented. In other words, we need to provide students with an understanding of the relationships between equitable practice and learning, between equitable practice and school attendance, and between equitable practice and self-esteem. Administrators also must be cognizant of how gender and race affect administrative style and effectiveness. Finally, programs need to provide this content in an environment that supports and encourages women and minorities. Departments of educational administration have traditionally failed to deliver any of these three components of equity to their students.

Equity and Schooling

It is crucial that potential administrators understand the role that equity plays in effective schooling. Earlier chapters in this volume have presented in detail the relationship between equitable practice and school success. Administrators need to understand this relationship. Beyond understanding, administrators must be able to see equity as a problem of practice and must have the tools to develop policies and responses that ensure that all students will learn. It is not enough to acquaint students with the research on equity — although in most programs this would be a revolutionary addition — universities must also help administration students create equitable environments in the schools and districts in which they work.

Structure

Because administration students need to understand both the why and the how of equity, the best delivery system for this component is a required course in the administrative preparation sequence that examines both the relationship between equity and good schools and the role administrators have in creating an equitable culture. While research on equity should be incorporated into all classes in a preparation program, it is necessary to have one class the sole purpose of which is to examine equity. This separate course strategy is necessary for two reasons. First, the literature on race, gender, and class is voluminous; it cannot be covered adequately in a module or a class session. Second, students will not see equity as a primary responsibility of an administrator unless its importance is underscored by a course central to their program.

The best way to ensure that every administrative student is exposed to information on equity and schooling is to make this course a program requirement. Experience tells us that the students who most need to learn about equity issues will be the least likely to register for a course in this area. Unless this course is required to become an administrator, the majority of students will bypass it for other courses that they or their professors see as more central to an administrator's life.

There is an attitude about equity that goes something like this: "We did that in the sixties!" or "That's all taken care of now." This kind of reasoning fails to acknowledge that information about equity and schooling is something that must be taught every year to each new crop of prospective administrators. Just as every child somewhere at the beginning of her or his school career must learn the alphabet, so must every teacher and administrator be schooled in equity. Thus a required course devoted to this issue is absolutely critical in the preparation program of an administrator.

Content

To help aspiring administrators fully in dealing with the issues of equity in schooling, this required course should include at least the following topics: personal values; conceptual, philosophical, and societal issues of equity; equity in student treatment and placement; and equity in the curriculum.

One of the first steps in helping future administrators provide an equitable environment in their schools is to help them understand their own notions and beliefs about race and gender. Without some personal investigation, little else that is taught will have an impact. Time needs to be taken to help students explore their own biases and the ways these biases, most of which are subtle, affect behavior.

Conceptual, philosophical, and societal issues in equity are central to understanding not only what happens, but why it happens. Although most of us think we know what is meant by the term *equity*, it is important for students to be introduced to the large body of literature that has examined and defined equity. Administrative students need to be able to differentiate among the various policy definitions of equity and the actions attached to each. Those who wish to be administrators must understand the societal patterns outside of the school that have an impact on behavior within the school. These same students need to become acquainted with community and social service agencies that interact with children and to learn to develop working relationships with these agencies so that their own students can receive coordinated, comprehensive, and nonfragmented service.

The treatment and placement of students in schools is another area in which the sex, class, or race of a student plays a big role. Administrators need to understand how access to courses and curricular activities affect students' lives. Once they understand the implications of inequitable practices, aspiring administrators must be taught how to examine their own schools or districts for deficiencies, and they must be provided with strategies for overcoming the barriers to good schooling. For instance, we must teach future administrators the importance of examining enrollment patterns in elective math, science, and life-skills courses, and, if there are sex or race differences in these patterns, we must offer them strategies for changing these patterns. Not only do administrators need to know about effective discipline, they must also be able to examine these practices in light of race and sex issues. The research documenting that teachers interact differently with students based upon students' race and sex needs to be part of the working knowledge of both teachers and administrators, so that these interaction patterns can be changed. Additionally, administrators must be able to recognize racial and sexual harassment and abuse within their schools and districts by teachers and students and know how to create a culture in which all students feel safe.

Finally, this course should help future administrators understand how women and minorities have been left out of much of the subject matter that is taught within their schools. The relationship of language to achievement and the effects of sexist language must be part of what students in our programs learn. As administrators, they must be able to help conceptualize curriculums that cover the range of human experiences and to help teachers supplement textbooks where such absences occur.

Process

In my own experience teaching a course of this nature to prospective administrators, I have found that the most effective way to drive home the currency of the material as well as its centrality in an administrator's life is to include large segments of experiential learning. Unless students have current and local evidence that men and women and majority and minority students are treated differently in schools, many will not believe such practices occur. Therefore, I use exercises in class that require students to undertake the following activities: (a) Examine hiring practices over the past five years within their districts with regard to race and sex; (b) tape-record student-teacher interactions in their own classrooms and then analyze them, using worksheets I distribute that isolate teaching, disciplinary, and reward practices according to race and sex of student; and (c) gather information from their own students that would indicate whether or not these students hold stereotypic notions about themselves. For instance, one such exercise is to have administration students go back into their classrooms and ask their students to complete the following statement, "If I woke up tomorrow a member of the other sex, I would . . . ." The students in my class bring back the responses of their students and we analyze them according to sex of respondent. Because my students are primarily teachers preparing to be administrators and because they teach a range of ages, we have evidence within the class that students of all ages, in all kinds of classrooms, and with all types of abilities hold stereotypic views of what is appropriate for males and females. This exercise quiets any protests such as "Students today are different. They don't see the world like we did."

Implications of Race and Gender
for the Management of Schools

In addition to helping administrative students understand the role of equity in the delivery of effective schooling, departments of educational administration have a responsibility to acquaint them with the implications of race and gender for the management of schools. A number of studies of journals and textbooks in the field addressed to both theory and practice have documented that women and minorities are not the subject of these works (Nagle, Gardner, Levine, & Wolf, 1982; Schmuck, Butman, & Person, 1982; Shakeshaft & Hanson, 1986;

Tietze, Shakeshaft, & Davis, 1981). The majority of theory and practice literature is research that sees the world from the perspective of White males. If women and minorities behaved the same, were treated the same, and conceptualized the world in the same way as White males, this would not pose a problem. However, there is substantial evidence to the contrary that indicates that what is an effective management style for a White man may not be equally useful for a White woman or a minority person.

Although there are similarities in the backgrounds and experiences of male and female, minority and majority managers, it is also the case that they vary in important ways. The profiles of women and minority administrators and their history in administration are not the same as the profiles and history of White men in administration (Shakeshaft, 1987). Further, the legacy of discrimination and exclusion has shaped a world in which White women's and minorities' experiences and behaviors are often unlike those of White men.

My work on majority and minority women administrators illustrates some of these differences (Shakeshaft, 1987). In the area of supervision, for example, little has been written about the impact of gender and race on successful supervision. This issue seems particularly salient given the sex and race structuring in schools that results in an organization in which males most often supervise females and in which there are few minority people in either teaching or administration. Research tells us that the sex of participants affects what is communicated and how it is communicated, and that communication is very much affected by cultural and racial norms. The same words spoken by a male administrator have different meanings to male and female teachers, while for both women and minorities, language has the potential for becoming a "trigger" event that gets in the way of communication. Conversely, an interaction between a female principal and a male teacher is not the same as an exchange between a female principal and a female teacher. What impact might our understanding of gender and race issues have on supervision? Unfortunately, the theory and lore of the field offer few clues.

We know that men and women communicate differently and that majority and minority people may emphasize different content. It may be that in a supervisory conference in which a principal is discussing an instructional issue with a teacher, the woman participant is listening for the feeling and the man for the facts (Shakeshaft, 1987). It may also be, given what we know of the values males and females carry into their jobs in schools, that the woman is focused upon an instructional issue or a matter concerning the child, while the man has chosen to discuss an administrative problem.

Further, research tells us that there may be discomfort in communicating with a member of the other sex. Certainly, we know that male teachers exhibit more hostility in dealing with female administrators than do female teachers. We also know that women administrators have to work to get male teachers to "hear" them. Whether in job interviews or in determining job performance, women are initially evaluated less favorably than equally competent men. Knowing that women are rated as less competent or less effective than men is important for developing supervisory styles (Frasher & Frasher, 1980).

Although women are often seen in a more negative light, this view is seldom communicated to them directly. Studies tell us that male administrators are less likely to be candid with a female teacher than are female administrators. When a male subordinate makes a mistake, his supervisor tends to level with him, to "tell it like it is." When a female errs, she often is not informed; instead, the mistake is corrected by others. The results are twofold. For the male, learning takes place instantly. He gets criticism and the chance to change his behavior. He learns to deal with negative opinions of his work and has the option of improving. Females often never hear anything but praise, even if their performance is known to be less than ideal. This results in the woman being denied the opportunity for immediate feedback that would allow her to improve her performance. It also results in a woman's misconception of her abilities. If all she hears is that she is doing a good job, it comes as a shock to her when she is fired, demoted, or not promoted. Illustrative of this process is a sex discrimination case in California. A woman supervisor had been demoted because of poor performance, and it was clear from the record and from the woman's own accounts that she had not been an effective administrator. Yet all of her evaluations rated her in the highest category possible. Further, her supervisor, the assistant superintendent, revealed that he had never communicated his displeasure, but rather had "fixed her mistakes" without her knowledge. When she was demoted, she claimed sex discrimination, because she had received no feedback that would have given her another picture.

Interviews with women administrators and their supervisors indicate that this woman's case is not unusual (Shakeshaft, 1987). Women and minority people do not get feedback as often as do White men. In interviews with male superintendents and principals in which I asked them why they did not confront women, all expressed that one reason was their fear of women's tears. The threat of crying kept supervisors from giving important corrective feedback that would have allowed women to improve their performance as educators. Another reason given was fear that the woman would accuse them of sexist behavior, a reason similar to why white administrators felt uncomfortable confronting people of color about unsatisfactory work behavior. White administrators admitted that they feared they would be labeled racist if they gave critical evaluations of minority workers and so often did not offer the kind of feedback that would have given those workers an honest assessment of their output.

The example of how race and gender issues can and do affect supervisory style and effectiveness serves to show how all administration students — male and female, majority and minority — need to understand the role of race and gender in administrative style. Professors of educational administration do little to make sure this information is incorporated into the curriculum aimed at helping students become effective administrators.

In addition to including race and gender issues in courses in supervision, theory, and management, this information needs to be infused into already existing courses in a number of other areas. Law courses need to include explanations of laws related to equity. Personnel courses must make clear the laws and procedures allowable in hiring as well as equitable policies for employees in school districts. Finance courses must discuss the concept of equity and financing.

The infusion of equity concepts and the addition of material that examines the lives and management practices of women and minorities will help all students develop more effective administrative styles, styles that work with all people.

Graduate School Climate

When white women and all minorities go to college to acquire administrative degrees, they often find a less than supportive environment. The majority of professors in educational administration are white males (McCarthy, Kuh, Newell, & Iacona, 1988). A number of studies support the notion that because of historical and societal factors, white women and all minorities need more encouragement from professors than do white men. Unfortunately, they do not receive it. In the best of circumstances, they receive equal amounts of positive attention as do white men; in the majority of cases they receive less. Studies confirm the hunch that if women and minority professors were more abundant, students would receive more support. Studies of women professors, for instance, find that women professors not only provide women students with more support, they provide men students with a more positive and nurturing environment than do men professors (Oller, 1979). One woman, discussing her experiences as a graduate student, said: "Isn't it interesting that the encouragement for my present activity in the program came from women, most of whom were relative strangers" (p. 2).

Silver (1976) discusses women's further isolation in graduate school, since they cannot identify with the male students, either:

> The male students have typically been more conforming, more compatible with the existing power structure, more able to visualize themselves as part of the administration group. Thus, there are likely to be personality clashes between men and women in the graduate school situation: the women tend to be older, in many cases having raised families during the intervening years; they also tend to be more experienced and more socially deviant than the men. (p. 12)

This interaction supports Adkison's (1981) notion that "men choose to sponsor women who conform to their stereotypes" (p. 323). University professors often do not find women who are acceptable as protégées, and, when they do, they may choose women who are least likely to be competent and successful; women who are "passive and nonthreatening, or at least capable of appearing so" (p. 323).

These same kinds of patterns result in an isolating environment for minority students in administrative preparation programs. The token minority student is always aware of her of his difference in a nearly all-white classroom. Professors often feel uncomfortable working with minority students, and, even when they do, they may choose to work only with those students who mimic or embrace white culture. This leaves many minority students isolated.

A not-so-subtle barrier for women and minority graduate students is the instructional material they must read. I have already discussed the lack of appropriate materials presenting the relationship of race and gender to effective administration, but even in race- and sex-neutral areas, discussions are most often presented using male pronouns, in textbooks or films illustrated with pictures of white males.

Equity Recommendations for
Administration Preparation Programs

Administrators obviously need to be prepared for a world that contains men and women from a variety of cultures and races. It becomes even more important to understand equity issues when one takes into account the legacy of discrimination and exclusion of women and people of color from positions of power and influence in our culture. If administrative preparation programs are to prepare aspiring administrators adequately to deal with the issues, the following guidelines need to be incorporated into programs.

(1) A course on equity and schooling should be a required part of the administrative preparation curriculum. This course should include at least the following topics: personal values; conceptual, philosophical, and societal issues of equity; equity in student treatment and placement; and equity in curriculum and instructional materials.

(2) Existing courses in the administrative preparation sequence should be expanded to include women's and minorities' experiences in administration. Where materials are unavailable to address these, they should be developed. UCEA, ASCD, AASA, and other administrative organizations should be involved in helping to prepare materials that focus on the relationships of gender and race to effective management.

(3) Women and minority administrators should be brought to the classroom to discuss issues relevant to female and minority students.

(4) Where possible, women students should intern with women administrators; minority students should intern with minority administrators.

(5) The number of women and minorities on faculties of educational administration should be increased.

(6) Research on the styles of women and minority administrators should be supported and encouraged.

(7) Workshops sponsored by UCEA and NCPEA should be developed to help professors of educational administration incorporate materials on equity into their courses.

These recommendations are rather modest; however, their implementation is necessary if we hope to make a difference in the next generation of administrators.

References

Adkison, J. A. (1981). Women in school administration: A review of the research. *Review of Educational Research, 51*(3), 311-343.

Frasher, J. M., & Frasher, R. S. (1980). Sex bias in the evaluation of administrators. *Journal of Educational Administration, 18*(2), 245-253.

McCarthy, M. M., Kuh, G. D., Newell, L. J., & Iacona, C. M. (1988). *Under scrutiny: The educational administration professoriate.* Tempe, AZ: University Council for Educational Administration.

Nagle, L., Gardner, D. W., Levine, M., & Wolf, S. (1982, March). *Sexist bias in instructional supervision textbooks.* Paper presented at the annual meeting of the American Educational Research Association, New York.

Oller, C. S. (1979, April). *Differential experiences of male and female aspirants in public school administration: A closer look at perceptions within the field.* Paper presented at the annual meeting of the American Educational Research Association, San Francisco.

Schmuck, P. A., Butman, L. A., & Person, L. R. (1982, March). *Analyzing sex bias in planning and changing.* Paper presented at the annual meeting of the American Educational Research Association, New York.

Shakeshaft, C. (1987). *Women in educational administration.* Newbury Park, CA: Sage.

Shakeshaft, C., & Hanson, M. (1986). Androcentric bias in the *Educational Administration Quarterly. Educational Administration Quarterly, 22*(1), 68-92.

Silver, P. F. (1976). *Women in educational leadership: A trend discussion.* Columbus, OH: University Council for Educational Administration.

Tietze, I. N., Shakeshaft, C., & Davis, B. N. (1981, April). *Sexism in texts in educational administration.* Paper presented at the annual meeting of the American Educational Research Association, Los Angeles.

17

Teacher Preparation for Equity

GENEVA GAY

Purdue University

Traditionally, teacher education programs have operated on the assumption that certain generic competencies characterize effective classroom teaching. These are generalizable to all local school settings and to specific groups of students irrespective of their ethnic, social, and cultural backgrounds. The exceptions to this rule are students who are handicapped, gifted, or talented. Otherwise, "average" students do not require any unique preparation simply because they belong to ethnic, racial, and social groups that are not part of the dominant culture. Although more teachers from these groups are needed to serve as role models, instructionally, all students should be treated the same. This is the best way to guarantee equal educational opportunities for everyone. Implicit in these assumptions are beliefs that teaching is a value-free and culture-neutral process that is transcendent of any given social or cultural context and student population. Claims that these beliefs are grounded in solid educational research, theory, and practice do not make them any the less naive and unrealistic.

In fact, teaching is a sociocultural process. Its effectiveness with culturally different groups of students is due as much to social and cultural competence as to pedagogical capabilities. Therefore, this discussion will explain some of the skills teachers need in order to make their pedagogical efforts more functionally effective with poor and ethnic minority students, and thereby make educational success more accessible to a wider variety of students. These skills include (a) conceptualizing equity as the comparability or equivalence of learning opportunities for diverse learners instead of as the same treatment for everyone; (b) becoming consciously aware of routine teaching behaviors that militate against educational equity; and (c) learning how to make regular instructional procedures more accommodating to culturally different students. Thus *teacher preparation for equity* means learning how to differentiate the means of instruction to make high-status knowledge and academic success as accessible to culturally, ethnically, and socially different students as to students who are members of the majority culture. In the classroom, "teaching with equity means first helping children gain fluency in their natural and individual ways of knowing — ways of studying, asking, answering, understanding, cogitating, expressing, and engaging with others — and then challenging and assisting them to learn other forms to broaden their repertoires" ("Teaching Diverse Students," 1989, p. 4).

Perspective on Equity and Teacher Education

Teaching and learning involve interactions among teachers and students who are conditioned to perceive, believe, value, behave, and assign meaning to stimuli by their prior cultural experiences. The school experiences students undergo initiate them into the culture of the classroom, and serve as preparation for life in the larger society and culture. They include rituals, ceremonies, symbols, values, habits, and patterns of social relationships that form the context in which knowledge and skill learning takes place. These tend to be more attitudinal and procedural than pedagogical, but their mastery is as imperative as the academic knowledge and skills themselves. For example, teachers expect students to learn the importance of order and ranking, follow set rules of procedure and decorum, develop self-reliance and self-maintenance, compete for scarce resources, adhere to regimentation, be autonomous in personal behavior, and accept responsibility (Johnson, 1985). Frequently, mastery of these "procedural protocols" is a prerequisite of learning academic skills. Understanding the culture of the classroom and how it affects the educational opportunities of culturally different students is a logical place to begin the process of preparing teachers to be more equitable in their instructional behaviors.

The legacy of American education theory and practice is biased in favor of Eurocentric cultural practices and middle-class social standards. Embedded in this legacy are negative attitudes and behaviors toward the cultural experiences, social values, and intellectual capabilities of students from racial minority groups and low socioeconomic backgrounds. These biases and misconceptions militate against teachers who provide minority students with educational opportunities comparable to those of majority students. As Goodlad and Oakes (1988) suggest, "Deep-seated myths and prejudices regarding the distribution of ability to learn contribute strongly to the differentiation of students' access to the array of knowledge schools provide. . . . As one confronts increasing evidence of inequities, one simultaneously encounters a growing proportion of minority and economically deprived white children and youth" (p. 17).

Even when teachers try conscientiously to control their ethnic, racial, and social biases, they still may discriminate against culturally different students. The typical conceptions and criteria of instructional normalcy are culturally determined by middle-class, Anglocentric orientations. Students whose ethnic identities and cultural backgrounds predispose them toward similar standards have a distinct learning advantage over those who are different. Comparisons of the activity styles of Anglo and Afro-American students illustrate this point. Most middle-class Anglo students can perform adequately in the large group, relatively passive, and teacher-controlled activity mode typical of classroom instruction. This success is not as prevalent for Afro-Americans. Their cultural socialization is more kinesthetic, and it emphasizes multimodal, simultaneous sensory stimulation. They perform better in learning environments with highly interactive and frequently varied stimuli or activities (Boykin, 1979, 1983; Goodlad & Oakes, 1988).

These and other differences among students in personal characteristics, cultural experiences, and ethnic identities make equal treatment an untenable criterion of educational equity. Instead, educational equity should be conceptually understood as the comparability of learning opportunities and experiences to make high-status knowledge and school success more accessible to students who are diversified by culture, race, ethnicity, class, and gender. Operationally, this requires teachers to differentiate the methods and means of teaching and learning while maintaining high standards of knowledge and skill mastery for all students.

This conception of equity can be problematic for teachers because of a tendency to confuse educational means and ends and to equate differentiating instructional methods with lowering educational standards. For instance, the same value and significance attached to teaching reading skills are often extended to the materials used. Measuring academic achievement and taking norm-referenced standardized tests are interchangeable. Teaching and learning methods should be highly flexible and negotiable, depending upon who is to be taught what, where, when, and under what conditions. However, expected performance outcomes and standards of achievement are nonnegotiable. They are universally applicable to all students. While all students should be expected to master basic skills, critical thinking, and problem solving, materials and methods used to teach these skills should be diversified. The simple fact is that all students do not learn in the same way. Therefore, they cannot be taught identically and still be given comparable opportunities for quality education and academic success.

How students learn is significantly influenced by who they are ethnically, culturally, and socially. But what and whether they learn is largely determined by the kinds of opportunities and experiences available to them. Many poor and ethnic minority children have learning styles that are clearly distinct from that of Anglo middle-class students. This does not mean that their intellectual capabilities are not comparable. They are limited only to the extent that classroom teachers minimize learning expectations and opportunities. The patterns of perception, stimulus response, cue selection, and information processing (the fundamental components of learning styles) of culturally different students must be employed in instructional interactions to make knowledge and learning more accessible to them. Thus educational equity and ethnic and cultural diversity are inextricably interwoven.

Specific Program Components

Three categorical needs are essential to prepare teachers to provide educational equity for diverse learners. First, teachers need to become knowledgeable about the interactive relationships among cultural conditioning, ethnic identity, the teaching and learning process, and academic achievement. Second, they should learn how to analyze common educational practices and beliefs to determine why and how they facilitate the achievement of some students and inhibit the performance of others. Third, preparation programs should provide opportunities for teachers to practice translating knowledge about cultural diversity into action strategies for instructional reform. Each of these categorical needs has many specific programmatic implications. The scope of this chapter prevents elucidating all of them, but five of them are discussed below to clarify further the parameters of preparing teachers to make learning more equal and accessible to culturally different students. These are the management of instruction, the use of textbooks and other instructional materials, teacher attitudes and expectations about different students' abilities, teaching styles, and the assessment of student achievement.

These five elements are all part of what teachers routinely do as they work with students. Their selection is symbolic of a basic premise about how teacher education should be structured. That is, preparing teachers to work more effectively with culturally different students is more successful when proposals for change are tied directly to what is routinely done in the role of instructional leader. This emphasis counterbalances the commonly held misconception that making education more successful for diverse learners requires teachers to do something extraordinary and far beyond their regular routines. The challenge is not so much to do more as it is to perform routine functions differently in order to engage fully a wider range of students in the substantive dimensions of teaching.

Managing Instruction

One of the first steps in educating teachers for equity is to develop in them a conscious awareness of routine practices used to manage and facilitate instruction, how various students respond to these procedures, and the relationship between educational opportunities and protocols of instruction. Observing teachers in naturalistic settings, recording their behaviors, and explaining those behaviors according to some established conceptual principles are useful ways of identifying the most salient elements of the instructional process and classroom culture. Observations may be from actual classroom interactions, interviews with teachers and students, and analyses of videotapes of teaching. The function of this exercise should be to isolate teacher behaviors and other dimensions of instructional routines that prevent culturally different students from being fully engaged in teaching-learning interactions. The results will create a reality construct for assessing the feasibility of various ideas and techniques for making the instructional process more accessible to both majority and minority group students. The Cross-Cultural Outline of Education, developed by Jules Henry (1960), is a useful tool for observing and analyzing classroom culture. It includes specific elements about the focus of the educational process (values emphasized), how information is communicated (teaching methods), how students and teachers participate in the educational process (attitudes and behaviors), discontinuities in the process, what limits and facilitates the information students receive, techniques used to conduct control (discipline), the relationship between educational intents and results, and how self-concepts are reinforced.

Teachers need to understand how and why grouping practices commonly used in schools and classrooms are inherently discriminatory to racial minority and poor students. The overrepresentation of these students in low skill performance reading and math groups, special education, low-ability academic classes, and vocational education and their underrepresentation in gifted and college preparatory programs are not chance occurrences (Gay, 1989; Oakes, 1985). These assignments are the result of decisions based on biased perceptions about the distribution of intelligence and ability among students, and the use of evaluation criteria and techniques that do not capitalize on the strengths of poor Anglos, Hispanics, American Indians, Afro-Americans, and other minorities. Tests of intelligence, ability, and achievement systematically limit some students' access to knowledge by ranking and sorting out who will receive enriched educational opportunities and who will be relegated to low-level academic participation (Keating & Oakes, 1988). These inequities are transmitted through irrelevant test content, testing structures and styles, teacher attitudes, instructional quality, and program concentrations.

A disproportionate number of Afro-American, Hispanic, American Indian, and poor students are assigned to low-ability groups and receive lower status, less socially valued knowledge and skills. Instruction in low-ability groups tends to emphasize rote learning, workbooks and kits, easy materials, discipline, and social adjustment skills. Furthermore, academic mobility is highly constrained since it is virtually impossible for students to move from low-ability to high-ability program placements (Chunn, 1987-88; Keating & Oakes, 1988; Oakes, 1985). These instructional biases derive from assumptions that racial minority and poor students have limited intellectual capabilities because of their ethnic identities, social status, and cultural backgrounds. Asian Americans are an exception to this pattern. They are often perceived as a monolith of model students and high achievers. This positive stereotype causes Asian American students who need corrective and remedial interventions, such as special education and basic skill repair, to be overlooked and underserved (Yu, Doi, & Chang, 1986).

At the other end of the spectrum is the underrepresentation of poor and minority students in high-ability, gifted and talented, and college-preparatory programs. Thus they are denied access to the instructional benefits usually associated with these programs. These include higher-quality instruction, higher teacher expectations for performance, better qualified and more conscientious teachers, lower student-teacher ratios, better materials and resources, more instructional time devoted to academic tasks, and concentration on higher-order and more socially valued skills such as critical thinking, independent questioning, and decision making (Chunn, 1987-88; Keating & Oakes, 1988; Morgan, 1977; Oakes, 1985; Persell, 1977; Rosenbaum, 1976).

Tracking of this kind is a common phenomenon in most public schools. Whether done formally through school policy or informally through teacher attitudes, expectations, and management expediency, the effects are the same. The assignment of students to instructional program options perpetuates social biases and inequities that exist in the larger society (Morgan, 1977). This situation can be rectified, and more students given greater access to equal status knowledge, if teachers learn (a) to use a wider variety of multimodal tools and techniques to diagnose students' needs and abilities, (b) to clarify their own attitudes and values about the functional effects of cultural pluralism in teaching and learning, (c) to develop more positive expectations about the educational rights and capabilities of culturally different learners, and (d) to replace tracking with different forms of heterogeneous grouping for instruction. These emphases should be complemented with skills in using alternative instructional arrangements, such as heterogeneous and multiage grouping, cooperative learning, peer teaching, and self-paced contract learning.

Research shows that "when the classroom is structured in a way that allows students to work cooperatively on learning tasks, students benefit academically as well as socially" (Slavin, 1987, p. 26). Cooperative learning strategies improve academic achievement in a variety of grade levels and subjects, interracial relations, relationships between handicapped and normal-progressing students, self-esteem, liking for school, and students' feelings of control over their own fate in school. The effects of cooperative learning are not limited to low-achieving students, do not compromise the performance of high achievers, and are particularly strong for Black and Hispanic students regardless of their achievement levels (Cohen, 1986; Slavin, 1987). The alternative methods and general techniques for designing cooperative learning experiences offered by Slavin (1983b, 1987) and Cohen (1986), and how to modify these for maximal effect with diverse students, should be essential components of teacher preparation for equity.

Textbook Use

Another routine element of classroom instruction that can be either an obstacle or a conduit to educational equity is that of the textbooks used in teaching. Textbooks hold a virtual monopoly on the contents of instruction and the value attached to what is taught. They are the single most frequently used instructional resource: 75-90% of all classroom instruction is based on textbooks (Davis, Ponder, Burlbaw, Garza-Lubeck, & Moss, 1986; Woodward, Elliott, & Nagel, 1986). Only occasionally do teachers deviate from information, assignments, discussions, activities, and test-related items prescribed by textbooks. In most classrooms the curriculum and the textbook are indistinguishable. This is true irrespective of subject area or skill being taught, or school level (Powell & Garcia, 1985).

When textbooks do not give comparable treatment to the heritages, experiences, perspectives, and contributions of all ethnic, cultural, and social groups in the United States, they practice intellectual discrimination and educational inequity. This is accomplished in at least two major ways. First, the omission of culturally pluralistic content distorts disciplinary truth and social reality. The deleterious effects of these distortions and omissions are felt by all students in varying degrees and differing manifestations. Children of color learn to feel alienated and inferior when exposed to learning environments and instructional materials that do not affirm their background experiences. Majority students learn a false sense of superiority, and are insulated from the realities of an increasingly pluralistic world. Second, biased textbooks are not of equal relevance and utility to all students. The information presented, which composes the context for the mastery of academic skills, is not as meaningful to the life experiences and frames of reference of poor, Afro-American, Asian American, Hispanic, or American Indian students as it is for middle-class Anglo students. Since interest appeal and relevance of materials used for instruction have a positive effect upon skill mastery (Au & Jordan, 1981), textbooks that do not include cultural diversity create unequal access to learning for diverse students.

Although some real progress has been made over the last two decades in making textbooks more inclusive of social, cultural, ethnic, and gender diversity, they are still far from flawless. Minority groups are not portrayed as accurately or comprehensively as they should be; residues of gender stereotyping persist; urban life is stigmatized as chaotic, violent, and destructive; and the social experiences included tend to cluster close to the middle-class, suburban ideal.

Three recent studies document these trends. Davis et al. (1986) conclude their study of 31 secondary U.S. history textbooks with these observations: "Overall, treatment of Hispanics, Asians, and American Indians perpetuates their invisible roles in building this nation. . . . Similarly, women . . . must be recognized more than these books do for their impressive and continuing contributions" (p. 10). Powell and Garcia (1985) analyzed visual illustrations in 7 commonly used elementary science textbooks. Their results indicate that female children are represented with greater frequency than males. Adult females are shown in a variety of science and nonscience careers, but not as frequently as males. Minority adults and children are represented less frequently than nonminorities, and the minority adults are rarely shown in science-related roles. The majority of the 12 secondary economics textbooks included in a study by Ellington (1986) do not deal realistically and in depth with the economic realities of minority groups. They tend to ignore ethnic groups that are not prospering in the American economic system, do not establish any direct relationship between the ethnic photographs used and the topics discussed, and contain no analytical passages about Afro-Americans and Hispanics in the narrative content. These books fail to meet standards of pedagogical rigor with respect to the treatment of minorities because "the greater the amount of text material where readers compare, contrast and analyze cause and effect relationships, the more students learn about a given subject; the greater the correlation between text photographs and narrative, the better the overall level of student understanding of subject matter" (Ellington, 1986, p. 66).

Students who do not see and hear their ethnic and cultural groups portrayed in positive, significant, and vital roles in instructional materials and processes face an additional barrier to learning. A major conduit through which learning occurs becomes as abstract as the skills to be mastered. Therefore, diverse students have the dual task of finding personal meaning in unfamiliar materials and learning the skills being taught. Majority students can concentrate their efforts only on learning the skills, since the instructional materials are compatible with their cultures and experiences. In addition to making skill mastery more difficult for culturally different learners, biased textbooks militate against educational equity in another significant way. They transmit a very potent symbolic message that the cultures and life experiences of some groups are more significant and worthy than others. Knowledge that is primarily monocultural limits the opportunities for culturally diverse students to confirm and improve their individual and communal self-images (Swartz, 1989). When internalized by poor and minority students, these negative messages can have a destructive impact upon their feelings of personal competence, their academic effort, and their actual achievement.

Teacher preparation programs can facilitate instructional equity by teaching techniques for analyzing and evaluating textbooks for cultural, racial, and social bias, making instructional materials more culturally fair, and developing new materials that are inclusive of the cultural diversity that exists in American society and the world. Familiarity with the existing research on textbook evaluations will provide (a) valuable case study examples on how and why textbooks discriminate against different groups of people, (b) models of how to recognize biases in content, and (c) tested criteria to use in evaluating textbooks. Three such reference sources are *Looking at History* (Davis et al., 1986), *Biased Textbooks* (Weitzman & Rizzo, 1974), and the *Ethnic Studies Materials Analysis Instrument* (Social Science Education Consortium, 1975).

The practical application of these skills requires a solid knowledge base about the life-styles, heritages, cultures, and contributions of different ethnic, racial, and social groups. Operationally, this means that prospective teachers should take humanities, social science, and fine arts courses that deal specifically with cultural diversity. Such courses might include ethnic histories, cultural anthropology, sociolinguistics, cultural communications, ethnic literature, developmental and social psychology of ethnic groups, and sociology of ethnicity. Teachers should also take culturally pluralistic content courses within their subject matter concentrations, such as ethnic politics and economics for social studies majors; Afro-American, Hispanic, and Asian American literature for English majors; and ethnic contributions in the sciences for natural sciences majors.

Teacher Attitudes and Invitations to Learning

Extensive research (Dusek & Joseph, 1983; Good & Brophy, 1984; Purkey, 1978) and experiential anecdotes attest to how teacher expectations minimize the learning opportunities of some students and maximize those of others. If teachers believe students are academically capable and socially desirable, they create learning situations that challenge those students' abilities, facilitate their performance, and celebrate their achievement. Conversely, those who believe students are intellectually limited and socially undesirable tend to have lower performance expectations, provide less challenging instruction, create fewer opportunities to participate in qualitative interactions, offer less praise for performance, and give more criticism for failure. A significant pattern of these attitudes and behaviors occurs along ethnic, racial, economic, and social lines. Poor, Hispanic, American Indian, and Afro-American students are asked fewer questions about the substantive content being taught, given less wait time for responses, and offered fewer prompts and cues to elicit response clarification and elaboration. Children who are perceived to be physically unattractive and who are dialect speakers also are often perceived to have less academic ability (Dusek & Joseph, 1983; Gay, 1974; Good & Brophy, 1984; Greenbaum, 1985; U.S. Commission on Civil Rights, 1973).

Negative teacher attitudes and expectations, or "protocols of interactive behavior" (Chunn, 1987-88), toward culturally different students create serious "disinvitations to learning" (Purkey, 1978). Students can also be disinvited from learning by being constantly overlooked; through labeling and grouping patterns; by disciplinary practices that remove them from the substantive core of instruction; by teacher behavior that embarrasses, frustrates, or alienates them; and through the use of instructional materials, teaching styles, and evaluation procedures that do not tap into their personal strengths. When students are rejected for simply being who they are, their very sense of worth is called into question. Frequently these disinviting attitudes and expectations toward economically disadvantaged and ethnic minority youths are so deeply entrenched in instructional behaviors that teachers are not conscious of their existence. Yet their detrimental effects upon educational opportunities and access to high-status knowledge are astronomical. They block equal access to the instructional process by withholding teacher endorsement, lowering performance expectations, creating personal insecurities in students (Purkey, 1978), and exposing them to lower-status academic knowledge and skills.

By comparison, invitations to learning imply that students are capable, valuable, and expected to learn, and that teachers are conscientious about facilitating their maximum achievement. They function as conduits to higher performance by affirming personal worth, building personal confidence, transmitting teacher confidence in student capabilities, and providing entry into the heart of classroom interactions, where the essence of instruction resides.

Educational equity can be advanced by sensitizing teachers to the characteristic traits of learning disinvitations and by helping them to develop skills in invitational teaching. Four specific techniques should be employed to achieve these goals:

(1) using research findings, personal observations, and anecdotal records to document and describe different teaching attitudes, expectations, and behaviors that constitute invitations and disinvitations to learning;

(2) practicing techniques for observing, recording, and analyzing learning invitations and disinvitations exhibited in culturally pluralistic classroom interactions;

(3) determining what constitutes appropriate invitations to learning for various kinds of culturally different students; and

(4) developing and practicing strategies for making teaching more invitational for culturally different students.

Instructional Styles

The implications of the instructional style commonly used in classrooms for providing equal access to education constitute another major component of teacher preparation for equity. Most teachers teach as they have been taught, according to established precedent, or in ways that are consistent with how they learn best — that is, their own learning modalities. Learning modalities are channels through which individuals receive, process, and retain information. They are composed of sensations, perceptions, cue selections, and memory (Barbe & Swassing, 1979; Shade, 1982). The major kinds of learning modalities are visual, auditory, and kinesthetic.

The models, precedents, and modalities that shape classroom teaching styles have similar structural features, participation patterns, and content emphases. They express a preference for visual learning and are manifested in the form of didactic teaching. Telling, lecturing, and monitoring homework and seatwork predominate (Keating & Oakes, 1988). Teaches do most of the talking, control and direct the learning activities, and unilaterally decide who will participate in instructional exchanges (when and under what conditions). Students are expected to do as they are told, work individually, compete for rewards and recognitions, and engage in interactions in a serialized fashion (Allameh, 1986; Boykin, 1983; West, 1984).

These interactional patterns, which Philips (1985) calls a "switchboard participation structure," reflect mainstream Anglocentric values of order, authority, status, power, and interpersonal relations. Students whose presentational styles, participation structures, and learning modalities are compatible with those teachers use have more access to knowledge and learning than students with different interactional styles. Students violate fewer instructional protocols in the act of learning, and, therefore, receive more invitations to engage in the substance of teaching (Barbe & Swassing, 1979; Boggs, Watson-Gegeo, & Mcmillen, 1985).

The cultural experiences of many economically poor and racial minority students emphasize interactional styles and stimulus-response patterns that translate into auditory and kinesthetic learning modalities. They have to adjust their personal interactional styles to the classroom norm *before* they can effectively attend to the demands of academic tasks. Thus for culturally different students to succeed in school, social competence must precede academic competence (Holliday, 1985). These dual demands can seriously impede access to equal status knowledge and school success by significantly increasing the incidence of poor and racial minority youths being disinvited from learning.

Six components should be included in teacher education to correct the disparities in educational opportunities caused by incompatibilities between teaching and learning styles. Information should be provided in each of the following areas:

(1) values and behaviors that characterize commonly used instructional styles
(2) salient characteristics of different cultural groups' participation structures, performance styles, and learning modalities
(3) how to diagnose learning modality preferences and strengths
(4) the modalities through which different students learn best, and which instructional styles are most compatible with them
(5) how to avoid confusing failure to comply with the social and structural protocols of teaching and learning with intellectual limitations
(6) how to modify dominant classroom participation structures and instructional styles to accommodate culturally different students

There are several available instruments and procedures for diagnosing performance styles and learning modalities that are useful for preservice teachers. Among these are the Swassing-Barbe Modality Index (Barbe & Swassing, 1979), the Learning Style Inventory (Dunn & Dunn, 1975), and the Field Sensitive/Field Independent Behavior Observation Instruments (Ramirez & Castaneda, 1974). Prospective teachers should also have the opportunity to practice alternative teaching strategies, such as cooperative learning, role playing, tutoring, team learning, demonstrating, coaching, problem solving, and nondirective teaching (Keating & Oakes, 1988).

An impressive body of literature is emerging that describes characteristics of culture-specific participation structures and performance styles, and the effects of these upon educational opportunities and academic achievement. It constitutes a fundamental knowledge base for helping teachers to understand better how culturally different students go about the process of learning and demonstrating what they have learned. This literature deserves a prominent place in teacher education curricula. It includes Kochman's (1981) and Smitherman's (1977) analyses of Afro-American and Anglo communication styles; the research of Au and Jordan (1981), Boggs et al. (1985), Boykin (1982), and Foster (1987) on the positive effects of matching teaching styles with the learning styles of culturally different students; Grossman's (1984) recommendations on how to use the cultural characteristics of Hispanic students in classroom instruction, management, and performance assessment; Sue's (1973) and Tong's (1978) portrayals of Asian American cultural values that may facilitate adjustment to the instructional procedures and academic achievement; and the conflicts that often occur in cross-cultural interactions between mainstream and minority individuals depicted in the video series *Valuing Diversity* (Copeland-Griggs, 1987; although the specific incidents portrayed take place in business settings, the general principles and messages they symbolize are applicable to teaching and learning, too).

Student Evaluation

The extent to which the techniques teachers use to assess student achievement reflect diversities in performance styles and learning modalities is a strong indication of equal access to learning. Certainly, using a single form of evaluation, or even many, with a style, focus, and content that are predominantly visual, didactic, and Anglocentric discriminates against students with different cultural heritages, learning modalities, and performance styles.

The device most commonly used to evaluate student achievement, and to direct subsequent instruction, is pencil-and-paper tests. Whether norm or criterion referenced, standardized or teacher-made, local or national, the standards of performance acceptability on tests are based on criteria that are not significantly influenced by culturally diverse input. Achievement is measured primarily by mastery of facts and isolated details. Little emphasis is placed on process skills such as problem solving, critical thinking, analysis, and creative expression. Moreover, teachers tend to believe that how students perform on tests is entirely a function of their intelligence or skill mastery. In fact, these are only two of many types of variables that influence test scores. Others include the technical quality of the test itself, who is being tested, and the test-taking process. Specific human factors affecting test performance include race, gender, socioeconomic status, motivation, prior experiences, ways of thinking, personal interests and learning preferences, and styles of performance presentation. Among the environmental or contextual factors affecting test scores are the expectations and beliefs of the tester, physical surroundings, the psychoemotional dispositions of the test takers, and the mode, timing, and pacing of the test presentation (Johnson, 1987-88).

Students whose performance styles match the structural, perceptual, and sensory priorities (e.g., didactic, visual, and cognitive) of tests used by teachers demonstrate higher levels of content and skill mastery than those whose presentational styles differ. The latter category includes students whose cultural backgrounds emphasize auditory, kinesthetic, tactile, gestalt, and affective sensations in learning and demonstrating competence (such as Afro-Americans, American Indians, Hispanics, and poor students). Having to demonstrate the knowledge and skills they have acquired in a performance style that is not compatible with their own culturally induced ones can impede mastery and lead to misevaluations. Thus what often appears to be academic inability may in fact be context or procedural problems caused by the fact that the students are unable to shift successfully from one style of performance to another. For example, the same Afro-American students who exhibit high levels of verbal artistry and dexterity in social situations may not be able to construct simple sentences when asked to write a composition. American Indian youths who know, in great detail, the intricate vegetation patterns of local forests may be unable to apply the classification system of plants taught in a science class.

To avoid perpetuating the inequities inherent in using traditional intelligence, ability, and achievement tests to assess student knowledge and skill mastery, teachers should be taught how to design, evaluate, and use alternative evaluation techniques. Several guidelines should be applied to direct these efforts. First, teachers should be able to teach diverse students style-shifting, modality-adjustment, and test-taking skills so that they can function better on traditional evaluation tools. Second, teachers should learn how to select alternative evaluation techniques that are more auditory, tactile, and kinesthetic. Third, the organizational structures provided for students to demonstrate performance should be varied to include individuals, small groups, teams, and large groups. Fourth, continuous progress reporting on both traditional performance styles and academic content achievement expedites learning for culturally different students by providing early diagnosis and treatment of problems. Fifth, computers, videotapes, and tape recorders can accommodate kinesthetic and auditory performance styles more easily than written tests.

Since the mystique and aura surrounding testing are so strong, teacher preparation programs should apply a fourfold approach in this dimension of education for equity. Programs should clarify the value and legitimacy of using alternative evaluation techniques with culturally different students, distinguish variability in methods of assessment from commonality of performance expectations, identify specific techniques that are appropriate for use with diverse learners, and incorporate the practice of analyzing, using, and interpreting different evaluation devices. Some techniques that are potentially more effective with students from various ethnic, cultural, and social backgrounds are sociodramas, role playing, behavior observations, oral testing, interviews, demonstrations, creative expressions, anecdotal records, and videotape logs of progressional skill development. This variety provides students with auditory and kinesthetic learning modalities better opportunities to demonstrate their substantive achievement without being unnecessarily handicapped by performance structure and style features of the evaluation tools being used.

Conclusion

The suggestions discussed above for preparing teachers to provide better access to learning for culturally different students illustrate some basic value beliefs and assumptions about the interactions among culture, ethnicity, and education. One of these beliefs is that many of the things teachers routinely do in the act of teaching interfere with diverse students' equal access to knowledge and opportunities to learn. Another belief is that techniques for delivering instructional equity should be strategically placed throughout the routine components of teacher preparation programs. Explorations of philosophies of education should include the additional factors of how race, ethnicity, gender, and class affect notions about what knowledge is worth acquiring, how it is best acquired, and the role of schools in this process. Questions about their applicability to diverse students should be integral to the teaching of psychological principles and theories of human development, cognition, motivation, and learning. No student should complete a teacher education program without having acquired a knowledge base about the contributions of different cultural groups to his or her area of subject-matter specialization. Various methods of teaching, selecting instructional materials, diagnosing students' needs, and evaluating achievement should be scrutinized for the appropriateness of their use with different cultural, social, and ethnic students. These integrative efforts need to be complemented by separate courses that deal more comprehensively with teaching diverse students. Among these might be cross-cultural counseling, multicultural curriculum, culturally fair testing, and methods and materials for teaching cultural diversity in content areas.

Finally, the ideas and arguments presented in this chapter assume that teacher education programs value cultural diversity, are committed to change, and are willing to hold themselves and their graduates accountable for quality instruction appropriate for the students being taught. These value orientations must permeate the policies of admission and graduation, the variety of learning experiences available, and the knowledge and skills acquired. They are prerequisite conditions of teacher accountability for instructional equity in elementary and secondary classrooms.

References

Allameh, J. (1986). *Learning about culturally different populations.* (ERIC Document Reproduction Service No. ED 273 137)

Au, K.H.P., & Jordan, C. (1981). Teaching reading to Hawaiian children: Finding a culturally appropriate solution. In H. T. Trueba, G. P. Guthrie, & K.H.P. Au (Eds.), *Culture and the bilingual classroom: Studies in classroom ethnography* (pp. 139-152). Rowley, MA: Newbury House.

Barbe, W. B., & Swassing, R. H. (1979). *Teaching through modality strengths: Concepts and practice.* Columbus, OH: Zaner-Bloser.

Boggs, S. T., Watson-Gegeo, K., & Mcmillen, G. (1985). *Speaking, relating, and learning: A study of Hawaiian children at home and at school.* Norwood, NJ: Ablex.

Boykin, A. W. (1979). Psychological/behavioral verve in academic task performance: Pretheoretical considerations. In A. W. Boykin, A. J. Franklin, & J. F. Yates (Eds.), *Research directions for Black psychologists* (pp. 351-367). New York: Russell Sage Foundation.

Boykin, A. W. (1982). Task variability and the performance of Black and White school-children: Vervistic explorations. *Journal of Black Studies, 12,* 469-485.

Boykin, A. W. (1983). The academic performance of Afro-American children. In J. T. Spencer (Ed.), *Achievement and achievement motives: Psychological and sociological approaches* (pp. 321-371). San Francisco: W. H. Freeman.

Chunn, E. W. (1987-88). Sorting Black students for success and failure: The inequity of ability grouping and tracking. *Urban League Review, 11,* 93-106.

Cohen, E. G. (1986). *Designing groupwork: Strategies for the heterogeneous classroom.* New York: Teachers College Press.

Copeland-Griggs, Inc. (Producer). (1987). *Valuing diversity* [video series]. San Francisco: Author.

Davis, O. L., Jr., Ponder, G., Burlbaw, L, M,, Garza-Lubeck, M , & Moss, J. (1986). *Looking at history: A review of major U.S. history textbooks.* Washington, DC: People for the American Way.

Dunn, R., & Dunn, K. (1975). *Learning style inventory.* Lawrence, KS: Price Systems.

Dusek, J.. & Joseph, G. (1983). The bases of teacher expectancies: A meta-analysis. *Journal of Educational Psychology, 75.* 327-346.

Ellington, L. (1986). Blacks and Hispanics in high school economics texts. *Social Education, 50,* 64-67.

Foster, M. (1987). *It's cookin' now: A performance analysis of the speech events of a Black teacher in an urban community college.* Paper presented at the Symposium on Afro-American Perspectives on Issues of Learning, Ethnicity and Identity, at the annual meeting of the American Anthropological Association, Chicago.

Gay, G. (1974). *Differential dyadic interactions of Black and White teachers with Black and White pupils in recently desegregated classrooms: A function of teacher and pupil ethnicity.* Washington, DC: National Institute of Education.

Gay, G. (1989). Ethnic minorities and educational equality. In J. A. Banks & C.A.M. Banks (Eds.), *Multicultural education: Issues and perspectives* (pp. 167-188). Boston: Allyn & Bacon.

Good, T. L., & Brophy, J. E. (1984). *Looking in classrooms* (3rd ed.). New York: Harper & Row.

Goodlad, J. L., & Oakes, J. (1988). We must offer equal access to knowledge. *Educational Leadership, 45,* 16-22.

Greenbaum, P. E. (1985). Nonverbal differences in communication style between American Indian and Anglo elementary classrooms. *American Educational Research Journal, 22,* 101-115.

Grossman, H. (1984). *Educating Hispanic students: Cultural implications for instruction, classroom management, counseling and assessment.* Springfield. IL: Charles C Thomas.

Henry, J. (1960). A cross-cultural outline of education. *Current Anthropology, 1,* 267-305.

Holliday, B. G. (1985). Towards a model of teacher-child transactional processes affecting Black children's academic achievement. In M. B. Spencer, G. K. Brookins, & W. R. Allen (Eds.), *Beginnings: The social and affective development of Black children* (pp. 117-130). Hillsdale, NJ: Lawrence Erlbaum.

Johnson, N. B. (1985). *West Haven: Classroom culture in a rural elementary school.* Chapel Hill: University of North Carolina Press.

Johnson, S. T. (1987-88). Test fairness and bias: Measuring academic achievement among Black youth. *Urban League Review, 11,* 76-92.

Keating, P., & Oakes, J. (1988). *Access to knowledge: Breaking down school barriers to learning.* Denver: Education Commission of the States.

Kitano, H.H.L., & Kikumura, A. (1980). The Japanese American family. In R. Endo, S. Sue, & N. N. Wagner (Eds.), *Asian-Americans: Social and psychological perspectives* (pp. 3-16). Palo Alto, CA: Science & Behavior.

Kochman, T. (1981). *Black and White styles in conflict.* Chicago: University of Chicago Press.

Morgan, E. P. (1977). *Inequality in classroom learning: Schooling and democratic citizenship.* New York: Praeger.

Oakes, J. (1985). *Keeping tracks: How schools structure inequality.* New Haven, CT: Yale University Press.

Persell, C. H. (1977). *Education and inequality: A theoretical and empirical synthesis.* New York: Free Press.

Philips, S. U. (1985). Participation structures and communicative competence: Warms Springs children in community and classroom. In C. B. Cazden, V. P. John, & D. Hymes (Eds.), *Functions of language in the classroom* (pp. 370-394). Prospect Heights, IL: Waveland.

Powell, R. R., & Garcia, J. (1985). The portrayal of minorities and women in selected elementary science series. *Journal of Research in Science Teaching, 22,* 519-533.

Purkey, W. W. (1978). *Inviting school success: A self-concept approach to teaching and learning.* Belmont, CA: Wadsworth.

Ramirez, M., III, & Castaneda, A. (1974). *Cultural democracy, bicognitive development and education.* New York: Academic Press.

Rosenbaum, J. E. (1976). *Making equality: The hidden curriculum in high school tracking.* New York: John Wiley.

Shade, B. J. (1982). Afro-American cognitive style: A variable in school success? *Review of Educational Research, 52,* 219-244.

Slavin, R. E. (1983a). *Cooperative learning.* New York: Longman.

Slavin, R. E. (1983b). *Student team learning: An overview and practical guide.* Washington, DC: National Education Association.

Slavin, R. E. (1987). *Cooperative learning: Student teams* (2nd ed.). Washington, DC; National Education Association.

Smitherman, G. (1977). *Talkin' and testifyin': The language of Black America.* Boston: Houghton Mifflin.

Social Science Education Consortium. (1975). *Ethnic studies materials analysis instrument.* Boulder, CO: Author.

Sue, D. W. (1973). Ethnic identity: The impact of two cultures on the psychological development of Asians in America. In S. Sue & N. N. Wagner (Eds.), *Asian-American psychological perspective* (pp. 140-149). Ben Lomond, CA: Science & Behavior.

Swartz, E. (1989). *Multicultural curriculum development: A practical approach to curriculum development at the school level.* Rochester, NY: Rochester City School District.

Teaching diverse students with equity: A "Tomorrow's School Seminar." (1989). *Holmes Group Forum, 2,* 4-8.

Tong, B. R. (1978). Warriors and victims: Chinese American sensibility and learning styles. In L. Morris, G. Sather, & S. Scull (Eds.), *Extracting learning styles from social/cultural diversity: A study of five American minorities* (pp. 70-93). Norman, OK: Southwest Teacher Corps Network.

U.S. Commission on Civil Rights. (1973). *Teachers and students.* (Mexican American Education Study, Report No. 5: Differences in teacher interaction with Mexican American and Anglo students). Washington, DC: Author.

Weitzman, L. J., & Rizzo, D. (1974). *Biased textbooks: Images of males and females in school textbooks in five subject areas.* (ERIC Document Reproduction Service No. ED 119 114)

West, B. E. (1984). *Culture before ethnicity.* (ERIC Document Reproduction Service No. ED 258 716)

Woodward, A., Elliott, D. L., & Nagel, K. C. (1986). Beyond textbooks in elementary social studies. *Social Education, 50,* 50-53.

Yu, E.S.H., Doi, M., & Chang, C. F. (1986). *Asian American education in Illinois: A review of the data.* Springfield: Illinois State Board of Education.

18

Teacher Education
That Enhances Equity

JAMES B. BOYER

Kansas State University

Teacher education in the United States has had a long and legendary history. It is one of academia's most significant elements, in that the education of the American teacher is the gateway to literacy, the framework from which young children gain a view of life, and the channel through which almost all thinking is influenced. Other than the electronic media, no group of professionals influences the young minds of America more than do classroom teachers. The education of the classroom teacher, then, becomes more and more significant as the complexity of American life continues to increase.

Teacher education is broad and multifaceted. No longer is it limited to the ivory tower of the university. Almost every community in America now has televised university-level courses for credit, correspondence course availability, in-service credits for upgrading, staff development activities, and scores of other channels for continuous education. Initial teacher certification in the United States, however, is primarily acquired as a result of university- or college-level credit hours — earned in rather traditional degree programs made up of approximately 125 to 135 credits built into three blocks. In reviewing most of those programs over a 20-year period as a teacher educator, I have found them woefully traditional and almost 100% Eurocentric in perspective; they also seem to assume that all who come for preparation as teachers represent a single profile.

Not only have many of our programs reflected subtle messages of traditional conceptualizations, but they have been viewed as detached, separate entities through which one can travel without being philosophically touched. There are courses, experiences, and readings, and clinical settings and laboratory exploration and experimentation, but the degree to which these experiences have left teacher education candidates limited in the areas of ethnic literacy, racial and cultural contributions, and a philosophical respect for human diversity leaves much to be desired.

The reform movement, particularly the massive response to *A Nation at Risk* (National Commission on Excellence in Education, 1983) and many reports that followed, has failed to address changes in the American demographic picture, changes in the perspective of those in the American population who happen not to have a European heritage, and the age of consumerism in which we now find ourselves. Not until such reports as Harold Hodgkinson's *All One System* (1985), the Carnegie Foundation for the Advancement of Teaching's *Mixed Blessings* (1988), the National Alliance of Black School Educators' *Saving the African American Child* (1984), and the National Coalition of Advocates for Students' *Barriers to Excellence* (1985) were published did we begin to notice the major changes occurring in the American consumer population.

These changes and their implications suggest that teacher education must be upgraded if it is to keep up with the demands of a society such as ours. Demographic changes and concurrent assessments of achievement all present a bleak picture of success in the 25 largest school districts in the United States that employ teachers as they complete initial preparation for a teacher's license. Most strikingly, the number of Caucasian or majority teachers who will be teaching people who are racially or ethnically different from themselves will continue to rise dramatically. To underscore this reality, I would like to share a few statistics with you:

- As of 1984, the number of children per Cuban American woman of child-bearing age was 1.3; per Euro-American woman, 1.7; per Puerto Rican woman, 2.1; per African American woman, 2.4; and per Mexican American woman, 2.9.
- As of 1985, the median age of all Euro-American women was 31; of African American women, 25; and of all Hispanic women, 22.
- As of 1987-88, California had a 52% school enrollment of children who were something other than European-White (often called "minority enroll-

ment"); Texas had 47% such enrollment. In half of the states, 25% of the enrollment is now made up of culturally, racially, or ethnically different students. All 25 of the largest school districts in the United State have such learners at levels above 50%.

Among other general data that affect the way in which teacher education must upgrade service delivery, we find the following:

- Asians represent 44% of all immigrants currently admitted into the United States.
- The average Japanese American in school today speaks English as a first language. However, the Indochinese, for the most part, do not have English as a first language, and must be served with bilingual education, English as a second language, or multilingual programs. There are 31 million Americans for whom English is not a first language (Olsen, 1987).
- New York City's population is now 30% foreign-born (Copeland-Griggs, 1988).
- Detroit is 63% Black, and there are 8,000 people named Hmong in Minneapolis and St. Paul.
- Many of our cities are more multicultural, multiracial, and multilingual than they have ever been, and the trends suggest that there is no reversal in sight.

Traditional Patterns in Teacher Education

Historically, teacher education programs at the undergraduate level have included the following three steps:

(1) *lower division:* core curriculum, general education, or preprofessional
(2) *upper division:* professional education courses, readings, exposure
(3) internships and clinical or laboratory experiences as prerequisites to initial service

Considering the above-mentioned changes in the American populace, teachers must be prepared to meet the challenge — not with fear, anxiety, frustration, or discussions of "standards" (in the traditional ivory-tower sense), but with the expectation of a celebration as we improve teacher education to serve a pluralistic population. Equity and ethnic diversity both require new analyses of programmatic delivery to include procedural reviews, substantive content, intensive synthesis of the human service delivery role of the American teacher, and professional academic endeavors of all kinds.

The State of Multicultural Emphasis
in Teacher Education: 1989

Considering the wave of the future, it seems that course experiences, instruction, research, and programs designed for service will all be in need of upgrading. Twenty years ago, many people were struggling with the concept of racial desegregation. Over the past twenty years, a few professionals at the advocacy level have attempted to educate the profession on multicultural education, its philosophy, its theoretical framework, its research, and its role in the mosaic of American education. Today, this effort is still under way. Multicultural education is not a stopgap for racially motivated crises, but a serious area of academic study in which the teacher candidate must confront stereotypes, race relations, ethnic relations, language diversity, academic ethnocentrism, ethnic literacy, and the consuming social ills of racism and sexism.

Some program planners have attempted to respond to the need for multicultural teacher education with one required course or one elective course, by infusing the subject into foundation or curriculum courses, or by simply ignoring its reality. This has resulted in a resurgence of racist behaviors on U.S. college campuses—where prospective teachers are undergoing preparation to enter America's classrooms, which are populated by culturally different children. Using terms like *systems approach* and *monitored quality in program design*, we have ended up with programs that are ethnically homogeneous and that tend not to address cross-racial, cross-ethnic teaching and learning at all. According to the National Coalition of Advocates for Students (1985), in 1980-81, nearly 25% of all public school teachers in the United States had students with limited English proficiency in classes, but only 3% of those teachers had formal academic preparation or language instruction to enable them to teach their LEP students. The overriding assumption of many programs of teacher education is that different backgrounds and language constitute deficits to be corrected rather than strengths upon which to build.

In a recent study, Tracy, Sheehan, and McArdle (1988) report that stakeholders in teacher education programs prefer status quo programs when asked about such factors as alternate certification, fifth-year programs, and additional content area studies. It is interesting to note that in this report no mention is made of the critical areas of cross-racial and cross-ethnic teaching and learning.

The Age of Academic Consumerism

Because even teacher education candidates of my generation were almost always prepared with a European curriculum, more than 85% of the American school curriculum taught is about the beauty of European factors — including Bach, Beethoven, Brahms and the wonders of Shakespearian literature and drama. As a result, little is known about the three or four major groups of Americans who do not have European ancestry, and whose motivation to study in school can be directly tied to the nature of content, attitude, and experiences that provide some degree of ancestral connectedness.

In this age of American academic consumerism, culturally different students are beginning to demand a new kind of academic/ethnic empowerment. They will no longer adopt a European perspective without any vocal reaction. It is now understood that one needs one's own cultural, ethnic, and gender reinforcement in negotiating the curriculum of any endeavor. The same is true of teacher education curriculum. (The case of the student body at Gallaudet College — a college for the deaf — rising up and demanding a deaf college president, as they did last year, is a major example of the kind of consumerism that is under way.)

The curriculum/instructional factors that are available are somewhat different from those that are accessible. What is mandated is deliberate in American teacher education — we are very organized. We have reached the period in our academic and social history when those learners who are not psychologically accommodated are choosing to walk away from programs rather than experience cultural and ethnic assault. The professorship that has assumed instruction expertise and sophistication for all students is now being assessed seriously by this culturally different population who will make up almost 50% of students in public schools in just a few years.

Teacher Education's Responsibility
for Instructional Discrimination

Instructional discrimination can be found in any pedagogical act, practice, or behavior that results in unfair or inappropriate response to the varied learning styles of students. Further, the assumption that persons learn most effectively from listening to the teacher — regardless of what that teacher represents in ethnicity, culture, language, race, or gender — constitutes instructional discrimination. Equal instructional opportunity or equal learning opportunity results when varied teaching approaches are employed so that varied learning styles are accommodated (Boyer & Boyer, 1975).

At the teacher education level, one must ask how the profession is dealing with the cross-racial, cross-ethnic factors that enter into the instructional setting. The lack of recognition of racial/ethnic differences is evidence of the significance the profession assigns to such powerful variables. There is an assumption that all learners learn best from the analytical learning style (as described by Hale, 1982, in her book, *Black Children*), which is considered the best and most appropriate. Any learner bringing a different approach to the classroom is immediately referred for special classes and labeled as having a learning disability or as being retarded or behavior disordered. These programs are essential for some learners, but not for the masses of culturally different children who are placed in them. Teachers prepared in traditional teacher education programs are responsible for those referrals. The general incompatibility of the professorial instructional style and student learning styles based primarily on ethnic/racial differences must become a factor in teacher education programs, so that attention to this problem can be transmitted to the classrooms of American schools.

In a brilliant article, James A. Anderson (1988) discusses cognitive styles and multicultural populations. He builds a rationale from the study of culturally different college students. Few teacher educators have stopped to provide components that help prospective teachers understand that the White, male, European learner experiences a linear, self-reinforcing course of action from birth to family, to school, to workplace. Only recently have we begun to deal with the low self-concept of the suburban White male in America. I do not want to imply that the self-concept of the student is America's great problem — although that may be a small part of the reality of teacher education — but I am interested in dealing with the profession of teacher education and its serious attention to cross-racial, cross-ethnic teaching and learning. Indeed, this will be much of the experience of most people now undergoing initial training for our profession.

Curriculum Bias in Teacher Education

Curriculum bias is inherent favoritism in the curriculum toward one economic or racial group over another. This is usually reflected in textbooks, instructional materials, standardized tests, and various artifacts that constitute the substance of school curricula in the United States. Bias exists when groups who are not substantively reflected in school programs are called on to respond as though they were so reflected. Curriculum bias is most reflected in the substance of content and the framework of thinking promoted through instructional delivery, choices about textbooks, films, film strips, and the various forms of content/information employed by those whose professional life involves instruction as a primary activity (Boyer & Boyer, 1975).

According to the National Coalition of Advocates for Students (1985), many textbooks remain culturally biased, both in their presentation of material and in their omission of material on the culture, history, or achievement of many of the national and cultural groups represented in the U.S. school population.

Further, use of the term *dropout rate* should be discontinued. A recent *New York Times* article reported that Hispanic students with B averages are leaving school before graduation; this suggests that we should rethink the reality of school leaving. I am involved in waging a campaign to change the term *dropout rate* to *cultural departure rate*; this phenomenon should be viewed as an indicator of the quality of a program, indicating the degree to which school curricula meet the consumer needs of cultural and linguistic minority students. The cultural departure rate should lead us to focus on the failure of the American teacher to meet the ethnic, racial, cultural, and economic needs of a large percentage of America's student population.

Curriculum Materials for Ethnic Diversity

In a booklet published through the University of Kansas Center for Black Research and Leadership, I have detailed what I call the "Eight States of Ethnic Growth" through which an individual goes based on the extent to which the curriculum experience respects, integrates, and utilizes the ethnic, racial, and cultural profile the learner brings to the classroom (Boyer, 1989a). Many teacher educators are involved in writing, researching, creating, and evaluating these materials, and it is the collective wisdom, attitude, and expertise of teacher educators that must be held partly accountable for this limitation.

Research, Research Topics, Policy, and Findings

Researchers in teacher education have not been negligent or lazy. The libraries are loaded with the written word expounding on the virtues of teacher education reform in both procedures and credit-hour generation. Teacher education must now address the changes needed in the monocultural materials employed in most programs across the country. Teacher education is a profession that attempts to build its practice primarily on the best that is known from the collective philosophies and research available. We must begin to reexamine the assumptions that historically have been made in teacher education:

- Culturally influenced learning styles are insignificant, if they exist at all.
- A good teacher is a good teacher for any learner or any cultural variation — whether or not that teacher has been professionally educated along those lines.
- Traditional assessment instruments (standardized tests) are infallible, culturally adequate, unbiased ethnically or linguistically, and highly sophisticated — in other words, they are unquestionable.

The celebration is on its way because the Association of Teacher Educators and other similar groups are beginning to respond to academic demands in a different way. The profession of teacher educators now is beginning (a) to see curriculum change as preventive of crisis-level realities, rather than as a modification of standards; (b) to understand that accountability to the larger consuming public means that ethnic diversity is a reality in that public; and (c) to realize that university faculty staff development is also a reality or necessity for these rapidly changing times — particularly as it relates to racial, ethnic, economic, and linguistic differences.

Teacher Education in the United States: The 1990s

Teacher education must take into account the historical, economic, and geopolitical context of the preparation curriculum as it affects culturally different people. Part of this involves greater self-knowledge along psychological and sociological lines. It also involves accurate social knowledge (cross-racial, cross-ethnic) and knowledge of the patterns of negative interpretations of human reality. The age of consumerism means that people now define themselves.

Teacher Education That Embraces
Affirmation of Ethnic Differences

The celebration of which I write is on its way. It comes with the realization that not all Americans have been psychologically embraced in the current teacher education curriculum. It comes with understanding and competence in providing instruction that takes account of the fact that individuals need their own cultural, ethnic reinforcement. It embraces the discovery of culturally influenced learning styles. The celebration comes with the affirmation of the real experience, beauty, intelligence, power, courage, creativity, and contributions of culturally different people.

I have frequently been asked about models of teacher education that are exemplary of this quest for celebration. I regret that there are no known models that have reached the level of which I speak. Several individual programs are beginning their serious study, but few have really demonstrated the comprehensive level of competence and substantive curriculum within teacher education. We must remember that there can be no excellence without equity, and this means confronting the Eurocentric view of equality.

Some Celebration Factors

What are some of the celebration factors? How can we upgrade teacher education to yield a more equitable society? How can we begin this quest for real excellence for all of America's teaching population? What staff development elements must be put into place in order to begin movement toward this celebration? We must begin with recognition of the rapid changes facing us. Denial is the most serious form of arrogance. Ignorance (or lack of information) is a curable disease; arrogance is almost always fatal. Our multicultural society now demands recognition as the most basic level of inclusiveness.

Following is a list of proactive behaviors, considerations, and concerns that might begin to lead toward the celebration of which I speak. It should be realized that this discourse is directed to those of us in universities and colleges, where we have limited much of our activity concerning direct instruction of prospective teachers. However, it is addressed equally to policymakers in state departments of education, to superintendents and to personnel officers who interview and employ teacher education graduates, to agencies such as the National Council for the Accreditation of Teacher Education, to AACTE, and, above all, to the membership of the Association of Teacher Educators.

(1) Since 1636, American education (and teacher education) has been an experience in the Eurocentric indoctrination of what the American curriculum is and should be. The celebration begins when we expand our narrow definition of a good education.

(2) There are connections among teacher education, the quality of life in the United States, limitations on patterns of thought, and which instructional profiles should be enhanced.

(3) There must be authentic and basic research/literature. In other words, including the profiles under study must become a priority.

(4) Exposure to the work of culturally different researchers who have been successful in confronting cultural dislocation must become a major part of the preparation of teachers for the future.

(5) No teacher should ever complete a teacher education curriculum in the United States without direct exposure to the work of culturally different researchers who have been successful in confronting cultural dislocation within the curriculum.

(6) The National Alliance of Black School Educators (1984) has implied that testing a culturally different student (and this includes the teacher education student) with alien cultural content is a scientific error and is equivalent to professional malpractice (pp. 26-28).

(7) Teacher education in the United States must begin to research noncognitive factors adequately. Decisions about admissions, graduation, and licensing should not rest entirely on a single test score, as seems to be the case in many states.

(8) Teacher education as a profession must rethink both the instructional and the broader contexts in which it operates. This is indeed a political entity.

(9) Teacher education as a profession must reassess curriculum materials, including teacher education textbooks, supplementary materials, and required readings.

(10) In its efforts to become more of an exact science, teacher education has emphasized emotional detachment. The future, the celebration, the new and upgraded ethnic diversity standards demand some degree of emotional engagement with the art and science of cross-ethnic, cross-racial teaching and learning.

(11) Teacher education must confront all aspects of the scientific racism that embraces many research assumptions and much policy formation.

(12) There must be greater emphasis on the substantive content of teacher education degree programs, disaggregated for information and perspectives on the American academic consumers who have experienced (a) the highest rates of cultural departures from the schools; (b) the greatest loss of human dignity as a result of attention in textbooks, courses, and required experiences; and (c) the least success with the Euro-American curriculum provided at every level of schooling.

(13) Teacher education must engage in creative dialogue that causes each of us to confront his or her own academic biases and racial and ethnic histories, and the extent to which these are reflected in professional behaviors, writings, instruction, policy, curriculum, and personal lives.

(14) Teacher education must fight the battle of poor self-image. Within the university structure, teacher education has historically been defined as the stepchild of higher education curriculum by those outside the profession. We must no longer accept that designation, and we must be assertive in redefining ourselves and our place within that structure.

(15) Teacher education must transform its rather sophisticated techniques and skills into an equitable level of humanity that embraces the ethnic, racial, economic, linguistic, and gender differences within the American populace.

(16) Europe, European perspectives, and the masculine gender of all profiles have dominated the world for some 500 years, but there is a new coalition of humanity, prepared for excellence, as it redefines teacher education, and, indeed, the American curriculum.

(17) Teacher education must reduce academic ethnocentrism and become more ethnically literate. Within the past two years, Allan Bloom, with *The Closing of the American Mind* (1987), and E. D. Hirsch, with *Cultural Literacy* (1987), have offered rather convincing arguments for a renewed attachment to a Eurocentric curriculum, but they both fall short of the goal of academic equity in teacher education.

(18) Teacher education needs to develop a new and precise code of ethics especially for teacher educators, with specific attention to preventing bias in the classroom. (Perhaps new attention to racial harassment is needed.)

(19) Teacher education needs to move beyond racial and ethnic tolerance in perspective, in policy, and in behaviors to a position of shared inclusiveness. This could involve the creation of a new kind of teacher education council, with systems for confronting incidents of racial, ethnic, economic, and linguistic intolerance and discrimination.

Research Directions in Teacher Education

(20) As far back as 1980, some of us were concerned with the direction of research activity in teacher education. We now make a strong recommendation that research activities stop concentrating on the low status of teacher education. In the age of consumerism, there is a need for us to accept external definitions of the professional identity. We are our own best friends — not the politicians, not the chief executive officers of the institutions in which we work, and not our colleagues in other disciplines — and we must place a very high premium on what we do, who we are, and what our contributions to the American way of life are — in or out of academe.

(21) Teacher education must adopt the following as top priorities for the 1990s: (a) producing teachers who are reflective, perceptive practitioners, not just technicians who can pass standardized tests; and (b) producing teachers who understand the ethical dimensions of ethnic, racial, and cultural diversity, and who have increased ethnic literacy and skill in cross-racial, cross-ethnic service delivery.

(22) Teacher education may need to develop task forces on equity issues that will enhance much of staff initiative toward equity. Our profession must become even more accountable for how we are delivering on our public responsibility, including how we are addressing the demographic change in the American populace.

(23) Teacher education must begin to address the mentality of teaching candidates and teacher educators so that there is more rapid movement from dependency to empowerment. This includes the need to deliver skills in valuing, organizing, and communicating from different cultural perspectives.

(24) Teacher education must work to reverse its historical failures in the areas of minority client affirmation, cross-cultural literacy, and cross-cultural communication.

(25) Teacher education must embrace more of the following kinds of leadership and research endeavors: (a) Kathleen Ross at Heritage College has found that there are major teacher education concerns with Native American prospective teachers having to do with whether they are first-generation college students or place-bound prospective teachers, and that communication distortion is the single most common factor inhibiting ethnic growth and academic development (see Ross, 1988); (b) Ray Barnhardt of the University of Alaska found a positive achievement difference when Native American children were taught by Native American teachers; some of this he attributes to communication nuances when there was no cross-ethnic element involved between teacher and learner (see Barnhardt, 1988).

(26) Teacher education researchers must refuse to participate in any further research that essentially blames the victim. Instead, they must go about fixing the system in which success has not been attained by those the system is meant to serve.

(27) Teacher education must embrace the concept of multicultural education as the primary vehicle through which majority teachers become competent in approach. This includes how one thinks about cultural diversity, not just teaching about customs and artifacts.

From Public Policy to Local Action

In our movement toward this celebration, perhaps we need to be even more proactive with some of the following ideas — most of which can be initiated without major additional economic resources:

(28) Teacher education must aim for substantive change rather than cosmetic change in program design.

(29) Teacher education must lead the way in the development of ethnic research centers especially to serve the population of teacher education candidates.

(30) Teacher education must avoid implying that the study of one's own ethnic identity (in the case of ethnic minority students) is a negative endeavor not worthy of academic respect.

(31) Teacher education must be more deliberate in the study of learning styles of economically poor learners — White, Black, Hispanic, Native American, and others.

(32) Teacher education must include the study of practices of institutional racism in its foundation-level work with prospective teachers.

(33) Teacher education must begin to pluralize children's literature, music in the elementary school, science in the secondary school, art, drama, and all the other essentials of the programs in which we work.

(34) Teacher education must become more deliberate in its emphasis on the dynamics of cross-racial, cross-ethnic teaching and learning (Boyer, 1983).

(35) Teacher education must make an urgent priority of the development of competencies associated with cross-racial, cross-ethnic parent conferencing.

Final Thoughts

Teacher education in the United States has served the country well in many instances. The production of new teachers has kept pace with the growth in student populations by our traditional formulas. However, what was a good teacher education program in 1969 is certainly not an adequate program for 1989. The 1990s will be significantly different from the 1970s. Teacher educators are charged with one of the highest callings of any professional group serving the American consumer. Let us accept that calling with renewed vigor, greater energy, and a broader conceptualization of all humankind than ever before. Academic racism, academic sexism, child maltreatment, professional malpractice, and teacher education as a Eurocentric experience are all factors that must be eliminated before the celebration can really get under way.

In the meantime, teacher educators can experience the optimism that results from measuring how far they have already come. They can believe that it is possible to develop the kind of teacher education system that creates the equitable teacher, a teacher with knowledge and skills adequate to the changes that have taken place in the American academic community.

References

Anderson, J. A. (1988). Cognitive styles and multicultural population. *Journal of Teacher Education, 39*(1), 2-9.

Association of Teacher Educators. (1986). *Guidelines for professional experiences in teacher education: A policy statement.* Reston, VA: Author.

Banks, J. A., & Banks, C. M. (1989). *Multicultural education: Issues and perspectives.* Boston: Allyn & Bacon.

Barnhardt, R. (1988, October 4). Informal presentation at Rural Education Clearinghouse Project, Kansas City, MO.

Bloom, A. (1987). *The closing of the American mind.* New York: Simon & Schuster.

Boyer, J. B. (1981). *Multicultural instructional inventory for enhancing college-university curriculum: A self-improvement inventory.* Manhattan: Kansas State University.

Boyer, J. B. (1983). The ten most critical dimensions of cross-racial, cross-ethnic teaching and learning. *Educational Considerations, 10*(3).

Boyer, J. B. (1985). *Multicultural education: Product or process?* Kansas City, KS: Urban Education Center.

Boyer, J. B. (1988). The other side of gender equity: Black males in America. *Educational Considerations, 15*(1), 15-17.

Boyer, J. B. (1989a). *Curriculum materials for ethnic diversity: Rationale and perspective.* Lawrence: University of Kansas, Center for Black Research and Leadership.

Boyer, J. B. (1989b). Ethnic literacy as an aspect of multicultural education: A perspective on the education of teachers. In R. M. Duhon (Ed.), *Educational excellence through the implementation of education that is multicultural.* Reston, VA: Association of Teacher Educators.

Boyer, J. B., & Boyer, J. L. (1975). *Curriculum and instruction after desegregation.* Manhattan, KS: Ag Press.

Carnegie Forum on Education and the Economy. (1986). *A nation prepared: Teachers for the twenty-first century.* New York: Author.

Carnegie Foundation for the Advancement of Teaching. (1988, May). *Mixed blessings.* Princeton, NJ: Author.

Copeland-Griggs, Inc. (Producer). (1988). *Valuing diversity* (part III) [videotape]. San Francisco: Author.

Hale, J. E. (1982). *Black children: Their roots, culture, and learning styles.* Provo, UT: Brigham Young University Press.

Hirsch, E., Jr. (1987). *Cultural literacy.* Boston: Houghton Mifflin.

Hodgkinson, H. (1985). *All one system: Demographics of education* — kindergarten through graduate school. Washington, DC: Institute for Educational Leadership.

Kitano, H.H.L. (1974). *Race relations.* Englewood Cliffs, NJ: Prentice-Hall.

National Alliance of Black School Educators. (1984). *Saving the African American child.* Washington, DC: Author.

National Coalition of Advocates for Students. (1985). *Barriers to excellence: Our children at risk.* Boston: Author.

National Commission on Excellence in Education. (1983). *A nation at risk: The imperative for educational reform.* Washington, DC: Government Printing Office.

Olsen, C. S. (1987). *Teacher student interaction and its relationship to the socialization of female children.* Unpublished manuscript, Kansas State University.

Palulston, C. B. (1980). *English as a second language.* Washington, DC: National Education Association.

Ross, K. (1988, October 4). Informal presentation at Rural Education Clearinghouse Project, Kansas City, MO.

Tafel, L., & Christensen, J. (1988). Teacher education in the 1990's: Looking ahead while learning from the past. *Action in Teacher Education, 10*(3), 1-6.

Tracy, S. J., Sheehan, R., & McArdle, R. J. (1988). Teacher education reforms: The implementers' reaction. *Action in Teacher Education, 10*(3).

William T. Grant Foundation Commission of Work, Family and Citizenship. (1988). *The forgotten half: Pathways to success for America's youth and young families.* Washington, DC: Author.

19

Educating Society for Equity

CARLOS E. CORTÉS

University of California, Riverside

New Year's Day, 1989, brought the national broadcast of the television docudrama *The Karen Carpenter Story*, about the talented young singer who died from a heart attack brought on by anorexia nervosa. The following day, Philadelphia's Renfrew Center, which specializes in eating disorders, received more than 1,000 telephone calls from persons seeking information about the disease.

* * *

Later that month, the California Governor's Committee for the Employment of Disabled Persons presented the Media Access Award for the year's best feature film to *Gaby*, the powerful story of Gabriela Brimmer, the renowned Mexican author who wrote an acclaimed autobiography although paralyzed by cerebral palsy. In addition, a special merit award went to the television series *L.A. Law*, for its sensitive portrayal of Benny Stolwitz, a mentally rewarded young man who works effectively as a messenger for a Los Angeles legal firm. In the process, he overcomes the doubts of some firm members as to his competence and his ability to serve the firm with dignity. Other groups representing mentally retarded Americans have also commended actor Larry Drake, who brilliantly portrays Benny, for his contributions to improving the image of mentally retarded persons.

* * *

In August 1988, the release of Universal's motion picture adaptation of Nikos Kazantzakis's novel *The Last Temptation of Christ* caused an explosion of controversy throughout the United States and the rest of the world. A war of words erupted involving the film's director, Martin Scorsese, studio executives, community groups, and spokespersons for various religious groups (who split in their reactions to the film, some condemning it as blasphemy, others defending it as a potential strengthener of religious faith). Those opposing the film's release and calling for a boycott argued that the movie distorted Jesus, particularly by suggesting that he entertained sexual fantasies about Mary Magdalene as he hung from the cross. Moreover, they asserted, these distortions could weaken the beliefs and religiosity of viewers. The protest itself even developed anti-Semitic overtones, as some opponents showered ethnic epithets on Lew Wasserman, chairman of MCA, which owns Universal. The protesters apparently lost sight of the fact that director Scorsese was Roman Catholic, screenwriter Paul Schrader was Dutch Calvinist, and author Kazantzakis was Greek Orthodox.

* * *

On September 18, 1986, the popular daytime television game show *The $25,000 Pyramid* was being shown. On this program, competition involves two pairs of contestants. For each pair, words appear on a screen in front of one contestant, who then gives clues to try to get the partner to identify the correct words. On that day the word *gangs* popped up on the cluer's screen. Without hesitation, he fired out the first thing that came to his mind: "They have lots of these in East L.A." (a heavily Mexican American section of Los Angeles). Responding at once, his guest celebrity partner answered, "Gangs." Under competitive pressure, two strangers had immediately achieved mental communion, linking East L.A. with gangs and transmitting their ethnic stereotype to a national audience.

* * *

Women's groups have challenged media portrayals, with much of their vehemence directed against sexual violence in music videos. Such videos, these groups have argued, legitimize sexual violence against women and desensitize men to these depredations. MTV, the popular music video cable network, responded by establishing a policy of deleting what it deems to be the more offensive portions of videos it plays.

* * *

The Cosby Show and *Golden Girls*, both major audience hits, have become the subjects of considerable analysis because they portray two societal groups — Blacks and older women — in ways far different from their traditional treatment on entertainment television. By presenting the viewing public with well-educated, cerebral, financially successful Blacks and intelligent, active (including sexually) female seniors, these two shows have expanded the spectrum of television's racial, gender, and age depictions.

Yet even these two popular, much acclaimed shows have generated controversy. Some viewers have expressed reservations about *The Cosby Show* on the grounds that its concentration on well-heeled Blacks might unintentionally encourage viewers to ignore the tremendous social and economic problems faced by the majority of American Blacks. A recent audience study of *Golden Girls* revealed that a significant minority of viewers found these articulate seniors to be insensitive, immature, and excessively bawdy (Cassata & Irwin, 1989).

* * *

The above examples have several things in common. They all emanate from the mass media; they all involve efforts to entertain; and they all show how entertainment media can teach, whether intentionally or unintentionally (although viewers may draw varying, sometimes conflicting, messages from the same entertainment "textbook").

As informal teachers, entertainment media participate in the complex process of educating society for equity (and inequity) by disseminating images and ideas about different societal groups — ethnic, racial, gender, religious, age, and of varying physical and mental characteristics, for example. These cases also reveal that persons, groups, and institutions outside of the media recognize the media's teaching power, particularly their power to reinforce, modify, and sometimes even create public images of societal groups. Finally, these examples demonstrate that people outside of the media have responded — sometimes challenging media depictions, sometimes attempting to improve images, sometimes trying to mitigate negative treatment, and sometimes complimenting the media for providing positive messages that promote better intergroup understanding and thereby help educate society for equity.

The Societal Curriculum

However, the mass media constitute only part of the education for equity challenge and must be considered within the larger context of the educational process taken as a whole. Discussions of education often, and mistakenly, use schools and education as synonymous concepts. Certainly schools constitute an important part of education, but they do not have a monopoly on education, nor could they even if they wished.

Students learn through schools, but people also learn outside of schools. They learn language. They learn culture. They learn attitudes and patterns of behavior. They learn about gender roles and religion, about race and ethnicity. They learn about themselves and others. They learn about our nation and about other nations and cultures. Most important for the issue of equity, they learn about the many types of groups that make up our society.

Moreover, nonschool learning covers a time span that well exceeds the temporal grasp of schools. Young people learn before they ever begin school. While they go to school, students continue to learn in society. Finally, for most of us school days will end, but learning in society will continue as long as we live. Schools, then, should help prepare students to deal effectively and analytically with the process of lifelong learning.

If school educators are to engage the issue of educating society for equity adequately, they need to address equity education in its lifelong societal dimensions. In particular, educators need to examine the relationships between school and societal education and build pedagogical bridges between the two educational spheres. Four educational relationships between school and society need continuous attention:

(1) societal education's implications for equity (or inequity), including its potential influence on current students;

(2) the importance of school education for increasing intergroup understanding in order to foster societal equity;

(3) the preparation of students for lifelong societal learning related to equity; and

(4) the direct influence of schools and school educators on societal teaching concerning equity.

In grappling with these four relationships between school and societal learning, I have developed the concept of the societal curriculum — that massive, ongoing, informal curriculum of family, peer groups, neighborhoods, churches, organizations, institutions, mass media, and other socializing forces that educate all of us throughout our lives (Cortés, 1981). This societal curriculum may be viewed as operating in four general, overlapping, and interacting curricular sectors:

(1) *the immediate curriculum:* the powerful educational influences emanating from family, home, peer group, neighborhood, and community
(2) *the institutional curriculum:* the formal and informal educational curriculum that resides within such diverse institutions and organizations as religious institutions, youth groups, social organizations, professional associations, and special interest entities
(3) *the serendipitous curriculum:* the incidental, sometimes accidental, education that occurs through individual experiences in each person's life
(4) *the media curriculum:* the educational messages disseminated intentionally and unintentionally through the various media — newspapers, magazines, motion pictures, television, radio, and the like

As do schools themselves, each of these nonschool sectors teaches about societal groups, thereby contributing to both the strengthening and the weakening of equity. Through the multicultural societal curriculum people learn — for better and for worse — about such equity-related themes as race, ethnic diversity, religion, the significance of gender, the implications of age, and the potential of persons of different physical and mental attributes. They also learn about relations among individuals, groups, and institutions.

The immediate curriculum serves as each individual's first school, although family and neighborhood residents may not think of themselves as teachers. Parents and other family members may talk about different groups, sometimes in serious discussions, sometimes in offhand remarks (such as negative epithets or stereotypical generalizations). They model behavior and attitudes toward people of different groups, while families also socialize members concerning gender and generational roles and expectations. Neighborhood peers informally build up and transmit collective norms of attitude, belief, and behavior concerning various elements of society. The emergence of skinheads and other groups grounded in bigotry provides only the most obvious evidence of such peer education. Immediate curriculum teaching may be both positive and negative, will probably combine both factual accuracy and distortion, will range from restrained group generalizations to gross stereotypes, and may contribute to attitudes conducive to or contrary to societal equity. Before children reach school, while they are in school, and after formal education has ended, each person continually participates, as both teacher and learner, in the multicultural immediate curriculum concerning diversity and societal equity.

The institutional curriculum, consisting of a wide variety of nonschool institutions and organizations, forms the second major component of nonschool education. Religious institutions, using channels ranging from sermons to religious school classes, inculcate beliefs and attitudes while also establishing a baseline of similarities to and differences from persons of other religious or nonreligious backgrounds. Social organizations explicitly and implicitly teach about diversity and give lessons concerning equity (or the lack of it) through their established rules of conduct and membership. People belong to groups organized around diverse special interests, from the National Rifle Association to the Sierra Club, from the National Organization for Women to the Eagle Forum, and from the National Association for the Advancement of Colored People to the Ku Klux Klan. Through conferences, meetings, lobbying, publications, and mailings, these groups attempt to educate their members and others on behalf of their beliefs. Name an organization or institution, and you can be certain that it provides some formal or informal teaching about diversity, with implications for the quest for or opposition to societal equity.

The serendipitous curriculum may be the area most resistant to "content analysis." Whether within the United States or in travels to other nations, each of us undergoes individual experiences that influence our perceptions of different groups. These experiences vary widely among individuals, as do the ways that people perceive, interpret, react to, remember, and make these experiences part of their own beliefs and value systems. Moreover, such experiences can help propel people in various directions in their attitudes, beliefs, and behavior concerning societal equity.

Finally comes the media curriculum, my special research interest. (I am currently working on a two-volume study of the multicultural implications of motion pictures. The first volume will examine the history of the U.S. feature film treatment of ethnicity; the second volume will address the history of the American movie depiction of foreign nations and cultures.) The teaching power of the mass media has long drawn the attention of scholars and concerned societal groups. Moreover, other nations have debated this issue, addressing both the role of the media within their own borders and the educational implications of transnational communications — a particular concern to Third World nations, who fear the growing cultural and ideological influence of wealthy, high-tech Western media.

The educational impact of motion pictures has been an issue since the early days of the twentieth century. Studies have shown that movies influence intergroup beliefs and attitudes, sometimes reinforcing them and sometimes modifying them (Raths & Trager, 1948). In a pioneering study, Peterson and Thurstone (1933) discovered that viewing the classic 1915 silent film *The Birth of a Nation*, which includes a degrading portrayal of post-Civil War Reconstruction-era southern Blacks, increased student prejudice toward Black Americans. In contrast, Rosen (1948) found that the 1947 anti-anti-Semitism film *Gentleman's Agreement* actually improved student attitudes toward Jews, even though most of the targeted students stated that the film *had not* influenced their attitudes.

Television, including cable, has recently received the most attention. While the extent of television viewing defies precise verification, analysts concur that it has been growing around the world. Within the United States, average household TV viewing time has climbed from five hours per day in 1956 to six hours per day in 1971 and to seven hours per day in 1983. As early as 1961, one study reported that young Americans between the ages of 3 and 16 devoted one-sixth of their waking hours to television (Schramm, Lyle, & Parker, 1961). According to another estimate, by the time of high school graduation, the average student will have spent 12,000 hours in the classroom and 15,000 hours in front of the television set. Sometimes movies and television blend into one, particularly as TV, cable, and videocassettes become prime recyclers of theatrical motion pictures.

People learn from their exposure to the entertainment media, often absorbing ideas conducive to or contrary to societal equity. Likening television to schools and television programs to school courses, Gans (1967) writes:

> Almost all TV programs and magazine fiction teach something about American society. For example, *Batman* is, from this vantage point, a course in criminology that describes how a superhuman aristocrat does a better job eradicating crime than do public officials. Similarly, *The Bever-*

ly Hillbillies offers a course in social stratification and applied economics, teaching that with money, uneducated and uncultured people can do pretty well in American society, and can easily outwit more sophisticated and more powerful middle-class types. . . . And even the innocuous family situation comedies such as *Ozzie and Harriet* deal occasionally with ethical problems encountered on a neighborhood level. . . . Although the schools argue that they are the major transmitter of society's moral values, the mass media offer a great deal more content on this topic. (pp. 21-22)

Some studies have concluded that entertainment media learning varies among societal groups. For example, based on their examination of studies of the perceived reality of television, Greenberg and Reeves (1976) conclude that "economically disadvantaged homes, black children, younger children, female children, and those with a higher frequency of watching have all indicated more belief in the true-to-life nature of TV entertainment" (p. 88). This raises serious equity issues in the realm of societal education.

However, in examining the media curriculum — in fact, all aspects of nonschool teaching — we need to remain aware that teaching and learning are not the same. Teachers know that from their own experience. We teach — in the classroom and through homework assignments — only to discover great student variation in the extent and quality of learning. If teaching and learning were synonymous, we would never have to give examinations; we would simply evaluate teacher presentations and textbook content.

In order to assess school learning, we have to examine learners themselves. This also applies to nonschool learning. Research has demonstrated conclusively that the societal curriculum teaches about diversity and contributes to both societal equity and inequity. Yet, while we know that this learning occurs, it is impossible to determine precisely what each individual learns from society and to what societal curriculum messages about diversity each person has been exposed. When researchers have examined specific instances of societal curriculum learning, they have encountered varying learner responses (Pingree & Hawkins, 1982). Two landmark television presentations, the comedy series *All in the Family* and the powerful TV docudrama *Roots*, demonstrate the phenomenon of contrasting viewer interpretations.

Norman Lear's popular television series *All in the Family* provides a prime example of variable learning. Inaugurated in 1971, the series portrayed Archie Bunker as the classic bigot — racist, sexist, and just about every other kind of anti-"ist" imaginable. By making his views appear absurd and laughable, the show attempted to critique bigotry. It succeeded — for some viewers. But others identified with Archie, finding his beliefs and prejudices a confirmation of the validity of their own (Leckenby & Surlin, 1976). For example, Vidmar and Rokeach (1974) confirmed the "selective perception hypothesis" by determining that "high prejudiced viewers" tended to admire Archie and to condone his racial and ethnic slurs.

The eight-night January 1977 broadcast of Alex Haley's *Roots*, the epic television docudrama on the experience of Black slaves, attracted numerous scholars (Howard, Rothbart, & Sloan, 1978; Hur, 1978) who assessed the reaction of a variety of audiences. While viewers did not polarize as sharply as with *All in the Family*, responses did vary. For example, one study conducted in Austin, Texas, reported that Mexican Americans and Anglos, far more than Black viewers, considered *Roots* to be an accurate presentation of slavery, while Mexican Americans, far more than Blacks and Anglos, found the depiction of Whites to be accurate (Balon, 1978).

An Agenda for Action

The societal curriculum, then, has played and continues to play a critical role in the education of society for and against equity. Therefore, if schools hope to educate students for societal equity, they need to focus their attention on the critical teaching relationship between schools and society. One way of evaluating and improving school effectiveness in contributing to societal equity and creating equity-oriented future citizens is by examining our schools' role in addressing the four school-society relationships — awareness of societal teaching about equity-related concerns, school education for societal equity, preparation of students for societal learning, and educator activism in influencing societal teaching concerning equity — as they apply to the four sectors of the societal curriculum.

Schools deal with the student products of the immediate curriculum. Students come with values and beliefs, positive attitudes and prejudices, knowledge and ignorance, understanding and stereotypes. This creates challenges and opportunities for school educators. It creates the challenge of understanding the immediate curriculum education being experienced by students in their daily nonschool lives. It also creates an opportunity for equity-oriented curricular innovation by making the local community, including its various cultures, a topic for classroom examination. Moreover, schools can help instill in students the importance of the role they can play as immediate curriculum teachers — both as peers in the present and as family and community members of the future — in improving societal equity.

But beyond dealing with students as products of and potential teachers within the immediate curriculum, schools can deal directly with that curriculum. Parent education workshops can inform parents of the nature of the school's multicultural, equity-oriented educational efforts, enlist parental support in this quest, and even provide them with training on how to become educational allies in striving for societal equity. My own work with parents, in workshops ranging from multicultural media analysis to intercultural understanding, has proven to be extremely rewarding.

The institutional curriculum provides different challenges and opportunities. Most communities have myriad institutions, each with its own agenda and teaching process, no matter how informal or unrecognized. Yet these institutions will likely have an educational impact on students and certainly will have an impact on adults. The first challenge for teachers is to become aware of what institutions exist in their communities and, to the degree possible, to develop an understanding of their lessons on diversity and equity. Students may learn from religious institutions, from youth groups, or from ethnic organizations, bringing this institutional curriculum learning into the classroom. That learning may interact with school teaching, may filter school education, or may even inject conflicting perspectives. Awareness of this societal institutional teaching will help equip teachers to recognize and deal with it.

Moreover, as with the immediate curriculum, the institutional curriculum may be incorporated into the classroom. Many states now mandate the teaching of comparative religion, so that students will develop an understanding and, one hopes, a greater sensitivity to diversity of religious views. The study of ethnic groups should include the types of organizations and institutions that they form to help maintain group cohesiveness, transmit cherished cultural beliefs and practices, and foster group progress. The study of U.S. institutions and organizations — governmental and private, political and social, public service and special interest — can help students become aware of the enormous range of beliefs and values that are being propounded in the "free (to a degree) marketplace of ideas."

But schools should go further in preparing students for a life as a part of the institutional curriculum. School educators can help students realize that they, too, will serve as educators as they become part of the institutional curriculum — as members and possibly as leaders. Moreover, students should understand how they can use that role both to increase intergroup understanding and to work toward societal equity or, conversely, how some organizations, such as the Ku Klux Klan and the Aryan Brotherhood, have provided an institutional curriculum that challenges progress toward societal equity.

In recent years, considerable time and effort have been devoted to trying to provide postschool institutional remedial education for equity — for teachers and administrators, for business leaders, for government employees, for participants in public and private organizations, and for members of civic groups and religious institutions. How much better if schools can educate students for intergroup understanding and to be contributors to equity through the institutional curriculum, rather than having to try to remedy problems later!

The institutional curriculum can serve as a great ally in educating society for equity. Teachers and administrators can become more effective multicultural, equity-oriented educators if they can enlist the support of other institutions. For example, I have given multicultural talks and workshops for religious institutions, civic groups, and a wide variety of other organizations. In addition, for the past decade I have been giving multicultural workshops for business executives and supervisors, helping their companies become better models of intercultural equity in action and demonstrating how they can better use diversity as a strength rather than confronting it as a problem.

Schools can also play a role in the serendipitous curriculum. Certainly school educators cannot anticipate each and every intercultural and intergroup experience their students will encounter throughout their lives. Nor can educators inoculate students against misunderstanding and ignorance-based reactions to such experiences. However, we can help to prepare them for the future. The first steps are awareness and understanding. The classroom can become a place for students to share their experiences relating to diversity and equity. Student travel overseas or visits to culturally different settings within the United States, for example, can be discussed, examined, and interpreted. Chance meetings or experiences, both positive and negative, can be subjects for exploration. The goal should not simply be to have students report and analyze, but also to help them recognize the amount of serendipitous learning they experience, and to prepare them to deal more sensitively and accurately with future intergroup experiences.

Through an equity-oriented, multicultural education, we can help students develop a more knowledge-based understanding of different societal groups and foreign nations. We can help them learn strategies for interpreting the values and behaviors of groups and cultures with which they are less familiar — in particular, learning to restrain themselves from inappropriately injecting their own cultural interpretations into multicultural situations and from making hasty definitive judgments. We can also help them learn to become comfortable in situations in which they have to deal with unfamiliar cultural cues.

Finally, we have the media curriculum. Here, again, educators can deal both directly and indirectly with the curriculum. They can deal with it directly by becoming involved in attempting to improve media. They can deal with it indirectly by helping young people develop better critical media literacy.

The media furnish fascinating subject matter both for personal enlightenment and for school education about the media curriculum. In my multicultural courses and long-range workshops, I begin by giving teachers the assignment of keeping a media curriculum notebook of the media teaching they encounter about ethnicity, foreign cultures, genders, religions, age cohorts, and other societal groupings — whether that teaching is intentional or unintended, whether fictional or nonfictional. My goal is not to try to turn them into instant experts, but to help them develop media awareness and the habit of thinking critically about the media curriculum to which their students are exposed. I also train them in techniques for bringing the media curriculum into the classroom and for raising student awareness of the media curriculum.

Moreover, the careful use of media can help to heighten the significance of classroom subjects, such as priming students for the school investigation of critical topics, including many related to societal equity. For example, two recent productions, the 1988 feature film *Mississippi Burning* and the 1989 television docudrama *Unconquered*, have received justifiable criticism because of their overemphasis on the role of Whites in the civil rights movement in the South during the 1960s, with Blacks being shoved into the background and presented mainly as relatively passive victims. Yet the very controversy over these two presentations heightens their potential as teaching devices. Teachers could use these two films, including the controversy surrounding them, as a basis for motivating students to study the civil rights movement. I have found this approach — media as motivators for school investigation — to be one of the most effective ways of getting students to engage important social issues.

But media analysis should go even further. While school education will end someday for most students, the media curriculum will continue, including media teaching relating to societal equity. Therefore, a vital part of educating society for equity should be educating students to be analytical media consumers. This includes becoming sensitive to the ways in which media contribute to intergroup understanding and societal equity as well as to the ways in which they intentionally or incidentally work against these goals.

Finally, educators can help make the media curriculum a stronger force for seeking equity. For example, the national antiprejudice program A World of Difference has made effective use of local television stations and newspapers in its public educational activities. As part of the development of critical thinking skills, teachers can have students analyze newspaper and television coverage of various societal groups and even report their findings to the media, thereby helping the media become more aware of their educational role in the area of intergroup understanding and equity.

Conclusion

Schools play a critical role in educating society for equity, but school educators can become even more effective by addressing the four components of the multicultural societal curriculum and by emphasizing the four types of school-society educational relationships discussed above. Teachers should continually be cognizant of the content of the societal curriculum. They can bring it into their classrooms to enrich, motivate, provide social context, and heighten the significance of school subjects. They can help prepare students to be more enlightened learners in the societal curriculum and more sensitive, equity-oriented participants and leaders. Finally, they can work directly with elements of the societal curriculum — from parents to organizations to mass media — in order to help improve them as forces for intergroup understanding and social equity.

School effectiveness in contributing to future leadership and equity cannot and should not be evaluated in school achievement terms alone. The bottom line for schools is their contribution to society. Will our students of today, our leaders of tomorrow, become agents for social equity and intergroup understanding? That is our challenge. Only the future is at stake.

References

Balon, R. E. (1978). The impact of "Roots" on a racially heterogeneous southern community: An exploratory study. *Journal of Broadcasting, 22*(3), 299-307.

Cassata, M., & Irwin, B. (1989, Winter). Going for the gold: Prime time's sexy seniors. *Media & Values*, pp. 12-14.

Cortés, C. E. (1981). The societal curriculum: Implications for multiethnic education. In J. A. Banks (Ed.), *Education in the 80's: Multiethnic education.* Washington, DC: National Education Association.

Gans, H. J. (1967). The mass media as an educational institution. *Television Quarterly, 6*, 20-37.

Greenberg, B. S., & Reeves, B. (1976). Children and the perceived reality of television. *Journal of Social Issues, 32*(4), 86-97.

Howard, J., Rothbart, G., & Sloan, L. (1978). The response to "Roots": A national survey. *Journal of Broadcasting, 22*(3), 279-287.

Hur, K. K. (1978). Impact of "Roots" on black and white teenagers. *Journal of Broadcasting, 22*(3), 289-298.

Leckenby, J. D., & Surlin, S. H. (1976). Incidental social learning and viewer race: "All in the Family" and "Sanford and Son." *Journal of Broadcasting, 20*(4), 481-494.

Peterson, R. C., & Thurstone, L. L. (1933). *Motion pictures and the social attitudes of children.* New York: Macmillan.

Pingree, S., & Hawkins, R. P. (1982). What children do with television: Implications for communication research. In B. Dervin & M. J. Voigt (Eds.), *Progress in communication sciences* (Vol. 3). Norwood, NJ: Ablex.

Raths, L. E., & Trager, F. N. (1948). Public opinion and "Crossfire." *Journal of Educational Sociology, 21*(6), 345-368.

Rosen, I. C. (1948). The effect of the motion picture "Gentleman's Agreement" on attitudes toward Jews. *Journal of Psychology, 26*, 525-536.

Schramm, W., Lyle, J., & Parker, E. B. (1961). *Television in the lives of our children.* Stanford, CA: Stanford University Press.

Surlin, S. H. (1978). "Roots" research: A summary of findings. *Journal of Broadcasting, 22*(3), 309-320.

Vidmar, N., & Rokeach, M. (1974). Archie Bunker's bigotry: A study in selective perception and exposure. *Journal of Communication, 24*(1), 36-47.

About the Authors

James E. Anderson received his Ph.D. from Ohio State University. His areas of specialization are multicultural education, teacher education, and administration in multicultural settings. He is the author of a college text on teaching in a multicultural society, and he consults on that topic throughout the nation. He is Director of the International Multicultural Education Institute.

H. Prentice Baptiste, Jr., currently is Professor and Chair of the Department of Educational Leadership and Cultural Studies, University of Houston. He earned his B.S. from Lamar State College of Technology and his M.A.T. and Ed.D. degrees from Indiana University. His research has centered on multicultural education, effective school indicators, and science magnet schools. He served as coeditor of the *Journal of Educational Equity and Leadership* and publishes regularly in the field. He has worked extensively in staff development for urban schools faculty, and has edited a trainer's guide, *A Cross-Cultural Intervention Model for Refugees*. He currently is involved in an innovative principal preparation program funded by the Danforth Foundation.

James B. Boyer, Professor of Curriculum and Instruction and former Director of the Institute on Cultural Understandings at Kansas State University, holds a B.A. degree in business education, a master's degree in school administration, and a Ph.D. degree at Ohio State University. A member of Phi Delta Kappa and Kappa Delta Pi educational honorary societies, he is also a member of the Manhattan Human Relations Board, the Association for Childhood Education, and the Association for Supervision and Curriculum Development as well as the Association for Study of Afro-American Life and History. He has been a recipient of the Open Window Television Teacher Award and the Martin Luther King Award for Contributions to Higher Education, and was named Suwanee County Teacher of the Year. His recent books include *Curriculum and Instruction after Desegregation* and *Curriculum Desegregation in Public Schools: An Action Manual.* He has also written more than twenty articles, including "Curriculum Diversity for the Urban Economically Disadvantaged."

Carlos E. Cortés is a Professor of History at the University of California, Riverside. Among his many publications are *Three Perspectives on Ethnicity* and *A Filmic Approach to the Study of Historical Dilemmas.* He has also edited three major book series on U.S. Hispanics and has written documentary films. He is currently writing a two-volume study of the history of the U.S. motion picture treatment of ethnic groups and foreign nations. The recipient of the California Council for the Humanities' 1980 Distinguished California Humanist Award, he has lectured widely throughout the United States, Latin America, and Europe on such topics as media literacy, multicultural education, global education, and the implications of diversity for education, government, and private business. He has also appeared as guest host on the PBS national television series *Why in the World?*

Christian Faltis is Associate Professor of Second Language and Bilingual Education at the University of Nevada, Reno. Prior He was formerly on the faculty of the University of California, Davis, and the University of Alabama. He has also held a Fulbright Professorship at the University of Honduras in Tegucigalpa, and has taught in Ecuador, Colombia, and the Dominican Republic. His research interests include effective bilingual instruction, teachers with LEP students in regular classrooms, and second language socialization.

Adam Gamoran is Assistant Professor of Sociology and Educational Policy Studies at the University of Wisconsin — Madison. He received his Ph.D. from the Department of Education at the University of Chicago in 1984. His research focuses on stratification and resource allocation in school systems. Currently he is involved in a two-year study of ability grouping, instruction, and achievement in eighth- and ninth-grade English and social studies classes. With Robert D. Mare, he is the author of the article "Secondary School Tracking and Educational Inequality: Compensation, Reinforcement, or Neutrality?" (*American Journal of Sociology*, March 1989).

Geneva Gay is Professor of Education at Purdue University, where she teaches courses in curriculum and multicultural education. She has written many articles and book chapters on program planning and teacher education for ethnic and cultural diversity. She is the coeditor of *Expressively Black:The Cultural Basis of Ethnic Identity.*

J. Jerome Harris is Superintendent of Atlanta Public Schools. Although his accomplishments are numerous, none exceeds his impact on the academic performance of the students in Community District 13. Under his leadership, Community School District 13 became the only decentralized school district in New York City with a predominantly minority student population where more than 60% of the students performed at or above grade level on standardized reading and mathematics tests. He was one of the founders of the New York Association of Black Educators. He has received numerous honors for advocacy, initiative, and action in advancing the well-being of minority educators and students throughout the New York City Public School System.

Mae A. Kendall has been a classroom teacher and a Ford Foundation Leadership Fellow. She has taught young children, college students, and nonreading adults. She has presented papers and conducted workshops at the ASCD, the National Association for the Education of Young Children (and served on the NAEYC Governing Board from 1979 to 1983), and the International Symposium on Curriculum Development. In July 1986, she was named Outstanding Educator by the Georgia Association of Educational Leaders, and the State Board of Education honored her by bestowing upon her its Medallion of Excellence.

Stephanie L. Knight has been the recipient of several awards. Her recent honors include the 1988 Outstanding Research Award from the Southwest Educational Research Association and one of Phi Delta Kappa's eight national awards for Outstanding Dissertation. The results of her research have been presented at numerous national and international conferences and have been published in several journals and books, including the *Journal of Educational Research, Journal of Educational Equity and Leadership, National Reading Conference Yearbook, The Study of Learning Environments, Sociology and Social Research, The Reading Teacher, TESOL Quarterly*, and *School Climate.*

Jane McCarthy is a faculty member of the Department of Curriculum and Instruction and Chairperson of the Teacher Education Program Area of the College of Education at the University of Houston. She has also taught at Rice University and has been a public school teacher in inner-city, rural, and suburban settings. She has worked as a consultant to schools in Germany and India. She is the author of publications and papers in the fields of classroom management and effective teaching skills and practices. She has served four terms as a member of the board of trustees of a local school district.

Martha M. McCarthy is a Professor of Education and Director of the Consortium of Educational Policy Studies at Indiana University. Previously Associate Dean of the Faculties at I.U., she has also been a public school teacher and central office administrator. She has served as President of the National Organization on Legal Problems of Education (1984-85) and the University Council for Educational Administration (1985-86). She has authored or coauthored several books, including *Under Scrutiny: The Educational Administration Professoriate* and *Public School Law: Teachers' and Students' Rights.*

Yolanda N. Padron is Assistant Professor at the University of Houston, Clear Lake, where she teaches courses in bilingual education, English as a second language, and multicultural education. In addition, she has taught in the Houston public schools, both in conventional and bilingual classrooms. She has presented numerous papers at state, national, and international conferences and has published articles in journals such as *The Reading Teacher, TESOL Quarterly, Educational Horizons,* and the *Journal of Educational Equity and Leadership.* Her research has been concentrated in the areas of bilingual students' cognitive reading strategies and bilingual-bicultural education.

Hugh J. Scott has served as Dean of Programs in Education at Hunter College of the City University of New York since July 1, 1975. Prior to his deanship, he was a Professor of Education at Howard University in Washington, D.C. Before his superintendency, he served as Regional Assistant Superintendent in the Detroit Public Schools. He is an active writer and public speaker. His publications reveal major interests in the problems of educational leadership and the implementation of the concepts of equal educational opportunity and quality education. He is the author of *The Black School Superintendent: Messiah or Scapegoat.*

Charol Shakeshaft is Chairperson of the Administration and Policy Studies Department at Hofstra University. Her research has primarily focused on gender issues in both schooling and the administration of schools. A member of the editorial boards of *Educational Administration Quarterly* and the *Journal of Educational Administration*, she is also the recipient of the Jack A. Culbertson Award for contributions to theory in educational administration. Additionally, she has directed a program for women in school administration and is the author of *Women in Educational Administration.*

Barbara A. Sizemore has a B.A. and M.A. from Northwestern University and a Ph.D. from the University of Chicago. She has taught every grade (K-12) and has held both elementary and secondary principalships in Chicago. In 1969, she was appointed Director of the Woodlawn Experimental Schools Project, an experiment in community control. In 1972, she left to become the first woman and African American to serve as Associate Secretary in the American Association of School Administrators, from which she was recruited to become the first African American woman to head a big-city school system, Washington, D.C. She is now an Associate Professor in the Department of Black Community Education Research and Development, University of Pittsburgh.

Jane A. Stallings is Chairperson of the Curriculum and Instruction Department and Director of the Houston Center for Effective Teaching in the College of Education at the University of Houston. She is best known for her classroom research linking observed instructional strategies to student behavioral outcomes. Findings from this research form the basis for a staff development program called the Effective Use of Time for Teachers and Students. In 1987 she initiated an innovative school-college partnership with Houston Independent School District that established an academy school for collaborative teacher training. She is the author of *Learning to Look: A Handbook for Observation and Models of Teaching*, as well as numerous other publications.

Henry T. Trueba, who received his Ph.D. in anthropology from Pittsburgh University, is Professor of Educational Psychology, Director of Cross-Cultural Studies, and Director of the Office for Research on Educational Equity at the Graduate School of Education, University of California, Santa Barbara. He has received several awards from the American Educational Research Association for his work with linguistic minorities in the United States. He recently edited *Success or Failure: Learning and the Language Minority Student.* He is coeditor of *Language: Advances in Research and Theory* and *School and Society: Learning Content Through Culture.* He is the author of *Raising Silent Voices: Educating the Linguistic Minorities for the 21st Century.*

Herbert J. Walberg is Research Professor of Education at the University of Illinois at Chicago. A former Assistant Professor at Harvard University, he has served as an adviser on educational research and improvement to government and private agencies in the United States and a dozen other countries. He has written or edited more than 30 books and has contributed more than 300 articles to educational, psychological, and practitioner journals on such topics as educational productivity, giftedness, international comparisons, instruction, and parental education. He currently chairs the scientific committees of the National Assessment Governing Board and the Paris-based Organization for Economic and Cooperative Development.

Judith Walker de Felix received her B.S. from the University of Kansas and her Ph.D. from the University of Florida. She is Associate Professor and Associate Chair, Curriculum and Instruction Department, University of Houston. Her current graduate teaching includes courses in second language acquisition and research in second language classrooms. She is the author of articles and scholarly papers on classroom interaction, teacher characteristics, and background information in second language acquisition. She is currently coeditor of the *Journal of Educational Equity.*

Margaret Wang is Professor of Educational Psychology and Director of the Temple University Center for Research in Human Development and Education. She received her Ph.D. in child development and educational research at the University of Pittsburgh. She is a fellow of the Division of Educational Psychology of the American Psychological Association, is active in several professional organizations, and serves on the Secretary of Education's Task Force on Serving Students with Learning Problems. She has authored close to 100 articles and books. She is the senior editor of the three-volume *Handbook of Special Education: Research and Practice.*

Hersholt C. Waxman is Associate Dean for Research, Director of the Educational Research Center, and Associate Professor in Curriculum and Instruction at the University of Houston. He received his doctorate in educational research and evaluation from the University of Illinois at Chicago and his postdoctoral fellowship was from the Learning Research and Development Center at the University of Pittsburgh. He is currently President of the Southwest Educational Research Association and Research Representative for Phi Delta Kappa, University of Houston Chapter.

L. Dean Webb is the Associate Dean for Administration and Research for the College of Education at Arizona State University. She was the coeditor of the fourth (*School Finance and School Improvement: Linkages for the 1980's*, Ballinger, 1983) and fifth (*Managing Limited Resources: New Demands on Public School Business Management*, Ballinger, 1984) yearbooks of the American Education Finance Association and the coauthor of *Financing Elementary and Secondary Education, Personnel Administration in Education, School Business Administration*, and *Educational Administration Today*. She has served as journal editor and essay review editor of the *Journal of Educational Equity and Leadership* and currently serves on the Editorial Review Board of the *Journal of Education Finance.*